Tim Dörnemann

Supporting Quality of Service in Scientific Workflows

Tim Dörnemann

Supporting Quality of Service in Scientific Workflows

A Novel Approach to Workflow Quality of Service that utilizes Infrastructure as a Service (IaaS)-based Cloud Platforms

Südwestdeutscher Verlag für Hochschulschriften

Impressum / Imprint
Bibliografische Information der Deutschen Nationalbibliothek: Die Deutsche Nationalbibliothek verzeichnet diese Publikation in der Deutschen Nationalbibliografie; detaillierte bibliografische Daten sind im Internet über http://dnb.d-nb.de abrufbar.
Alle in diesem Buch genannten Marken und Produktnamen unterliegen warenzeichen-, marken- oder patentrechtlichem Schutz bzw. sind Warenzeichen oder eingetragene Warenzeichen der jeweiligen Inhaber. Die Wiedergabe von Marken, Produktnamen, Gebrauchsnamen, Handelsnamen, Warenbezeichnungen u.s.w. in diesem Werk berechtigt auch ohne besondere Kennzeichnung nicht zu der Annahme, dass solche Namen im Sinne der Warenzeichen- und Markenschutzgesetzgebung als frei zu betrachten wären und daher von jedermann benutzt werden dürften.

Bibliographic information published by the Deutsche Nationalbibliothek: The Deutsche Nationalbibliothek lists this publication in the Deutsche Nationalbibliografie; detailed bibliographic data are available in the Internet at http://dnb.d-nb.de.
Any brand names and product names mentioned in this book are subject to trademark, brand or patent protection and are trademarks or registered trademarks of their respective holders. The use of brand names, product names, common names, trade names, product descriptions etc. even without a particular marking in this works is in no way to be construed to mean that such names may be regarded as unrestricted in respect of trademark and brand protection legislation and could thus be used by anyone.

Coverbild / Cover image: www.ingimage.com

Verlag / Publisher:
Südwestdeutscher Verlag für Hochschulschriften
ist ein Imprint der / is a trademark of
OmniScriptum GmbH & Co. KG
Heinrich-Böcking-Str. 6-8, 66121 Saarbrücken, Deutschland / Germany
Email: info@svh-verlag.de

Herstellung: siehe letzte Seite /
Printed at: see last page
ISBN: 978-3-8381-3234-1

Zugl. / Approved by: Philipps-Universität Marburg, Diss., 2011

Copyright © 2013 OmniScriptum GmbH & Co. KG
Alle Rechte vorbehalten. / All rights reserved. Saarbrücken 2013

Acknowledgements

I would like to acknowledge the help of many people during my studies that led to this thesis.

In particular, I would like to thank my supervisor Prof. Dr. Bernd Freisleben for his permanent support – and sharing his knowledge, insights and experiences in numerous discussions – during the course of this thesis.

I would like to thank Prof. Dr. Thilo Kielmann from the Vrije Universiteit Amsterdam for acting as a reviewer for my thesis.

I am very grateful to my college Ernst Juhnke for long, fruitful, and motivating discussions, dedicated collaboration on our joint publications and the implementation of the BPEL-based workflow environment.

I also want to thank the following very knowledgeable and dedicated persons for helping to implement, test and improve the workflow system presented in this thesis (in alphabetical order): David Böck, Marian Harbach, Michael Heidt, Sergej Herdt, Sebastian Kirch, Thomas Noll, Stefan Schindelmann, and Bernd Wasmuth. I also thank the entire Distributed Systems Group (and former members) at the Philipps-University of Marburg for their work and collaboration, especially Dr. Matthias Schmidt, Dr. Markus Mathes, Roland Schwarzkopf, Dr. Matthew Smith, and Mechthild Keßler.

I have also benefited from discussions with various members of the scientific community on several occasions and the comments given by many anonymous reviewers who provided feedback on the subjects published during the research in the context of this thesis.

Finally, I would like to thank my family – especially my wife Marina and my brother Kay – for their support and for always being there for me.

Abstract

While workflow management systems have been utilized in enterprises to support businesses for almost two decades, the use of workflows in scientific environments was fairly uncommon until recently. Nowadays, scientists use workflow systems to conduct scientific experiments, simulations, and distributed computations. However, most scientific workflow management systems have not been built using existing workflow technology; rather they have been designed and developed from scratch. Due to the lack of generality of early scientific workflow systems, many domain-specific workflow systems have been developed. Generally speaking, those domain-specific approaches lack common acceptance and tool support and offer lower robustness compared to business workflow systems.

In this thesis, the use of the industry standard BPEL, a workflow language for modeling business processes, is proposed for the modeling and the execution of scientific workflows. Due to the widespread use of BPEL in enterprises, a number of stable and mature software products exist. The language is expressive (Turing-complete) and not restricted to specific applications. BPEL is well suited for the modeling of scientific workflows, but existing *implementations* of the standard lack important features that are necessary for the execution of scientific workflows.

This work presents components that extend an existing implementation of the BPEL standard and eliminate the identified weaknesses. The components thus provide the technical basis for use of BPEL in academia. The particular focus is on so-called non-functional (Quality of Service) requirements. These requirements include *scalability*, *reliability* (fault tolerance), data *security*, and *cost* (of executing a workflow). From a technical perspective, the workflow system must be able to interface with the middleware systems that are commonly used by the scientific workflow community to allow access to heterogeneous, distributed resources (especially Grid and Cloud resources).

The major components cover exactly these requirements:

Cloud Resource Provisioner Scalability of the workflow system is achieved by automatically adding additional (Cloud) resources to the workflow system's resource pool when the workflow system is heavily loaded.

Fault Tolerance Module High reliability is achieved via continuous monitoring of workflow execution and corrective interventions, such as re-execution of a failed workflow step or replacement of the faulty resource.

Cost And Data Flow Aware Scheduler The majority of scientific workflow systems only take the performance and utilization of resources for the execution of workflow steps into account when making scheduling decisions. The presented workflow system goes beyond that. By defining preference values for the weighting of costs and the anticipated workflow execution time, workflow users may influence the resource selection process. The developed *multi-objective* scheduling algorithm respects the defined weighting and makes both efficient and advantageous decisions using a heuristic approach.

Security Extensions Because it supports various encryption, signature and authentication mechanisms (e.g., Grid Security Infrastructure), the workflow system guarantees data security in the transfer of workflow data.

Furthermore, this work identifies the need to equip workflow developers with workflow modeling tools that can be used intuitively. This dissertation presents two modeling tools that support users with different needs. The first tool, DAVO (domain-adaptable, Visual BPEL Orchestrator), operates at a low level of abstraction and allows users with knowledge of BPEL to use the full extent of the language. DAVO is a software that offers extensibility and customizability for different application domains. These features are used in the implementation of the second tool, SimpleBPEL Composer. SimpleBPEL is aimed at users with little or no background in computer science and allows for quick and intuitive development of BPEL workflows based on predefined components.

Contents

1 Introduction   **1**
1.1 Research Contributions 6
1.2 Organization of this Thesis 11

2 Quality of Service Requirements   **13**
2.1 Introduction 13
2.2 Sample Applications 14
    2.2.1 Engineering Application 14
    2.2.2 Medical Application 15
    2.2.3 Systems Biology 17
2.3 Requirements Analysis 18
    2.3.1 Basics 18
    2.3.2 Quality of Service 20
    2.3.3 Development Support 24
2.4 Summary 24

3 A New Approach for Supporting Quality of Service in Scientific Workflows   **25**
3.1 Introduction 25
3.2 Related Work 26
    3.2.1 Scientific Workflow Systems 26
    3.2.2 Workflow Quality of Service 31
3.3 A QoS-supporting Workflow System Based on Standards .. 34
    3.3.1 Workflow Modeling Based on Standards 34
    3.3.2 Business Process Execution Language 35
    3.3.3 Execution Environment 37
    3.3.4 Development Environment 44
3.4 Summary 45

4 Automatic Infrastructure Scaling   **47**
4.1 Introduction 47
4.2 Technical Background 48
    4.2.1 Dynamic Resource Selection in BPEL 48
    4.2.2 Cloud Computing 50
4.3 Related Work 52
4.4 Cloud-enabled Auto-Scaling Architecture 53
    4.4.1 Extensions to the BPEL Engine 55

		4.4.2 Load Balancer	56
		4.4.3 Load Analyzer	58
	4.5	Implementation	58
		4.5.1 Extensions to the BPEL Engine	59
		4.5.2 Load Balancer	60
		4.5.3 Load Analyzer	64
	4.6	Experimental Results	64
	4.7	Summary	68

5 Improved Fault Handling in BPEL — 69

- 5.1 Introduction . . . 70
- 5.2 Fault Handling in BPEL . . . 71
  - 5.2.1 Status Quo . . . 71
  - 5.2.2 Improvements to the Handling of Infrastructural Errors 72
  - 5.2.3 Using Replication . . . 73
- 5.3 Related Work . . . 73
- 5.4 Design . . . 74
  - 5.4.1 Fault Tolerance Module . . . 75
  - 5.4.2 Dynamic Resolver . . . 78
- 5.5 Implementation . . . 79
  - 5.5.1 Fault Tolerance Module . . . 79
  - 5.5.2 Dynamic Resolver . . . 83
- 5.6 Fault-Tolerant and Auto-Scaling Deployment of the BPEL engine . . . 83
  - 5.6.1 Relevant Services of Amazon Web Services . . . 84
  - 5.6.2 Scenario Architecture . . . 86
  - 5.6.3 Configuration of the Required Services . . . 86
- 5.7 Experimental Results . . . 90
- 5.8 Summary . . . 95

6 Cost and Data Flow Aware Scheduling — 97

- 6.1 Introduction . . . 97
- 6.2 The Influence of Data Transfer on Workflow Runtime . . . 98
- 6.3 Related Work . . . 101
- 6.4 Design of CaDaS . . . 103
  - 6.4.1 Framework Components . . . 104
  - 6.4.2 Multi-Objective Scheduling Algorithm . . . 107
- 6.5 Implementation . . . 109
  - 6.5.1 Workflow Annotations . . . 109
  - 6.5.2 Workflow Execution . . . 110
- 6.6 Experimental Results . . . 117
- 6.7 Summary . . . 121

7 WSRF- and Grid-Related Extensions — 123

- 7.1 Introduction . . . 123
- 7.2 Technical Background . . . 124
  - 7.2.1 Web Services Resource Framework . . . 124
  - 7.2.2 Grid Security Infrastructure . . . 126

7.3	Related Work	127
7.4	WSRF Extensions	129
	7.4.1 Manual Invocation of WSRF Services	129
	7.4.2 BPEL Extension: GridInvoke	131
7.5	Support for Grid Security Infrastructure	133
	7.5.1 Status Quo and Requirements	133
	7.5.2 Security Extensions to BPEL	133
	7.5.3 Automatic Security Configuration	137
7.6	Implementation	139
	7.6.1 WSRF Extensions	139
	7.6.2 Support for Grid Security Infrastructure	141
	7.6.3 Automatic Security Configuration	145
7.7	Evaluation	147
7.8	Summary	151

8 Development Tools — 153
8.1	Introduction	153
8.2	Related Work	155
8.3	Design of the Development Suite	157
	8.3.1 Domain-adaptable Visual Orchestrator	157
	8.3.2 SimpleBPEL	162
8.4	Implementation of the Development Suite	167
	8.4.1 Domain-adaptable Visual Orchestrator	167
	8.4.2 SimpleBPEL	172
8.5	Use Cases	179
	8.5.1 Service-oriented Grid Computing	179
	8.5.2 Time-constrained Web Services for Industrial Automation	180
	8.5.3 SimpleBPEL	187
8.6	Summary	189

9 Conclusions and Future Work — 193
9.1	Summary	193
9.2	Future Work	195

List of Figures — 199

List of Tables — 203

List of Listings — 205

Bibliography — 207

Chapter 1
Introduction

Contents
1.1 Research Contributions 6
1.2 Organization of this Thesis 11

Scientists often need to develop and execute complex *in-silico* experiments, simulations, or (data) analysis applications with many (interdependent) tasks, which are to be executed sequentially or simultaneously. Those applications with connected tasks are typically referred to as *workflows*. According to the Workflow Management Coalition's definition [141], a workflow is "the automation of a business process, in whole or part, during which documents, information or tasks are passed from one participant to another for action, according to a set of procedural rules to achieve, or contribute to, an overall business goal."

Figure 1.1 contains the most important workflow-related terms. The grayed-out terms are not relevant for this thesis. The terms activity instance, (workflow) step and (workflow) task will be used synonymously in the following. Moreover, the terms workflow management system and workflow engine, as well as process and workflow are used synonymously.

While in enterprises workflow management systems (WfMS) have been utilized to support their businesses for almost two decades [117], the use of workflows in scientific environments was not common until recent years [77]. Traditional approaches for developing scientific workflows were based on techniques like scripting languages to tie application components (tasks) together. Writing those applications requires in-depth knowledge of a scripting language and becomes eminently complicated when the tasks need to be executed in distributed computing environments.

Nowadays, scientists use workflow systems to conduct scientific experiments, simulations and distributed computations. However, most scientific workflow management systems have not been built using existing workflow technology, but have been designed and developed from scratch. The main reason seems to be that scientists from different domains have diverging requirements concerning the capabilities of such workflow systems. There-

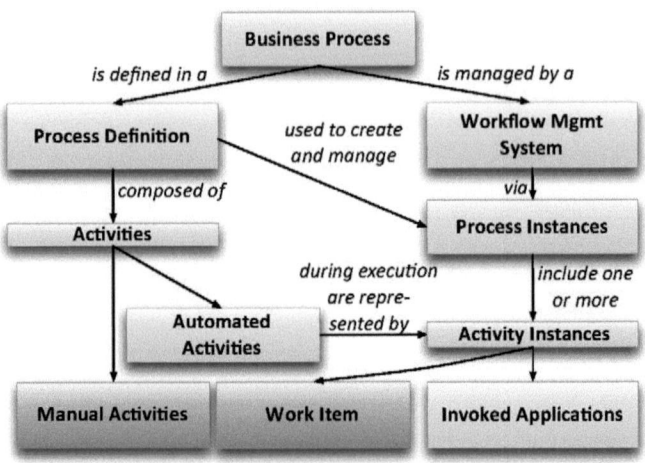

Figure 1.1: Relationship between basic workflow terminology. Based on [141]

fore, they tend to design and implement domain-specific systems that fit their needs. Building a workflow system from scratch is a tedious task since one has to define the language, verify it and implement a workflow engine for the given language. This is, at least partly, comparable to "reinventing the wheel." Due to the lack of generality of early scientific workflow systems, many domain-specific workflow systems have been developed. Generally speaking, those domain-specific approaches lack common acceptance, tool support and offer lower robustness compared to business workflow systems.

Gil et al. [77] have summarized some requirements that most scientific workflow users seem to share. The requirements include:

- "From an operational perspective, there is a need to provide solutions that are secure, reliable, and scalable."

- "The environments provided should also be flexible in terms of supporting both common analyses performed by many as well as unique individual analyses."

- "[...] scientists need easy to use tools that provide intelligent assistance for such complex workflow capabilities."

The principle of Service-Oriented Architectures (SOA) and Web services as the most widely used implementation technology of SOA are well-suited to help fulfill those requirements. As depicted above, scientists often need to model complex workflows with many tasks that are to be executed sequentially or simultaneously. Furthermore, flexibility is of great importance since researches might want to try different experimental setups. If the tasks a scientist wishes to incorporate into a workflow are modeled as components (i.e. Web services), they may be flexibly added to applications. The de-facto industry standard for developing Web service-based workflows is the Business Process Execution Language (BPEL for short [24]). This new way of writing (distributed) applications is often referred to as "Programming in the Large." In this context, BPEL can be seen as a programming language that allows developers to create applications by combining existing Web services. The control flow of the program/workflow is thereby defined using so-called structured activities, like *sequence*, *switch*, and *while* (refer to Section 3.3.2 for a detailed discussion).

Therefore, this thesis suggests the use of this de-facto industry standard for the development and execution of scientific workflows instead of defining domain-specific languages for different application domains. BPEL itself has an interesting feature that predestines it as a general-purpose workflow language: It has been proven that BPEL is Turing-complete and well-defined [47, 93], meaning that the language is expressive enough to model any kind of workflow. In contrast, the majority of scientific workflow languages are DAG-based (directed acyclic graph) and therefore do not allow users to define conditional loops, for instance.

BPEL enables the construction of value-added workflows that are composed of Web services, which act as the basic activities in the workflow. Access to a process is exposed by the workflow execution engine through a Web service interface (defined by the Web Services Description Language, WSDL [39]), allowing the process to be accessed by Web service clients or to be used as a basic activity in other processes. This implies another feature that is very useful when scientists wish to coordinate their work: both the Web services used as well as complete workflows may be shared[1] and accessed from almost any platform (because Web services operate independent of operating system and programming language). Due to its broad adoption in enterprises, a variety of both open-source and commercial software products exist to execute and model workflows.

Both in businesses and research, many problems that are to be solved using workflow technology are computationally intensive. Normally, one has to buy/lease and operate the IT infrastructure to carry out these computationally intensive tasks. Since many organizations do not have the financial resources to operate large data centers, these tasks can either not be computed at all or take a very long time to complete due to the lack of computing power.

There are different approaches to solving this dilemma. From a historical perspective, the basic idea was described by John McCarthy in 1955 in a speech given at the Dartmouth conference [82]:

> "If computers of the kind I have advocated become the computers of the future, then computing may someday be organized as a public utility just as the telephone system is a public utility... The computer utility could become the basis of a new and important industry."

McCarthy suggested that computer time-sharing technology might lead to a future in which computing power and even specific applications could be

---

[1] By simply providing URLs pointing to the Web services/workflow.

sold through the utility business model (like gas or electricity). While this idea was very popular in the 1970's, it more or less disappeared afterwards as it became clear that hardware, software and networking technologies were simply not ready. The idea has experienced a renaissance in the form of Grid and Cloud computing (since around 1998 and 2006, respectively).

Grid computing [31, 69, 71] describes the idea of resource sharing (e.g. computing power, storage, data sources, and special instruments) as easy as the distribution of electricity by plugging devices into the power grid. According to Foster [65], a Grid is a system that "coordinates resources that are not subject to centralized control," "[...] using standard, open, general-purpose protocols and interfaces," "[...] to deliver nontrivial qualities of service." This concept as well as actual implementations are further detailed in Chapter 7.

Similar ideas drive the related concept of Cloud computing [27, 133]. However, Cloud computing originates from commercial providers and does not focus on resource sharing, but on pay-per-use resource provisioning/consumption.

"Cloud Computing refers to both the applications delivered as services over the Internet and the hardware and systems software in the datacenters that provide those services. The services themselves have long been referred to as Software as a Service (SaaS). The datacenter hardware and software is what we will call a Cloud. When a Cloud is made available in a pay-as-you-go manner to the general public, we call it a Public Cloud; the service being sold is Utility Computing." [27]

While these approaches use different implementation technologies and have different (economic) backgrounds, they have a common goal [73]. They allow developers to solve more complex computational problems than ever before, while at the same time reducing cost by sharing resources or billing pay-per-use. For an in-depth comparison between Grid and Cloud computing, the reader is referred to a comparison conducted by Foster et al. [73].

Grid computing is quite well researched and adopted within the academic community; the access to Grid resources is supported by most scientific WfMS. However, Cloud infrastructures are at present mainly used by start-up companies (for instance, to react to peak-load in a pay-per-use manner) and not broadly supported by scientific workflow systems. The proposed BPEL-based workflow system strives to support access to both resource types, opening it to a larger audience. Furthermore, the system should fulfill certain other requirements. As stated by Gil et al. (see above), scientific workflow systems should be secure, reliable, and scalable. These kinds of non-functional requirements are commonly referred to as Quality of Service (QoS) requirements. According to Cardoso et al. [36], QoS requirements can be further sub-classified into quantitative (directly measurable) and qualitative requirements. While reliability and security are qualitative requirements, scalability (measurable by performance/execution time) and cost (of execution), which is mentioned by Cardoso et al. as another important requirement, belong to the category of quantitative requirements. Therefore, the second major objective of this thesis is to equip the workflow system with mechanisms to provide a certain level of QoS.

To achieve these objectives, a number of challenges must be taken into account and resolved. The system must, for instance, provide advanced fault handling mechanisms to improve *reliability*, since it is targeted for long-running and computationally-intensive workflows in a distributed environment that spans multiple administrative domains. When a workflow makes use of a number of machines that do not belong to a single Grid or Cloud site, one has to deal with unreliable network connections, for example.

To deliver constant performance to the workflow user, the system must be *scalable*. Scalability means that the system is able to handle an increasing amount of work with ease. This implies the capability of increasing the system's computing capacity. Scalability is often achieved by adding additional resources that run the same software as the system that is to be scaled-out. Given the possibility of on-demand resource provisioning in Cloud environments, the workflow execution system could take advantage of this feature in order to provide scalability.

Within a distributed infrastructure where the machines communicate using relatively slow network connections, another obstacle occurs. When workflow tasks are executed on (geographically) distributed machines and some steps depend on the results of preceding steps, the system must take data dependencies between workflow steps into account in order to operate to operate efficiently and *cost-effectively*, Not respecting these dependencies leads to two possible disadvantages: (1) The workflow system's throughput might be sub-optimal due to frequent data transfers between hosts (since workflow steps that depend on the results of preceding steps could be scheduled to different machines). (2) When Cloud resources are used in certain workflow steps, workflow execution might be costly, since data is transferred into and out of the Cloud frequently, which, depending on the business model of the Cloud provider, might induce data transfer costs.

A workflow execution engine that addresses all of the discussed challenges would be more stable and elastic to changing demand than existing workflow systems. Moreover, it could significantly reduce administration overhead and costs, as the infrastructure could be (completely or partly) provisioned (using machines from Cloud providers) at workflow runtime time without needing to manually set it up.

The aforementioned challenges focus on the complexity of executing workflows at runtime in heterogeneous Grid and Cloud environments. However, developing applications in distributed systems is a complex and laborious task. The inherent complexity introduced by the high degree of standardization[2] in the area of Web service further increases the learning curve for non-IT experts. A flexible and domain-adaptable development environment that is easy to use and allows users to abstract from technical details can at least help to decrease the learning curve for new workflow developers. On

---

[2]A high degree of standardization is required because Web services are an integration technology geared towards interoperability between different hardware and software systems.

that score, the third major objective of this thesis is not only to provide a BPEL runtime environment for Grid and Cloud infrastructures, but to also support fast and easy development of BPEL workflows by the means of development tools.

1.1 Research Contributions

Existing *implementations* of the BPEL standard are tailored towards the integration of public (business) services offered by different vendors which have different characteristics than services in scientific applications. One classic example for a business service-based workflow is making travel arrangements and reservations. A travel agency books different flights, hotel reservations, rental car services, and so on when booking trips for customers. These services are typically short-running, not data-intensive and installed in fixed locations. In contrast, scientific services tend to be long-running, data-intensive and are replicated over Grid and Cloud sites. Therefore, in this dissertation, missing components and concepts in current BPEL implementations are identified. Solutions are presented, accompanied by prototypical implementations.

The major research contributions of this thesis are:

- The general idea of developing a standard-based (BPEL) workflow system targeted at scientific users that seamlessly *integrates different infrastructures* like dedicated hosts, Grid sites and Cloud sites. While several researchers have previously investigated how BPEL can *generally* be used to model scientific workflows, this thesis presents the design and implementation of a system that solves the main obstacles that hampered the adoption of BPEL for scientists in the past. In particular, the systems uses several mechanisms to provide a high Quality of Service. Special emphasis is placed on performance/scalability, reliability/fault tolerance, and cost.

- This thesis presents a novel approach to scalability in workflow systems. It automatically scales out the workflow execution infrastructure (using machines from Cloud vendors) when demand increases; scale in is automatically performed when demand decreases to save cost. The system thereby configures the on-demand resources and deploys required software without requiring any user interaction.

- Scientific workflows are typically long-running (lasting anywhere from several hours up to several days), computationally intensive and executed on distributed resources. It is a known fact that failures in distributed systems is not an exception, but the common case. Therefore, software in distributed systems has to be engineered towards handling failures. Fault handling in long-running workflows is of special importance, since the failure of a single workflow step might lead to the entire workflow being abandoned, which would result in a loss of intermediate results and wasted CPU hours. Consequently, this thesis provides a fault handling component that is integrated into the workflow execution engine. The component identifies classes of faults that can be handled automatically and defines a policy language to configure automatic recovery behavior without the need for adding explicit fault handling mechanisms to the BPEL process. The approach provides automatic Cloud-based redundancy of services to allow the system to substitute defective services (or resources in general).

- When dealing with computationally and data intensive workflow applications, scheduling workflow tasks to resources is an important topic. The typical goal of scheduling in High Performance Computing (HPC) applications is to reduce the total execution time of the application. In workflows that utilize distributed resources for execution, data transfers between machines that execute dependent workflow steps have to be taken into account. Therefore, a *multi-objective* scheduling algorithm is presented that analyzes data dependencies within a workflow and performs the matching between workflow steps and resources based on the capabilities of the resources, data transfer times, and induced costs.

- The proposed system can be integrated into Globus Toolkit 4, the most-widely used Grid middleware. Special attention was paid to creating a solution that offers full support of the Grid Security Infrastructure (GSI), as none of the existing workflow systems do. Thereby, it is assured that all communication between the workflow engine and the Grid can be encrypted or signed to maintain privacy and prevent data manipulation.

- Application development in distributed systems is a complex and laborious task that is further aggravated by the inherent complexity of the standards and specifications in the Web service area. Since the workflow system developed in the course of this thesis is targeted towards end users from non-computer science domains, the complexity needs to be hidden. Therefore, a suite of highly integrated development tools is presented that facilitates BPEL workflow development on different levels of abstraction. One generic BPEL modeling tool named DAVO (Domain-Adaptable Visual BPEL4WS Orchestrator) is developed which features extensibility and flexibility, especially concerning the internal data model and visual representation of workflows. DAVO is the basis for domain-specific extensions (e.g., Grid and Cloud computing and industrial automation) and offers a low level of abstraction, meaning that the developer is confronted with BPEL building blocks and needs to know about the meaning and semantics of the language constructs. To further ease development for novice users and non-BPEL experts, SimpleBPEL is presented. It abstracts completely from BPEL and allows users to construct BPEL workflows from existing fragments without needing to be familiar with BPEL.

The following papers have been published as part of the research conducted within the context of this thesis:

1. T. Dörnemann, T. Friese, S. Herdt, E. Juhnke, B. Freisleben. Grid Workflow Modelling Using Grid-Specific BPEL Extensions. In *Proceedings of German e-Science Conference 2007*, pp. 1-9, 2007

2. T. Barth, K. Dörnemann, T. Dörnemann, B. Freisleben, T. Friese, M. Grauer, J. Jakumeit, C. Lütke Entrup, U. Müller, J. Reichwald, C. Schridde, M. Smith, F. Thilo. Supporting Engineering Processes Utilizing Service-Oriented Grid Technology. In *Proceedings of German e-Science Conference 2007*, pp. 1-10, 2007

3. T. Dörnemann, S. Heinzl, K. Dörnemann, M. Mathes, M. Smith, B. Freisleben. Secure Grid Service Engineering for Industrial Optimization. In *Proceedings of the 7th International Conference on Optimization: Techniques and Applications (ICOTA)*, pp. 371-372, 2007

4. J. Reichwald, T. Dörnemann, T. Barth, M. Grauer, B. Freisleben. Model-Driven Process Development Incorporating Human Tasks in Service-Oriented Grid Environments. In *Multikonferenz Wirtschaftsinformatik*, pp. 79-90, Springer-Verlag, 2008

5. M. Heidt, T. Dörnemann, K. Dörnemann, B. Freisleben. Omnivore: Integration of Grid Meta-Scheduling and Peer-to-Peer Technologies. In *Proceedings of the 8th IEEE International Symposium on Cluster Computing and the Grid (CCGrid '08)*, pp. 316-323, IEEE Press, 2008

6. T. Dörnemann, M. Smith, B. Freisleben. Composition and Execution of Secure Workflows in WSRF-Grids. In *Proceedings of the 8th IEEE International Symposium on Cluster Computing and the Grid (CCGrid '08)*, pp. 122-129, IEEE Press, 2008

7. M. Smith, M. Schmidt, N. Fallenbeck, T. Dörnemann, C. Schridde, B. Freisleben. Secure On-Demand Grid Computing. In *Journal of Future Generation Computer Systems (FGCS)*, pp. 315-325, Elsevier, 2008

8. T. Dörnemann, M. Smith, E. Juhnke, B. Freisleben. Secure Grid Micro-Workflows Using Virtual Workspaces. In *Proceedings of 34th Euromicro Conference on Software Engineering and Advanced Applications (SEAA)*, pp. 119-126, IEEE Press, 2008

9. M. Mathes, R. Schwarzkopf, T. Dörnemann, S. Heinzl, B. Freisleben. Orchestration of Time-Constrained BPEL4WS Workflows. In *Proceedings of the 13th IEEE International Conference on Emerging Technologies and Factory Automation (ETFA)*, pp. 1-4, IEEE Press, 2008

10. T. Dörnemann, M. Mathes, R. Schwarzkopf, E. Juhnke, B. Freisleben. DAVO: A Domain-Adaptable, Visual BPEL4WS Orchestrator. In *Proceedings of the 23rd IEEE International Conference on Advanced Information Networking and Applications (AINA)*, pp. 121-128, IEEE Press, 2009

11. K. Dörnemann, T. Dörnemann, B. Freisleben, Tobias M. Schneider, Bruno Eckhardt. A Hybrid Peer-to-Peer and Grid Job Scheduling System for Teaming Up Desktop Resources with Computer Clusters to Perform Turbulence Simulations. In *Proceedings of 4th IEEE International Conference on e-Science*, pp. 418-419, IEEE Press, 2008

12. T. Dörnemann, E. Juhnke, B. Freisleben. On-Demand Resource Provisioning for BPEL Workflows Using Amazon's Elastic Compute Cloud. In *Proceedings of the 9th IEEE/ACM International Symposium on Cluster Computing and the Grid (CCGrid '09)*, pp. 140-147, IEEE Press, 2009

13. M. Mathes, R. Schwarzkopf, T. Dörnemann, S. Heinzl, B. Freisleben. Composition of Time-Constrained BPEL4WS Workflows using the TiCS Modeler. In *Proceedings of the 13th IFAC Symposium on Information Control Problems in Manufacturing (INCOM)*, pp. 892-897, Elsevier, 2009

14. E. Juhnke, T. Dörnemann, B. Freisleben. Fault-Tolerant BPEL Workflow Execution via Cloud-Aware Recovery Policies. In *Proceedings of 35th Euromicro Conference on Software Engineering and Advanced Applications (SEAA)*, pp. 31-38, IEEE Press, 2009

15. J. Reichwald, T. Dörnemann, T. Barth, M. Grauer, B. Freisleben. Supporting and Optimizing Interactive Decision Processes in Grid Environments with a Model-Driven Approach. In *Lecture Notes in Business Information Processing (LNBIP)*, (to appear), Springer Verlag, 2009

16. E. Juhnke, D. Seiler, T. Stadelmann, T. Dörnemann, B. Freisleben. LCDL: An Extensible Framework for Wrapping Legacy Code. In *Proceedings of 11th International Conference on Information Integration and Web-based Applications & Services (iiWAS2009)*, pp. 646-650, ACM, 2009

17. M. Mathes, C. Stoidner, R. Schwarzkopf, S. Heinzl, T. Dörnemann, B. Freisleben, H. Dohmann. Time-constrained Services: A Framework for Using Real-Time Web Services in Industrial Automation. In *Service Oriented Computing and Applications*, pp. 239-262, Springer-Verlag, 2009

18. T. M. Schneider, F. De Lillo, J. Bührle, B. Eckhardt, T. Dörnemann, K. Dörnemann, B. Freisleben. Transient turbulence in plane Couette flow. In *Physical Review E*, pp. 15301-15305, American Physical Society, 2010

19. E. Juhnke, T. Dörnemann, R. Schwarzkopf, B. Freisleben. Security, Fault Tolerance and Modeling of Grid Workflows in BPEL4Grid. In *Proceedings of Software Engineering 2010, Grid Workflow Workshop (GWW-10)*, pp. 193-200, Springer-Verlag, 2010

20. C. Schridde, T. Dörnemann, E. Juhnke, M. Smith, B. Freisleben. An Identity-Based Security Infrastructure for Cloud Environments. In *Proceedings of IEEE International Conference on Wireless Communications, Networking and Information Security (WCNIS2010)*, pp. 644–649, IEEE Press, 2010

21. T. Dörnemann, E. Juhnke, T. Noll, D. Seiler, B. Freisleben. Data Flow Driven Scheduling of BPEL Workflows Using Cloud Resources. In *Proceedings of 3rd IEEE International Conference on Cloud Computing (IEEE CLOUD)*, pp. 193-203, IEEE Press, 2010

22. E. Juhnke, T. Dörnemann, S. Kirch, D. Seiler, B. Freisleben. SimpleBPEL: Simplified Modeling of BPEL Workflows for Scientific End Users. In *Proceedings of the 36th EUROMICRO Conference on Software Engineering and Advanced Applications (SEAA)*, pp. 137-140, IEEE Press, 2010

23. T. Dalman, E. Juhnke, T. Dörnemann, M. Weitzel, K. Nöh, W. Wiechert, B. Freisleben. Service Workflows and Distributed Computing Methods for 13C Metabolic Flux Analysis. In: *Proceedings of 7th EUROSIM Congress on Modelling and Simulation*, pp. 1-7, 2010

24. M. Harbach, T. Dörnemann, E. Juhnke, B. Freisleben. Semantic Validation of BPEL Fragment Compositions. In: *Proceedings of the 4th IEEE International Conference on Semantic Computing (ICSC2010)*, pp. 176-183, IEEE Press, 2010

25. T. Dalman, T. Dörnemann, E. Juhnke, M. Weitzel, M. Smith, W. Wiechert, K. Nöh, B. Freisleben Metabolic Flux Analysis in the Cloud. In: *Proceedings of the 6th IEEE Internal Conference on eScience 2010*, pp. 57-64, IEEE Press, 2010

26. B. Ihle, S. Kirch, E. Juhnke, T. Dörnemann, D. Seiler, B. Freisleben. A Workflow Management Platform for Media Analysis in BPEL-based Grid Environments. In: *Proceedings of CEUR Workshop*, pp. 1-6, 2011

27. E. Juhnke, T. Dörnemann, D. Böck, B. Freisleben. Multi-Objective Scheduling of BPEL Workflows in Geographically Distributed Clouds. In: *Proceedings of the 4th IEEE International Conference on Cloud Computing (IEEE CLOUD)*, pp. 412-419, IEEE Press, 2011

28. T. Dalman, T. Dörnemann, E. Juhnke, M. Weitzel, W. Wiechert, K. Nöh, B. Freisleben. Cloud MapReduce for Monte Carlo Bootstrap Applied to Metabolic Flux Analysis. In *Journal of Future Generation Computer Systems (FGCS)*, pp. (to appear), Elsevier, 2011

The paper *Omnivore: Integration of Grid Meta-Scheduling and Peer-to-Peer Technologies* received an IEEE Best Paper Award; the publication *DAVO: A Domain-Adaptable, Visual BPEL4WS Orchestrator* received an IEEE Highly Commended Paper Award.

1.2 Organization of this Thesis

This thesis is organized into nine chapters. The first part of Chapter 2 presents sample applications from different scientific domains (engineering science, medical research and biology) which are used to deduce requirements for a general-purpose workflow system. The requirements are analyzed in the second part, whereby special emphasis is placed on the analysis of requirements related to Quality of Service.

Based on the requirements that have been identified in Chapter 2, Chapter 3 describes the design of the proposed scientific workflow system from a bird's eye view. Before that, related approaches are introduced.

Chapters 4 to 8 discuss the different components of the architecture in a self-contained way, meaning that each chapter discusses the motivation for the development of a given component, then, where necessary, describes technical backgrounds, discusses related work, elucidates the design, sketches interesting implementation details, and presents an evaluation of the given approach.

Chapter 4 introduces a provisioning component that enables the workflow system to automatically scale in and out by provisioning resources from Cloud infrastructures. This feature equips the BPEL engine with the ability to react to increasing and decreasing loads and thus fulfills the QoS-requirement *scalability*.

Chapter 5 delineates a component that equips the workflow engine with an enhanced fault handling mechanism. A striking feature of the approach is that the provisioning component presented in Chapter 4 is utilized to provide Cloud-backed redundancy, eliminating the need for sparse hardware while at the same time improving the *reliability* of the system.

Chapter 6 discusses problems that arise when workflow tasks are assigned to (geographically) distributed resources. It further delineates the effect of task placement in Cloud environments on workflow execution *costs*. In the second part, a *multi-objective* scheduling algorithm is presented that takes both execution time and *costs* into account.

Chapter 7 presents an extension to the BPEL engine that is used as the basis in this work, which enables the workflow system to access Grid resources. Furthermore, Grid-specific *security* mechanisms are supported by the described extension.

Chapter 8 presents two development tools, which are tailored towards different groups of users. DAVO is intended to be used by BPEL/Web service experts who need full control and wish to make use of all available language features while modeling workflows. The second tool, SimpleBPEL is a new approach to modeling BPEL workflows based on pre-defined process fragments.

Chapter 9 concludes the thesis and outlines directions for future work.

Chapter 2
Quality of Service Requirements

Contents

2.1	**Introduction**	**13**
2.2	**Sample Applications**	**14**
	2.2.1 Engineering Application	14
	2.2.2 Medical Application	15
	2.2.3 Systems Biology	17
2.3	**Requirements Analysis**	**18**
	2.3.1 Basics	18
	2.3.2 Quality of Service	20
	2.3.3 Development Support	24
2.4	**Summary**	**24**

2.1 Introduction

This chapter first introduces sample applications stemming from projects and cooperations which have inspired this thesis. The sample applications have had a major impact on the development of the presented workflow system, since they defined the requirements and general conditions. The applications belong to different scientific domains (engineering science, medical research and biology) and led to the insight that a general-purpose workflow system, rather a domain-specific one, should be developed.

The rest of this chapter is organized as follows: In Section 2.2, the sample applications are described. Section 2.3 derives a list of requirements that the workflow system must fulfill. Special emphasis is placed on on the description of Quality of Service aspects. The chapter is summarized in Section 2.4.

The derived requirements are used to construct the architecture of the workflow system in Chapter 3.
Parts of this chapter have already been published [43, 44, 52, 84].

2.2 Sample Applications

2.2.1 Engineering Application

In this section, the engineering process for the creation of a metal casting process model is presented as a sample application. This sample application is a use case within the context of the "In-Grid" [41] research project, a community Grid project for engineering applications and part of the German "D-Grid" [42] research program. Companies working in the casting sector, a sub-domain of metal forming, are typically medium-sized businesses supplying large-scale industrial clients (automobile manufacturers, power station builders). Customers' quality requirements, e.g. allowed tolerances in a casting product's geometry compared to the specification, are constantly increasing. Therefore, the use of numerical simulation and simulation-based optimization is gaining importance since the creation of prototypes is prohibitively expensive and time consuming. Ideally, the simulation of mould-filling and solidification during casting requires the coupled calculation of flow, temperature distribution and mechanical deformation. Applying numerical simulation for this purpose introduces an extremely high demand for computational capacity since a single – sufficiently precise – simulation run typically lasts anywhere from several hours up to several days. Since many small and medium-sized engineering enterprises are not capable of acquiring and maintaining high performance computing resources, outsourcing of computationally demanding tasks is necessary.

Since many applications for simulation and optimization already exist in the engineering domain, there is a need to "wrap" these existing legacy applications, such that they can be utilized in workflow applications. A tool suite to encapsulate legacy code, the *Grid Development Tools (GDT)* [75], has been developed within the context of the InGrid research project. Legacy applications wrapped by Web service interfaces allow rapid design and flexible reconfiguration of engineering processes by composing the services to obtain new applications.

The concrete scenario in the InGrid project is as follows. After deploying the created services (several metal casting services in this case, each providing reusable parts of the application), an engineer may start with a definition of a problem which progresses through some iterations of model definition, simulation and refinement. The given definition of the problem is then modeled as an initial casting process model. Thereby, a numerical simulation expert typically combines metal casting services and sets required input parameters using a workflow modeling tool. During this model calibration phase, an optimization expert is also involved in creating model variants. When a single model is calibrated, the optimization of the model begins by automatically generating a number of n new models by varying the parameters in the casting process model. They can be evaluated simultaneously, and the results from the simulation runs flow back to the optimization algorithm. This procedure iterates until the optimized casting process meets the requirements set by the casting engineer.

The simulation workflow, which runs n instances simultaneously, requires distributed computing resources and therefore suggests the application of Grid technology. Security aspects are very important in this case because engineers often deal with confidential data which might be crucial for their business' success. When computations are performed in Grid environments, the input and output data has to be transferred using public networks (i.e., the Internet). Therefore, the workflow system must be able to guarantee data integrity and encryption. Furthermore, it must be able to interface with a special kind of Web services, namely stateful Web services. Stateful Web services have been specified by OASIS as the so-called Web Services Resource Framework (WSRF, see Section 7.2 for details).

2.2.2 Medical Application

The medical application described as a usage scenario for scientific workflow technology is a data analysis application in sleep research and sleep medicine developed in cooperation with physicians from the University of Marburg. The general objective of this research area include sleep and sleep disorders as well as the development of clinical diagnosis and therapy of sleep-wake disorders.

In sleep medicine, measurements of the patient's various body functions are taken throughout a sleeping period. Those measurements include the electrocardiogram (ECG), breathing activity and the patients' brain activity measured as the electroencephalogram (EEG). These data, continuously measured using sensors attached to the patient's body, are collected by a computer and are stored on disk using a standardized format, European Data Format (EDF). In a first step, the EDF file needs to be evaluated in order to reduce it to a sleeping protocol that describes the sleeping cycle of a patient as an order of different sleep phases with respect to a multi-level sleep classification system. Today, this classification is mostly done manually even though classification algorithms exist that can automatically deduce a sleeping protocol from a given sleeping cycle data record. This automatic deduction requires the application of various filter functions and transformations on the experimental data. The resulting sleep protocol can be used to help physicians to diagnose sleep disorders and possibly connect them with other diseases caused by the sleep disorders.

The implementation of the aforementioned filters and transformations is built on the Physio Toolkit [118], which is a common set of open source tools in the biomedical sciences. To carry out, for instance, an analysis of the recorded ECG signal, the following steps needed to be implemented. Since the data format (European Data Format, EDF) of the recorded vital signs is different from the format required by the Physio Toolkit (WaveForm DataBase, WFDB), a data conversion is needed (*InvokeEDF*). Afterwards, Q-S peaks are detected within the ECG signal (*InvokeWQRS*). The results are passed to the annotation reader component (*InvokeAnnotationReader*) that in turn decodes the input and passes the results to the beat detection component *InvokeBeatDetection*, which detects *R* waves within the signal. At the same time, the output of *InvokeWQRS* is passed to the apnoea detection component (*InvokeApnoea*) that analyzes the input signal and detects respiration dropouts (to diagnose the sleep apnoea syndrome). Figure 2.1 illustrates the control as well as the data flow of the workflow.

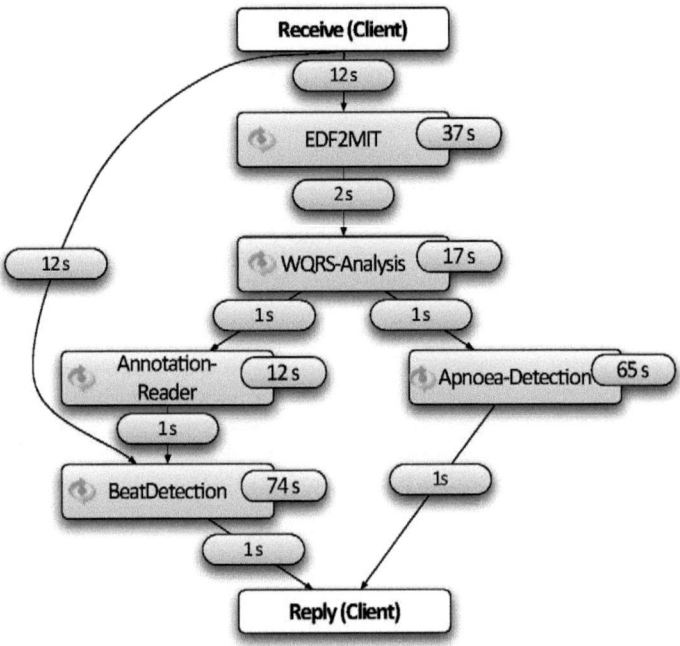

Figure 2.1: Simplified representation of an ECG analysis. Activities with orange background are to be executed, the gray ovals display execution times and data transfer times, respectively

The total amount of data to be processed per patient is approx. 258 MB. The net runtime of the different filter and transformation components on modern desktop PCs is about four minutes, if all steps are executed sequentially. While the runtime per patient is quite short, it should be noted that typically many patient records have to be analyzed at the same time. Therefore, the application would highly benefit from simultaneous processing.

2.2.3 Systems Biology

As a third sample application for scientific workflow technology, an application from systems biology is presented in this section. It originates from a cooperation with the Institute of Bio- and Geosciences (IBG) at Jülich Research Center.

Microorganisms convert substrates like sugars into products like amino acids. Understanding and optimizing this process is a challenging part of ongoing research in the field of Metabolic Engineering. In this field, isotope-based Metabolic Flux Analysis is a powerful method for accurately determining reaction rates within living microorganisms [139]. Roughly, this process consists of two steps:

1. **Carbon Labeling Experiment**: By using substrates that are labeled with ^{13}C at specific carbon locations, certain in vivo metabolic states become observable: Through a complex network of reactions and driven by metabolic activity, carbon atoms are distributed within the cell and characteristic labeling patterns emerge in intermediate metabolites. As soon as the labeling equilibrates, samples are withdrawn and isotopically labeled fractional enrichments are quantified with highly accurate measurement devices [128].

2. **Computer-based Evaluation**: The measured fractional labeling enrichments are then incorporated into an organism-specific network model that describes the fate of all carbon atoms. Assuming closed mass balances, a nonlinear mathematical model is deduced from which not directly measurable intracellular reaction rates, so-called fluxes, are determined by solving an inverse, nonlinear least-squares problem. Finally, the quality of these estimations is assessed using statistical methods [139].

For computer-based evaluation, high-performance simulation tools are readily available that have been well-suited for the evaluation of single data sets. In particular, the software 13CFLUX2 is used, the successor of the widely established 13CFLUX toolbox [138, 140]. 13CFLUX2 includes a set of applications for model generation, fast simulation of labeling patterns, sensitivity analysis, and parameter estimation of unknown fluxes. Moreover, built-in powerful sampling and non-linear optimization suites are accessible.

13CFLUX2 programs are implemented in a modular manner and compiled to run as command-line executables. Graphical interfaces are deliberately separated from the computational core components. Well-defined input/output semantics relying on XML-based documents, *FluxML* and *HDF5*, are generally used for describing and configuring models as well as measurements and for exchanging data [138]. Thus, all ingredients are available to easily integrate 13CFLUX2 programs into workflows in order to build automated simulation tasks.

Even the most basic applications in the context of 13C-MFA are complex; thus, the development of large-scale applications is not an easy task. Moreover, recent developments in experimental technologies created an increased need for a reliable higher-throughput MFA, i.e. automated processing of tens or hundreds of data sets. Thus, a software-aided workflow solution is needed.

2.3 Requirements Analysis

In this section, the presented sample applications are examined to deduce requirements for a scientific workflow environment. As the broad spectrum of application areas suggests, one cannot identify requirements that are equally important for all use cases. The goal of this thesis is to describe the design and implementation of a *general-purpose* scientific workflow system. Therefore, not the "lowest common denominator" of all requirements is important here, but uniting all of the requirements that do not conflict with each other.

First, basic requirements for a general-purpose scientific workflow are identified and described in detail, followed by a discussion of important QoS-requirements. The section closes with a definition of requirements for development tools.

2.3.1 Basics

2.3.1.1 Expressiveness of the Workflow Language

Expressiveness of a language in this context describes the strength of a workflow language. Thereby, two categories of languages exist: those which are only able to describe directed acyclic graphs (DAGs) and those which are powerful enough to describe cyclic graphs (typically called *non*-DAG). Simply put, the first category does not allow users to define loops that depend on a condition, while the latter allows users to define *while* loops (which means that the graph representation of the workflow would contain a cycle).

From a theoretical standpoint, the DAG-based workflow systems can be classified as using *loop* languages, which are not *Turing-complete*. In contrast, *while* languages are Turing-complete, meaning that they are able to model any problem that is computable (*Computability theory/Church-Turing thesis*). Since most scientific workflow languages have been designed with a concrete usage scenario in mind, they only support the control structures that are required for the application domain. According to Yu et al. [143], the majority of existing scientific workflow systems is DAG-based.

Turing-complete languages have the clear advantage that their expressive power is not limited; thus, they foster modeling of any kind of computational problem. If one needs a conditional loop in DAG-based systems, it has to be modeled within workflow tasks (in the source code of the invoked program). However, this may lead to different versions of the program, since looping might not be required in every case. When using a non-DAG based language, the conditional loop can be placed around the workflow step that executes a program. Then, the workflow system would evaluate the loop condition and, depending on the program's output, repeatedly invoke it until the condition is met.

Therefore, to build a general-purpose scientific workflow system, the language must be capable of defining conditional (*while*) loops, meaning that the resulting workflow graph is non-DAG.

Requirement 1: The workflow language must be as expressive as possible – Turing-completeness is required

2.3.1.2 Interface Standardization

All use cases clearly have in common that they are built on existing software. Each of the applications makes use of different pieces of software (called components in the following) to achieve a certain goal. Within each use case, the available components may be used in different orders (or some components might not be used at all) depending on the application's goal. For instance, the components of the medical application could also be used to help to diagnose heart attacks instead of respiration dropouts, if the component *Apnoea-Detection* were to be replaced by a component that detects anomalies within the ST-part of an ECG.

Technically speaking, the components differ in the given implementation technologies. Some of the mentioned components are written in Java, some in C/C++, Fortran or interpreted languages like Ruby, Python or bash. Furthermore, the components typically do not provide means for remote invocation. Remote invocation means that a component is "visible" from outside the operating system of the machine it runs on and may be started remotely. Hence, to allow for composition of these components into workflow applications, they need a common (remote) interface, such that the workflow system can start them, provide required input data and collect output data in a uniform way.

Requirement 2: Workflow components need a common interface

2.3.1.3 Utilization of Distributed Resources

The use cases described above are more or less computationally intensive. The application execution times range from minutes (medical application) to days or even weeks (systems biology), depending on the complexity of the given input. High demand for computational resources is, generally speaking, a property that many scientific applications share. *In silico* simulations, data analysis, and knowledge discovery – to only name a few – demand for more computational resources than a typical workstation can deliver. While the medical application could be run on a workstation in a reasonable time, it should be noted that the application is *instance intensive*, meaning that it is typically used by a group of researchers who concurrently perform data analysis. Therefore, many instances of the application may be run in parallel, resulting in a high computational demand.

All of the given sample applications would greatly profit from parallelization. There are at least two ways of implementing the sample applications in a parallel way: (1) parallelization within the application by distributing the components to different resources or (2) by distributing the execution of parallel workflow application instances to different resources.

All use case providers have the commonality that no or at least insufficient internal resources are available to perform the computations in a reasonable amount of time. Hence, they would benefit if the workflow system were enabled to use both local and remote resources offered by third parties. The use of additional resources acquired from Grid or Cloud environments provides several advantages: (1) the applications' runtimes could be reduced by adding additional resources and (2) the granularity of the simulation processes (especially relevant for the metal casting case and for systems biology) could be increased. This leads to more accurate results without increasing the total runtime if a sufficient amount of additional resources may be acquired.

Requirement 3: The workflow system should be able to utilize distributed computing environments

2.3.2 Quality of Service

The described use cases belong to different application domains and are applied in different organizational environments (small and medium sized enterprises, clinic, research facility). However, they share some QoS-requirements – partially for different reasons. According to Cardoso et al. [36], "Workflow QoS represents the quantitative and qualitative characteristics of a workflow application necessary to achieve a set of initial requirements." Thereby, quantitative characteristics are directly measurable – for instance workflow execution time (*performance*) and induced *cost*. Qualitative characteristics subsume features offered by the workflow system, such as fault-tolerance mechanisms (which can in turn be seen as mechanisms to achieve *reliability*) and *security*. Further details on the different QoS dimensions are given in Section 3.2.2.

In the following, first quantity-related QoS requirements are explained in further detail, followed by a discussion of qualitative requirements.

2.3.2.1 Performance

Workflow execution time is an indicator for the performance achieved by the workflow environment. Workflow execution time depends on several factors. First, it is determined by the performance of the resources that execute the workflow steps (tasks). The optimal performance (minimal execution time) is, of course, achieved when a workflow is executed on exclusively used resources, meaning that the resources do not have to be shared with others. However, this is an unrealistic assumption for most environments. Typically, researchers share a number of resources within their departments; resources are therefore either used concurrently or one is assigned a certain time slot in which the resources may be used exclusively. In Grid environments, concurrent access to and sharing of resources is not an exception, but the common case. In fact, resource sharing is one of the fundamental ideas behind Grid computing. Therefore, second, the workflow system has to deal with the fact that the available resources are shared, which influences workflow runtime. Furthermore, the workflows themselves may be shared and accessed concurrently, resulting in a higher use of resources (in particular on the machine hosting the workflow system).

To deliver a constant performance to the workflow user[1], the system must be *scalable*. Scalability means that the system is able to handle an increasing amount of work gracefully. This implies the capability of increasing the system's computing capacity. Scalability, or to be exact, horizontal scaling (*scale out*), is often achieved by adding additional resources that run the same software as the system that is to be scaled-out. By using *load balancing* techniques, the load is (equally) distributed to the pool of resources. Hence, the system should also automatically *scale in* (remove resources) when the load decreases.

To take advantage of the scalability of the underlying system and the resource pool, the workflow system must dynamically assign workflow steps to resources. Thereby, it has to factor in the workflow system's runtime measurements: resource utilization and network capacity. Workflow steps should not be assigned to busy machines, as this would increase the step's runtime compared to the execution on a free machine – or even lead to an abandonment of the workflow step (see Section 2.3.2.3 for details). Furthermore, the placement of dependent tasks influences the workflow runtime (and cost, see below), since unfavorable placement might lead to large data transfers over slow network connections.

Requirement 4: The workflow system should provide a load-independent performance, automatically scale in and out and perform advantageous resource assignment

2.3.2.2 Cost

Workflow execution cost represents the cost generated by using resources, resource setup and data transfer cost. As one can imagine, the cost associated with the execution of a workflow step typically depends on the hardware capabilities of the underlying resource. Simply put, a workflow task that is executed on a fast machine is typically more expensive than the same task executed on an slower machine. Even within enterprises, transfer prices are defined for the use of resources offered by different departments. An exception is the use of Grid resources: The principle here is resource sharing, meaning that one does not have to pay for using other user's resources, but one has to offer his/her own resources to other users for free as service in return. So, the use of Grid resources also comes at a certain price: one has to own and share resources. However, this price is hard to quantify. Furthermore, data transfer over the Internet costs money (paid peering between different providers). In particular, when Cloud resources are utilized within workflows, cost plays an important role. Use of Cloud resources is typically

---

[1]Ideally, he/she should have the illusion that he/she is using the workflow environment exclusively.

billed pay-per-use, meaning that factors like used CPU hours and data transfer to and from Cloud infrastructures also cost money.

Therefore, one needs mechanisms to estimate and limit workflow execution cost. There are at least two possible approaches.

Prior to workflow execution, it should be possible to estimate the workflow execution cost in order to guarantee that the workflow user's budget is not exceeded. Then, the user could decide whether or not he/she wants to execute the workflow.

A more advanced way of guaranteeing budget compliance is to let the user either define (1) a maximal price for the execution of a workflow or (2) preference values for the ratio between cost and execution time of a workflow. Both cases only make sense when a workflow task may be executed on more than one specific resource, meaning that the required component is present at more than one machine. Given this assumption, the workflow system could calculate a mapping between workflow steps and resources that respects the constraints defined in (1) and (2). The first case has both advantages and disadvantages. On the positive side, it guarantees that the user's budget is not exceeded. On the negative side, it makes the assumption that one can quantify the runtimes and uprising data amounts of each of the workflow steps a priori, which need to be known to exactly calculate the total cost. The assumption is unrealistic for many use cases, since scientific applications often consist of, for example, optimization problems, which are not exactly predictable (speed of convergence, etc.). The second case does not allow to guarantee budget compliance, but is applicable to scientific workflows. It allows the user to express his/her preference values concerning workflow cost and runtime. Given these values, the system can perform a matchmaking that best fits the preference values. For instance, it would select the fastest possible resources if workflow runtime had a high preference value and cost a low value. Otherwise, it would prefer cheaper (and possibly slower) machines if cost was dominant.

Requirement 5: The workflow user should be able to influence the workflow execution cost

2.3.2.3 Reliability

Reliability basically means that a software is able to perform its required functions under stated conditions [95]. The reliability is the overall measure of a component to maintain its service quality. It requires several other conditions to be met: The component must offer high availability, scalability and fault tolerance mechanisms since faults are much more likely to occur in distributed systems than in local systems. The following quotation paraphrases this fact in a humorous way:

> Failure is the defining difference between distributed and local programming, so you have to design distributed systems with the expectation of failure. Imagine asking people, "If the probability of something happening is one in ten to the thirteenth, how often would

it happen?" Your natural human sense would be to answer, "Never." That is an infinitely large number in human terms. But if you ask a physicist, she would say, "All the time. In a cubic foot of air, those things happen all the time." When you design distributed systems, you have to say, "Failure happens all the time." So when you design, you design for failure. It is your number one concern. [134]

In particular, when long-running or computationally-intensive workflows are to be executed, fault handling is very important, since the failure of a single component might lead to an abandonment of the entire workflow. This may lead to the loss of stability in the execution system; a high cost due to wasted CPU hours due to the loss of intermediary results of preceding process steps is another consequence.

Many faults can be corrected by either simply retrying the failed operation or by substituting an equivalent component for the failed one. A substitution can either be performed using equivalent components that are already running somewhere else or by deploying and starting the required components on-demand. On-demand provisioning is especially useful when no equivalent component is available. Cloud computing infrastructures are an ideal candidate for a possible solution since they can be used to host the required components, which guarantees the availability of failover components without the need for additional spare hardware.

Requirement 6: The workflow system should provide high reliability

2.3.2.4 Security

In computer science, security is a broad term. Restricted to distributed applications, or workflow applications in particular, it subsumes features like data protection (integrity and encryption) and access control (authentication, authorization, credential management). Data protection is particularly important here, since the proposed workflow system should be able to utilize distributed computing environments, such as Grids and Clouds. Hence, the input and output data of workflow steps has to be transferred using public networks (i.e., the Internet) that must be considered as insecure, since traffic can be eavesdropped and modified by third parties. While it might be acceptable for some use cases to take the risk of data manipulation or leakage, it is unacceptable for the presented use cases. In the engineering application, business secrets (and therefore money) need to be secured. In the medical use case, patient data has to be protected for legal and ethical reasons. On a technical level, the workflow system must support the authentication mechanism(s) of the target platform, for instance Grid Security Infrastructure (details are given in Section 7.2.2).

Requirement 7: The workflow system should take care of data protection and support access control mechanisms

2.3.3 Development Support

Scientific workflow systems are typically used by domain experts who are neither specialized in IT-related topics nor particularly interested in becoming IT experts. In addition, it is a clear understanding that the more advanced an application becomes, the more effort has to be made to model it as a workflow. At a certain level of complexity, a domain expert who is not familiar with the technical details of workflow modeling (since this is out of the scope of his/her research domain) would simply be overburdened by the complexity.

To put it simply, without tool support, the definition of workflows is quite error-prone and time-consuming. From this it follows that tool support is required to lower the entry burden into scientific workflow modeling and allow user-friendly development of complex workflow applications that run on (geographically) distributed resources. Ideally, the modeling tool would allow the user to work on different levels of abstraction and hide technical details where possible. It should also provide the ability to automate the generation of workflow parts with recurring patterns by allowing users to build a library of (domain-specific) shortcuts/building blocks.

Despite development tools, further tool support is required to allow users to work conveniently and efficiently with the workflow system. After modeling a workflow, a scientist would like to run the workflow, monitor its progress and potentially keep an eye on the infrastructure. Therefore, tools are required that, ideally, integrate into the development environment and allow to run, monitor and manage workflows and the infrastructure.

Requirement 8: A suite of highly integrated development tools that facilitate workflow development on different levels of abstraction is required

2.4 Summary

In this chapter, requirements for a scientific workflow system were derived from three sample applications from different scientific domains: engineering science, medical research and biology. Since this thesis thrives to develop a domain-agnostic, general-purpose scientific workflow system, not the "lowest common denominator" of all requirements is important here but uniting all of the requirements that do not conflict with each other.

The identified requirements ranged from the expressiveness of the underlying language (Turing-completeness is required) to the need for tool support to visually model workflows. It was argued why Quality of Service of workflow execution is important for a scientific workflow system. Moreover, the most important QoS requirements were identified and described: performance, cost, reliability, and security.

Chapter 3
A New Approach for Supporting Quality of Service in Scientific Workflows

Contents

3.1	Introduction	25
3.2	Related Work	26
	3.2.1 Scientific Workflow Systems	26
	3.2.2 Workflow Quality of Service	31
3.3	A QoS-supporting Workflow System Based on Standards .	34
	3.3.1 Workflow Modeling Based on Standards	34
	3.3.2 Business Process Execution Language	35
	3.3.3 Execution Environment	37
	3.3.4 Development Environment	44
3.4	Summary	45

3.1 Introduction

This chapter first discusses related work in the areas *scientific workflow* and *workflow quality of service*. After that, based on the requirements that were derived from the sample applications in Chapter 2, the architecture of the proposed workflow system is sketched. A detailed discussion of the architecture's building blocks is performed in the corresponding chapters.

The architecture consists of two building blocks: execution environment and development environment. Before the components of both building

blocks are described, a short introduction is given of BPEL, the workflow language used. The chapter is summarized in Section 3.4.
Parts of this chapter have already been published [51, 53–56, 84, 85, 87].

3.2 Related Work

In this section, an overview is given of related approaches in the area of scientific workflow systems. Furthermore, several methods to estimate workflow quality of service are discussed.

3.2.1 Scientific Workflow Systems

A variety of scientific workflow systems has been developed within the last decade. Yu and Buyya [143, 144] present a taxonomy of scientific workflow systems (with focus on Grid computing). This taxonomy will be used as the basis to classify existing workflow systems and to range in the proposed system. Due to the large number of scientific workflow systems (the taxonomy discusses 14 representatives), only two systems, which implement strongly divergent approaches, are discussed representatively.

3.2.1.1 Workflow Taxonomy

The workflow taxonomy developed by Yu and Buyya classifies workflow systems using four major aspects (see Figure 3.1): (1) workflow design, (2) workflow scheduling, (3) fault tolerance, and (4) data movement.

Workflow design subsumes the attributes workflow structure (DAG vs. non-DAG), workflow model, and composition system (development tools). The workflow model may either be abstract (meaning that the workflow's model does not contain bindings to resources) or concrete. The composition process in turn may be user-directed or automatic. In user-directed systems, one has to model the workflow directly using either text-based editors (language-based) or graphical editors (graph-based). Graph-based approaches have the clear advantage that they are "very intuitive and can be handled easily even by a non-expert user." Automatic composition means that the workflow system composes workflows automatically based on user-defined high level requirements.

Workflow scheduling is decomposed into four areas. The scheduling architecture may be centralized (one scheduler that makes all scheduling decisions), hierarchical (one central manager and multiple lower-level sub-workflow schedulers), or decentralized (multiple schedulers without centralized control). The authors believe that "the centralized scheme can produce efficient schedules [...]. However, it is not scalable [...]." Thereby, decision making can either be local (task-based) or global (workflow-based). While global decision making provides better overall results, it has a much higher complexity and therefore it takes more time to compute schedules on a workflow basis. When static planning is used, concrete workflow models have to

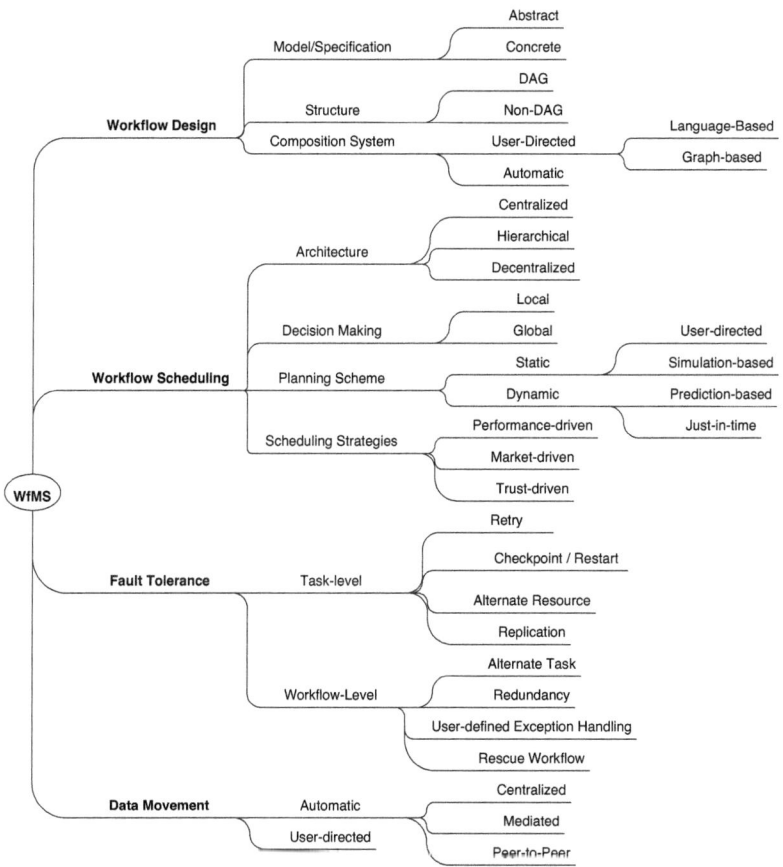

Figure 3.1: Graphical representation of the workflow taxonomy defined by Yu and Buyya. Source: [144]

be generated before the execution. This approach respects only information about the execution environment that is available at the time of decision making and ignores the dynamically changing state of the resources. Dynamic schemes, in contrast, use both dynamic and static information to make scheduling decisions at workflow runtime. The last area is scheduling strategy. Besides other categories, a scheduling strategy may be performance-driven, market-driven (cost-driven), or trust-driven. As the names suggest, the strategies directly influence the perceived workflow quality of service since they are tailored towards the optimization of certain QoS criteria.

Fault tolerance is the third major classification aspect. A "workflow management systems should be able to identify and handle failures and support reliable execution in the presence of concurrency and failures." The different mechanisms operate either on the task-level or the workflow-level. In contrast to task-level fault tolerance, the workflow-level mechanisms manipulate the workflow structure (such as execution flow). Task-level techniques can be further classified as retry, alternate resource, checkpoint/restart, and replication.

Data movement either has to be managed by the user (user-directed) or can be done automatically by the workflow system. The latter is further classified into centralized, mediated, and peer-to-peer approaches. Centralized approaches transfer data between resources via a central point (typically the workflow engine). In a mediated approach, the locations of the intermediate data are managed by a distributed data management system. A peer-to-peer approach transfers data directly between processing resources.

According to the authors, "centralized approaches are easily implemented and suit workflow applications in which large-scale data flow is not required." For applications which need to keep intermediate data for later use, mediated approaches are suitable and provide better scalability. Peer-to-peer approaches save transmission time significantly (since they avoid the data transfer to an intermediate) and reduce the bottleneck caused by the centralized and mediated approaches. Thus, "the peer-to-peer approach is more suitable for large-scale intermediate data transfer." In Table 3.1, the mapping of some widely used scientific workflow systems to the taxonomy is shown.

Representatively for the broad variety of existing scientific workflow systems, two approaches will be described in detail: Pegasus and Triana.

3.2.1.2 Pegasus

Pegasus (Planning for Execution in Grids) [46–48] is a framework that maps DAG-based scientific workflows onto distributed resources, in particular Grid resources running Globus Toolkit (see Chapter 7 for an introduction to Globus). Workflows are modeled abstract, whereby the workflow developer may choose between three different methods: (1) direct modeling, (2) using Chimera [72] to build workflows based on logical descriptions specified in Chimera's Virtual Data Language (VDL), or (3) using workflow editors such as the Composition Analysis Tool (CAT) [90]. In any case, the resulting workflow is not directly executable since the workflow steps need to be mapped onto resources for execution. Therefore, the main objective of Pegasus is to solve

Project	Workflow Design			Workflow Scheduling				Fault Tolerance	Data Movement
	Structure	Model	Composition	Architecture	Decision Making	Planning	Strategy		
DAGMan [40]	DAG	Abstract	User-dir. (language-based)	Centralized	Local	Dynamic (JIT[a])	Perf.-driven	Task-level (Migration, Retry) Workflow-level (Rescue)	User-directed
Pegasus [46]	DAG	Abstract	User-dir. (language-based) Automatic	Centralized	Local Global	Static (user-dir.) Dynamic (JIT)	Perf.-driven	Based on DAGMan	Mediated
Triana [129]	Non-DAG	Abstract	User-dir. (graph-based)	Decentralized	Local	Dynamic (JIT)	Perf.-driven	Based on GAT manager	Peer-to-Peer
Taverna [114]	DAG	Abstract Concrete	User-dir. (language & graph-based)	Centralized	Local	Dynamic (JIT)	Perf.-driven	Task-level (Retry, Alternate Resource)	Centralized
Askalon [61]	Non-DAG	Abstract	User-dir. (language & graph-based)	Decentralized	Global	Dynamic (JIT, prediction-based)	Perf.-driven Market-driven	Task-level (Retry, Alternate Resource) Workflow-level (Rescue)	Centralized User-directed
GridBus [142]	DAG	Abstract Concrete	User-dir. (language-based)	Hierarchical	Local	Static (user-dir.) Dynamic (JIT)	Market-driven	Task-level (Alternate Resource)	Centralized Peer-to-Peer
Proposed System	Non-DAG	Abstract Concrete	User-dir. (language & graph-based)	Centralized	Global	Static (user-dir.) Dynamic (JIT, prediction-based)	Perf.-driven Market-driven	Task-level (Retry, Alternate Resource)	Peer-to-Peer

Table 3.1: Mapping of workflow systems to the described taxonomy. Based on [144]

[a]Just-in-time

the workflow mapping problem. The authors define the problem as "finding a mapping of tasks to resources that minimizes the overall workflow execution time. The workflow execution consists of the running time of the tasks and the data transfer tasks that stage data in and out of the computation." [48] It is noteworthy that, in contrast to the mapping approach presented in Chapter 6 of this thesis, the reduction of the workflow execution time is Pegasus' only objective.

However, the mapping is conducted in a very sophisticated way. First, Pegasus contacts Globus' Monitoring and Discovery Service (MDS) to check which resources are available. Then, it contacts Globus' Replica Location Service (RLS) to locate replicas of required data and searches for intermediate data products produced by former workflow executions. The availability of such data products can reduce the execution time of succeeding workflows since these workflows might include steps that would produce the same data again. If the required data has already been produced, Pegasus removes the corresponding steps from the workflow. Furthermore, it also simulates whether it is more efficient to access data or recompute it (if appropriate). After these optimizations, the system actually selects the resources that will be used to execute the workflow using some standard algorithms (e.g., random and round-robin). In the last step, it adds data stage-in and -out operations (which use Globus' GridFTP [21] for data transfer) to the workflow and then produces the so-called *submit file* that can then be interpreted by workflow execution engines.

Once the submit file has been created, it can be executed using DAGMan (manages task dependencies) [40] and Condor-G (task execution) [74], meaning that Pegasus itself does not contain a workflow execution component, but relies on an existing solution. This is why Pegasus does not provide fault handling mechanisms, but relies on the mechanisms offered by DAGMan (see Table 3.1).

As this description shows, Pegasus is designed towards Grid environments (running the Globus Toolkit middleware). However, the developers of Pegasus also describe a way to utilize Cloud resources (Amazon EC2 instances) to execute the tasks of Pegasus workflows [88]. The setup requires a *submit host* with the software packages Pegasus, DAGMan and Condor installed running outside the Cloud and a virtual machine image preconfigured as a Condor worker. The complete worker software stack requires approx. 2 GB; two different versions for 32 and 64 Bit hardware have to be prepared. A step-by-step guide can be found on the Pegasus web site[1], which starts with the following effort estimation: "Using a cloud like Amazon EC2 to run a workflow application is relatively straightforward. In about a day you can be up and running with a basic configuration."[2]

3.2.1.3 Triana

Triana [48, 99] is a workflow system that was originally developed to perform data analysis in the gravitational wave field. Workflow composition

---

[1] http://pegasus.isi.edu/cloud
[2] Source: http://pegasus.isi.edu/cloud, Section "Getting Started"

is therefore based on the *data flow* between tasks and not the control flow (like in other systems and languages, like Pegasus, Askalon, and BPEL). This means that the dependencies between tasks are data dependencies, ensuring the data producer has finished before the consumer may start. Control structures like loops and conditional behavior are emulated through the use of specific components; a branch component with two or more output connections will output data on different connections, depending upon some condition. Loops are handled by making a circular (data) connection in the workflow and having a *conditional component* break the loop upon a finishing condition, outputting to continue normal workflow execution. According to the authors, the benefit of both of these solutions to control behavior in data flows is that the language representations remain simple. The downside is that the potential for running the workflow on different systems is reduced since the other system must have access not only to the workflow but to the components or services that perform the control operations.

In contrast, this thesis suggests to make use of a control flow-based language and to hide as much complexity as possible using sophisticated modeling tools and abstraction mechanisms like SimpleBPEL presented in Chapter 8. Generally speaking, workflow modeling in Triana is done graph-based; the system comes with a graphical user interface which contains a number of editing capabilities, wizards for on-the-fly creation of tools and GUI builders for creating user interfaces.

Triana's execution component is able to interface to a variety of execution environments using an abstraction library, the Grid Application Toolkit (GAT) [22], for task-based workflows and another abstraction library, the Grid Application Prototype (GAP) [130] for service-based workflows. Practically speaking, this means that GAT and GAP tasks to be invoked from a Triana workflow have to be wrapped as so-called *Triana units* before becoming visible in Triana's user interface, which requires workflow users to write Java code. However, Triana does not support Cloud infrastructures and is not able to dynamically provision additional resources.

Scheduling in Triana is performed on a per-task basis (locally) rather than workflow-based (globally); as described above, local decision making leads to worse execution plans compared to global decision making. The only objective is to reduce the execution time of workflows. Fault-tolerance is not an integral part of the design of the workflow system. However, both GAT and GAP allow to retrieve the status code of operations, e.g., Web service invocations or file transmissions using GridFTP. Based on the retrieved status code, the developer of the GAT/GAP service has to manually handle different fault conditions.

3.2.2 Workflow Quality of Service

Cardoso et al. [36] have contributed fundamentally in the area of quality of service of workflows. The authors define why being able to characterize workflows based on QoS has advantages. It allows for QoS-based design, QoS-based selection and execution of workflows, QoS monitoring, and QoS-based adaption (rescheduling to meet initial QoS requirements). These aspects play a significant role for the solutions related to workflow quality of service in this thesis.

According to the authors, workflow QoS represents the "quantitative and qualitative characteristics of a workflow application necessary to achieve a set of initial requirements." Their QoS model, which is in turn based on the investigation of related work, is composed of three dimensions: time, cost, and reliability.

Thereby, the *task response time* (T) for a task *t* is defined as:

$$T(t) = DT(t) + PT(t),$$

whereby *DT* is the delay time (queuing delay, setup time, etc.) and *PT* is defined as the process time (the time it actually takes to execute the workflow task). The scheduling algorithm presented in Chapter 6 uses this definition to compute the execution time of tasks (and entire workflows).

Task cost (C) for the execution of a task *t* is broken down into two components: enactment cost (EC) and realization cost (RC):

$$C(t) = EC(t) + RC(t).$$

Enactment cost refers to the cost induced by the management and the monitoring of workflow instances. Realization cost is the cost associated with the actual execution of the task. The cost model in this thesis differs: enactment cost is not explicitly factored in the cost calculation (it is seen as part of the realization cost since the management of workflow instances is highly automated using the capabilities of Cloud infrastructures), but data transfer cost (for required input data) is explicitly modeled as part of the total cost of the execution of a task.

Task reliability (R) models task failures and is organized into two main classes: system failures (SF) and process failures (PF). The first type consists of software and hardware failures which lead to a task terminating abnormally. Process failures consist of business process exceptions. Then,

$$R(t) = 1 - (SF\ rate + PF\ rate),$$

whereby system failure rate is calculated as #(unsuccessful executions) / #(called for execution). Process failure rate is computed analogously.

Based on these definitions, the authors define how QoS estimates for tasks can be computed. The basic idea is to let the workflow developer set QoS estimates for each task at workflow design time. Such an estimation is not always possible, because the QoS estimates might heavily depend on user input and the actual system environment. Therefore, the authors propose to study the workflow QoS under real operations and derive an *operational profile*, which partitions the input space and adds a probability of being selected during runtime to each partition. These values and actual input values given, one can compute predictions for all three QoS dimensions at workflow runtime. The same principle is applied to transitions in workflows: the workflow designer has to set transition probabilities, which are then re-computed at runtime. Using the values for all tasks and transitions, it is possible to estimate the QoS of entire workflows. The computation of the workflow's QoS metrics is based on Stochastic Workflow Reduction [35] and not further discussed here.

The presented approach is very interesting and useful to estimate workflow QoS. However, the solution only estimates workflow QoS and provides no means to actually *influence* it. In this thesis, a workflow system is proposed and developed that is able to improve workflow QoS by advanced fault handling mechanisms, automatic infrastructure scaling and cost-efficient scheduling of workflow tasks. Therefore, both approaches complement each other.

Canfora et al. [34] apply Cardoso's QoS model with minor modifications (especially the handling of loops differs from Cardoso's approach) in their BPEL-based middleware. Their goal is to compute a mapping between workflow tasks and resources that matches the user-defined QoS requirement's best. Thereby, a genetic algorithm is used to determine the best-matching mapping from a number of candidate mappings. A *fitness function* with weights for the different fitness factors (i.e., QoS dimensions) classifies all candidates. To simulate evolution, a crossover function randomly replaces services in existing candidate mappings by others in each iteration of the algorithm. The general idea of applying a genetic algorithm to a workflow matchmaking problem with QoS constraints is comparable to the approach presented in Chapter 6. However, the approach in this thesis goes further: it factors in several other scheduling criteria, like the delay induced by data transfers between resources, the costs induced by resource usage and data transfers, and utilization of resources. It further simulates whether the user-defined QoS requirements could be better met, if additional resources were provisioned.

Liu et al. [97] present an extensible QoS computation model for web service selection. The approach is based on an extended service broker (QoS registry) that can store both generic (such as price, execution duration, and reliability) and domain-specific QoS requirements. The actual QoS computation is done via matrix normalization. Each service thereby represents one row in the matrix, whereby the services's QoS parameters build the matrix' columns. By applying an array of user-preference values (for each QoS dimension) to the normalized matrix, a rating is computed.

Mukherjee et al. [111] describe an approach to determine the quality of service of BPEL workflows. The approach focuses on the QoS dimensions *Reliability*, *Response Time* and *Cost*. Thereby, it is required that the workflow developer defines certain parameters before the workflow QoS can be computed. Examples for these parameters are the probability of selecting workflow branches, the number of iterations of loops, and values for reliability, response time, and cost. The authors claim to support most workflow pattern that may be expressed by BPEL and argue that the approach by Cardoso (see above) cannot be applied, because "BPEL is semantically more powerful than workflow languages." To sum up, the approach allows users to compute the expected QoS for BPEL processes when all relevant input parameters have been set manually.

3.3 A QoS-supporting Workflow System Based on Standards

The following subsections sketch the architecture of the proposed workflow system. First, it is discussed why building new workflow systems on standards is beneficial; afterwards, some details on BPEL, the de-facto industry standard for workflow modeling, are given.

From a bird's-eye view, it is obvious that two different functional areas exist: an execution environment and an end-user oriented development and monitoring environment. These functional areas will be described separately in Sections 3.3.3 and 3.3.4.

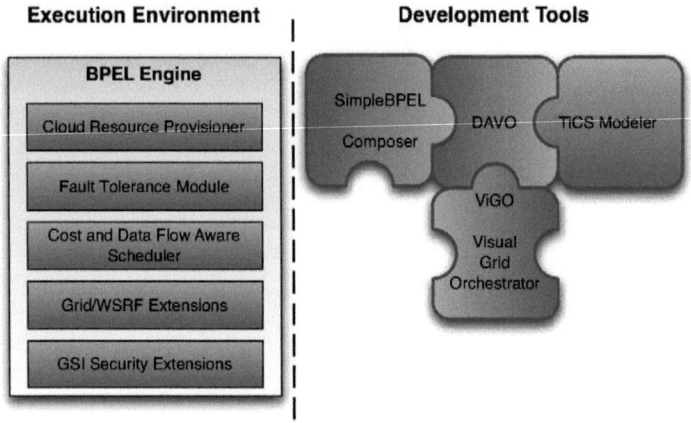

Figure 3.2: Overview of the development and runtime components of the proposed system

3.3.1 Workflow Modeling Based on Standards

This thesis suggests the use of proven (industrial) standards for scientific workflow modeling instead of defining domain-specific languages for different application domains. The latter is a tedious task since one has to define the language, verify it and implement a workflow engine for the language. This is – at least in part – comparable to "reinventing the wheel". Furthermore, building on existing standards has the advantage that integration with other standard-based systems is possible (without writing a lot of mediation code). A detailed discussion concerning the standardization topic can be found in a paper by Barker and van Hemert [28]. The authors state that one should stick to standards; they encourage workflow designers to use the *de facto* industry standard BPEL and to invest time in tool support for BPEL (like increased modeling abstraction for special domains) instead of inventing their own special-purpose workflow system.

Besides strong tool support (especially with respect to workflow execution engines), BPEL has one main advantage that perfectly fits into the idea of a general-purpose workflow system. It has been proven that BPEL is Turing-complete and well-defined [47, 93], meaning that the language is expressive enough to model any kind of workflow. Therewith, Requirement 1 (Turing-completeness) is fulfilled. A detailed introduction to the BPEL standard is given in the next subsection.

Therefore, instead of starting development from scratch, this work is based on BPEL and makes use of existing software wherever possible. The system sketched below is based on ActiveBPEL [1], the workflow enactment engine developed by ActiveEndpoints, a stable and well-documented software that is published under GNU Public License (GPL).

All entities to be arranged to a BPEL-based workflow need to be available as SOAP-based [19] Web services. Therewith, the components not only get a common, but also a standardized[3], interface that allows seamless integration with other standard-based software. As already sketched in Section 2.2, scientists would often like to combine existing software components to workflow applications. Typically, these programs are available as command-line driven binaries. So, they need to be equipped with a Web service interface first. A variety of development tools exist that allow users to easily "wrap" those existing applications. For instance, Java 6 (JAX-WS) allows to easily create Web services. Some tools that are created specifically for stateful Web services, a special kind of Web services, are the Grid Development Tools (GDT) [75], the Legacy Code Description Framework (LCDL) [87], both developed at the University of Marburg, and Globus Introduce [79]. Stateful Web services, implemented according to the Web Services Resource Framework (WSRF) [11] specifications, are detailed in Chapter 7. Using one of these tools, any existing legacy application can be wrapped into a Web service, resulting in a common interface for all components and the fulfillment of Requirement 2.

Section 3.3.2 summarizes the most important concepts of BPEL.

3.3.2 Business Process Execution Language

The Business Process Execution Language for Web services is the de facto (industrial) standard for Web service composition in business applications. It has emerged from the earlier proposed XLANG [16] and Web service Flow Language (WSFL) [17]. BPEL enables the construction of complex Web services composed of other Web services that act as the basic activities in the process model of the newly constructed service. Access to a *process* is exposed by the execution engine through a Web service interface (Web Services Description Language, WSDL [39]), allowing the process to be accessed by Web service clients or to be used as a basic activity in other processes.

---
[3]SOAP is a W3C specification[19].

BPEL offers a conceptual distinction between abstract processes that describe the external view on the process model and executable processes that describe the workflow of the compound service and can be executed by a process execution engine in order to provide the functionality of the compound service to a client. Access to the process is exposed by the execution engine through a Web service interface, allowing those processes to be accessed by Web service clients or to act as basic activities in other process specifications.

BPEL features several basic activities which allow for interaction with the services being arranged in the workflow. These activities include *invoke*, *receive* and *reply*. Furthermore, it is possible to wait for some time (*wait*), terminate the execution of the workflow instance (*terminate* activity), copy data from one message to another (*assign*), announce errors (*throw*), or just to do nothing (*empty* activity).

To allow users to compose complex operations, a variety of structured activities exists. *Sequence* offers the ability to define ordered sequences of steps, *flow* executes a collection of steps in parallel whereas the execution order is given by links between the activities. The *switch* activity allows branching, *pick* executes one of several alternative paths and loops can be defined using the *while* activity. A workflow can be represented as a *Directed Acyclic Graph* (DAG) or a *non*-DAG [143]. DAG-based workflows only allow for *sequence*, *parallelism* and *choice* as structural elements. Non-DAG workflows also allow workflow developers to define *conditional* loops. Loops are quite frequently used in both scientific and business workflows to express a task which is executed repeatedly (for instance, until a condition is satisfied). Since BPEL allows users to define conditional loops via *while*, it can be classified as a *non-DAG*-based workflow language. This makes BPEL much more expressive and versatile than most of the workflow languages and system presented in Section 3.2.

Furthermore, BPEL includes the feature of scoping activities and specifying fault handlers and compensation handlers for scopes. Fault handlers are executed when exceptions occur, for instance, through the execution of the mentioned *throw* activity. Compensation handlers are activated when faults occur or when compensation activities that force compensation of a scope are executed.

All entities orchestrated in a workflow are seen as so-called "partners" in BPEL. Partners offer their functionality via their WSDL [39] port type description. The syntactical element *partnerLink* contains two attributes apart from the partnerLinkType (which refers to the port type): *myRole* and *partnerRole*, which specify which roles are played by the composition and the partner. During runtime, partners are mapped to actual service instances by the workflow-enactment engine.

As this short introduction to BPEL clarifies, the language specification [24] does not specify deployment aspects and security-related settings of business processes. This means, that is up to the implementors of the standard to define the syntax of deployment descriptors and security settings. Regarded with favor, this leaves freedom to the implementors. This also incidentally opens many possibilities for extensions to a BPEL engine without breaking compatibility with the language standard.

3.3.3 Execution Environment

In the context of BPEL, the software that hosts and executes workflows is called BPEL engine or just engine for short. The proposed execution environment uses ActiveEndpoint's ActiveBPEL engine as the basis for further enhancements regarding the aforementioned requirements. As described above, the BPEL standard (and the standard-compliant implementation ActiveBPEL) already fulfill Requirement 1 and 2. Therefore, only the remaining six requirements need to be explicitly covered by this thesis.

In total, five enhancements to the execution environment are proposed (see Figure 3.3). They cover all aforementioned Quality of Service requirements for the execution environment. In the following sections, each extension is described briefly. Details on their architectures, implementations, and evaluations can be found in the respective chapters.

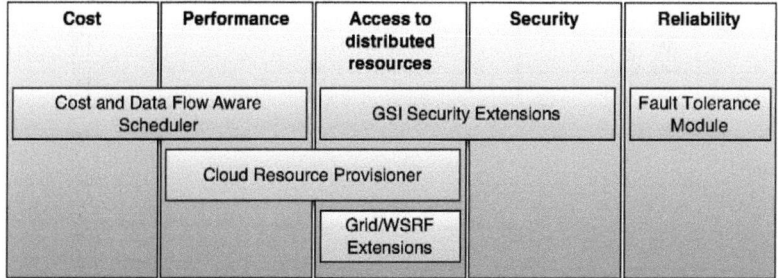

Figure 3.3: Extensions to the BPEL engine. Some extensions cover more than one requirement

The engine already provides several useful features. When a workflow is *deployed* (installed) to the engine, it automatically verifies whether it is syntactically correct[4]. Given a syntactically correct workflow description, it automatically generates a WSDL interface for the workflow such that it can be invoked using standardized mechanisms (SOAP protocol, HTTP). Furthermore, it already offers basic security mechanisms, namely symmetric encryption (HTTPS/TLS).

Due to the relatively large data sets (in all sample applications) there is a need for efficient data transfer. Web services communicate using the SOAP protocol [19], which defines the (XML-based) message format for data exchange between services. If one wishes to send binary data to a service (which is quite a common case), the binary data has to be encoded in order to be transmitted via a SOAP message. Binary data in SOAP messages is encoded as BASE64 – with the consequence that the encoded data in the message is 33 % larger than the original data itself. Another solution is to

---
[4]using static analysis

make use of SOAP with Attachments (SwA) [29]. It defines a way to attach binary data to a SOAP message (outside the SOAP envelope), which circumvents the conversion to BASE64 and thus the induced transmission overhead. Its successor, SOAP Message Transmission Optimization Mechanism (MTOM) [18], makes use of XOP (XML-binary Optimized Packaging) to further optimize of process of transporting binary data within an XML message. However, one major performance bottleneck still remains: All data is sent using the BPEL engine as an intermediary between the services that need to exchange data (see left side of Figure 3.4); the workflow taxonomy presented in Section 3.2.1.1 would classify this data movement method as *centralized*.

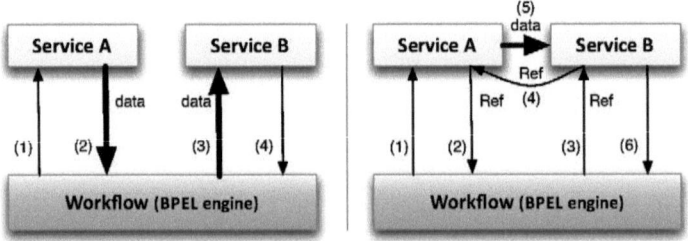

Figure 3.4: Normal transfer of data using SOAP compared to the Flex-SwA reference passing principle

A solution that both avoids the conversion to BASE64 and the transmission of all data through the BPEL engine is Flex-SwA developed by Heinzl et al. [80]. When Flex-SwA is used, only a reference to the actual data is transmitted via the SOAP message, and the binary data is transferred from host to host (bypassing the BPEL engine, turning it into *peer-to-peer* data movement) by the Flex-SwA middleware. Thus, the engine does not represent a bottleneck for transferring data. Therefore, Flex-SwA is used as the basis for data transfer between services in this work.

3.3.3.1 Cloud Resource Provisioner

Cloud computing is concerned with offering and using abstracted IT infrastructures in networked environments, typically the Internet. It is commonly agreed that three layers of abstraction exist: Software as a Service (SaaS), Platform as a Service (PaaS) and Infrastructure as a Service (IaaS) [73]. While SaaS providers typically run Web-based applications that clients may access using their Web browser and pay for them via subscriptions, PaaS and IaaS are less focused on end users. PaaS is tailored towards companies that want to offer services to customers, but do not want to host the services on their own. They can make use of PaaS offerings that allow them to deploy applications to hosting environments (such as .NET/Azure or Java/Google App

Engine) installed on the PaaS provider's resources. Especially IaaS-based Clouds are ideal environments for solving computationally demanding problems when no or insufficient local resources are available. IaaS-based Cloud computing delivers entire computing infrastructures (computing power, storage, etc.) based on a pay-per-use model. Users may access resources on-demand through simple interfaces such as Web services, without knowledge or control of the technology and the infrastructure used by the provider. Since virtualization technology is used by most providers, users can configure virtual machine images with customized operating systems and installed user applications that are stored in the Cloud infrastructure. Upon request, such a virtual machine is booted on a physical host in the infrastructure and it may be used like a dedicated physical host shortly after the request. The price varies depending on the requested configuration of the virtual machine (number of CPUs, amount of RAM, instance storage).

To take advantage of the flexibility induced by such infrastructures, the workflow system should be able to take advantage of on-demand resource provisioning and thereby automatically scale in and out using IaaS. This would allow the systems to react to increasing and decreasing demand and thus provide near-constant execution performance. The current market leaders in IaaS-based Cloud computing rely on SOAP-based Web services which, without any doubt, allows users to provision virtual machines from BPEL processes by invoking the corresponding provisioning service at the provider. However, this procedure would heavily clutter the workflow with non-functional aspects. Furthermore, the procedure would be even more complicated than manually invoking stateful services: After provisioning a new virtual machine, one would have to query its address, point the succeeding invoke operations to the retrieved address and so on. Moreover, a logic would be required to decide if and when virtual machines should be added to execute a workflow. This logic also would also have to be modeled in BPEL, further cluttering the workflow.

Therefore, a solution is proposed that combines the versatile and powerful composition and control mechanisms of BPEL with an adaptive runtime environment without breaking the compatibility with existing standards. The system seamlessly integrates dedicated resources and on-demand resources provided by Cloud infrastructures. Figure 3.5 sketches the general idea. The mechanism integrates into ActiveBPEL engine without needing to alter the language standard. Furthermore, the BPEL process itself remains unchanged. Within the deployment descriptor (refer to Section 3.3.2) of the corresponding workflow, the default invoke handler is replaced by a custom invoke handler (detailed in Section 4.4.1). For each invoke operation, the invoke handler (called *LoadBalancer* in the figure) is enquired to find a suitable machine. It contacts a scheduler[5] which is responsible for finding a machine that hosts the required service and is capable of carrying out the computation (i.e., it is not overloaded). If it does not find a suitable machine, it invokes the provisioning component, which in turn starts a new virtual machine, installs the required software and returns the machine's address as soon as it is ready.

---

[5] As discussed later, the scheduler is exchangeable.

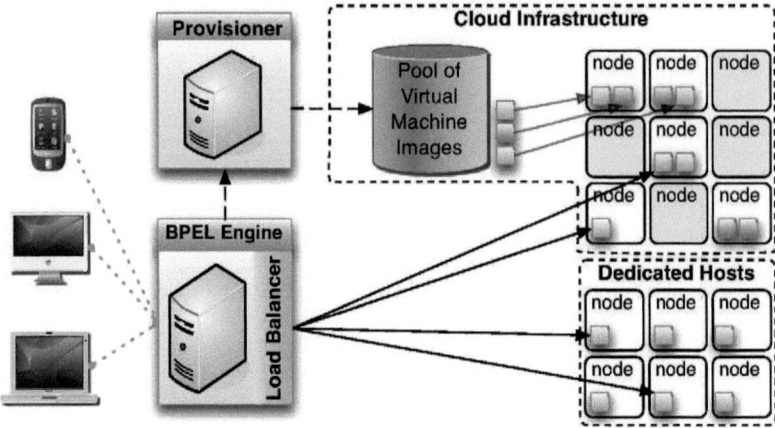

Figure 3.5: Topology of on-demand provisioning component

3.3.3.2 Improvements to Fault Handling

The development of software that follows the service-oriented architecture (SOA) concept differs from traditional approaches to software development. Web services, as the most-widely used implementation approach of components of SOAs and their composition to applications using workflow technology, allow developers to build distributed applications that have to deal with other sources of errors than non-distributed applications. Instead of tying application components together via (local) method calls in a programming language like Java or C, the components are loosely-coupled via message exchanges controlled by an execution engine, the BPEL engine to be precise.

Particularly in scientific domains, where long-running or computationally-intensive workflows are to be executed, fault handling is very important, since the failure of a single component might lead to an abandonment of the entire workflow. BPEL already offers a fault handling mechanism (*catch* activity) to react to faults. Within a catch block, arbitrary BPEL code to handle the fault may be executed. While it is perfectly reasonable to handle faults related to the "logic"[6] of the workflow using this mechanism, handling *infrastructural faults*[7] would clutter the composition logic with non-functional aspects. To simply retry a faulted invoke activity up to three times, one would have to place a loop that contains the invoke activity to be retried in the catch block of each invoke.

Consequently, this work identifies classes of faults that can be handled automatically and defines a XML-based policy language to configure automatic recovery behavior without the need for adding explicit fault handling mech-

---

[6]Those faults subsume all faults that are generated when there is a problem with the information being processed. Examples are: invalid input values given or requested data not found in database.

[7]Network timeouts, faults risen in middleware, server outages, etc.

anisms to the BPEL process. The approach provides automatic Cloud-based redundancy that allows substitution of defective services. A sample policy is depicted in Listing 3.1.

```
1 <Fault name="Middleware Fault (global)">
    <bycause value="MidlewareFault"/>
3   <OriginHost retry="true">
      <MaxTries value="3" />
5   </OriginHost>
    <Substitution resources="different">
7     <MaxTries value="1" />
    </Substitution>
9 </Fault>
```

Listing 3.1: A sample fault handling policy. Faults classified as MiddlewareFault will be recovered by retrying at most three times followed by the attempt to substitute the faulty service

The fault handling mechanism integrates into ActiveBPEL engine without needing to alter the language standard. Furthermore, the BPEL process itself remains unchanged. Within the deployment descriptor (refer to Section 3.3.2) of the corresponding workflow, the default invoke handler is replaced by a custom invoke handler that performs the fault handling (see Line 4 in Listing 3.2). As a parameter for the custom invoke handler, one simply has to add a file containing the desired fault handling policies (Lines 5–6). Since the custom invoke handler is added per partnerLink, one can configure per service if and how the fault handling mechanism should be used.

```
1 <partnerLink name="ecgAnalyzerPL">
    <partnerRole
3     endpointReference="dynamic"
      invokeHandler="java:FaultTolerantIH?
5                   GlobalPolicy="global.xml"
                    LocalPolicy="local.xml" />
7 />
```

Listing 3.2: Integration of a custom invoke handler into ActiveBPEL engine

While the proposed mechanism is capable of handling faults concerning the services (and hosts) that are orchestrated to workflows, it does not improve the overall reliability of the workflow system. The (machine hosting the) workflow engine remains a single point of failure and poses a potential performance bottleneck. The ActiveBPEL engine already features *process persistence*, which allows "processes to be automatically resumed after an engine shutdown by maintaining all process state information." [49] This feature is very helpful in the context of long-running workflows since it allows a system to resume workflows and therefore circumvents the loss of CPU hours (for workflow steps that finished before the system crash). However, it does not guarantee that, after a crash of the machine hosting the engine, the workflow engine is permanently available to workflow users. Furthermore, if many users run workflows in parallel, the machine might be overloaded and not be able to execute the requested workflows. To solve these issues, a deployment scenario for the workflow engine is presented that makes uses of features like load balancing, health monitoring and on-demand provisioning to guarantee the availability and prevent performance drops of the engine.

3.3.3.3 Cost and Data Flow Aware Scheduling

Workflow scheduling is an important topic because a workflow's total execution time (so-called makespan) strongly depends on the efficient usage of available resources. However, in distributed environments, the matchmaking[8] process must take data dependencies between workflow steps into account, since unnecessary data transmission between machines executing dependent workflow steps may heavily prolong the workflow execution time and thus increase the cost. Thereby, the services used by the workflow might be distributed in different ways: (1) some may run in Cloud A, some in Cloud B; (2) some may run on locally available resources, some on on-demand resources (Hybrid Cloud); (3) they might be distributed among different geographical regions/data centers of the same Cloud provider. Exactly the same problems occur when services are spread around different Grid sites.

To circumvent the disadvantages induced by distribution, a scheduling algorithm is proposed that takes resource utilization and data dependencies between workflow steps into account. It is Cloud-aware and is enabled to provision additional virtual machines from IaaS infrastructures, if beneficial. The algorithm belongs to the class of so-called genetic algorithms, which work heuristically and provide a good compromise between scheduling runtime (complexity of the assignment problem) and optimality of the assignment.

It is a multi-objective scheduling algorithm that takes both *workflow execution time* (consisting of computational time and data transmission time) and *cost induced by the resource selection* into account. Since multi-objective approaches produce *Pareto optimal* solutions, the workflow user can define weights for both criteria that lead to an unique solution.

The approach does neither require any changes to the BPEL standard nor do the workflows themselves have to be changed. However, some additional information has to be annotated to the edges and vertices of the workflow graph: expected execution time per invoke operation and expected amount of data to be transferred between steps. This data is, along with the custom invoke handler settings, used to integrate the algorithm into workflows, stored in the workflow's deployment descriptor.

3.3.3.4 WSRF-related Extensions

As detailed above, scientific workflow environments should be able to utilize distributed resources, such as Grid and Cloud environments. Access to Cloud resources is already covered by the Cloud Resource Provisioner extension. However, Grid systems have some peculiarities that require a different approach.

Modern Grid middleware environments like the Globus Toolkit 4 (GT4) [8], Unicore/GS [15] and gLite [7] are built on the Web Services Resource Framework (WSRF) specification which extends Web services. This allows the creation of so-called stateful Web services which can store the state of operations and other properties without breaking the compatibility to standard Web services. While it is also possible with "normal" Web services to

---

[8]Matchmaking basically means assignment of tasks to resources.

implement some notion of state, the WSRF specification defines a consistent and interoperable way to do so.

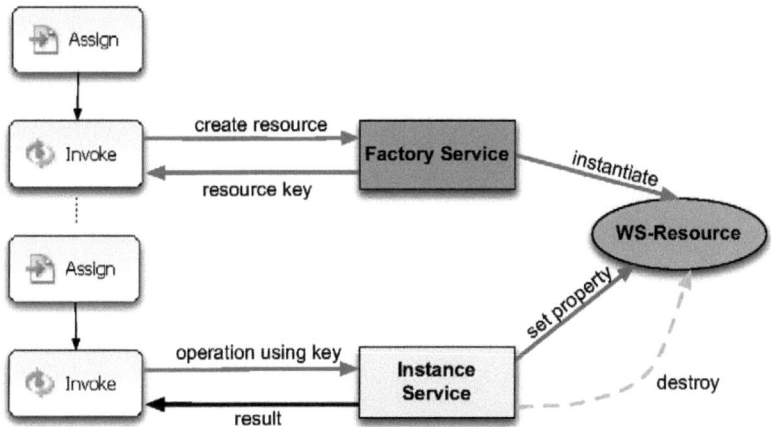

Figure 3.6: Invocation of WSRF service using standard BPEL operations

In the Grid environment, however, BPEL has a major drawback: it is not capable of dealing with WSRF-compliant services [38, 127] transparently to the workflow designer. The designer has to manually take care of creating resources, copying identifiers and so on (see Figure 3.6). This is a tedious task, as one has to manually deal with the (factory) pattern introduced by the underlying WSRF standard. The sequence of calls is as follows: (1) *assign* parameters to the call that invokes the factory service, (2) invoke the factory service to create a resource (which represents the state of the service), (3) assign the retrieved *key* that identifies the resource and copy it to into the following invoke operation, (4) invocation of the target operation of the stateful service.

Therefore, additions to the BPEL standard are proposed that reflect the *factory pattern* used by WSRF. Three additional activities are added to the language: (1) *gridCreateResourceInvoke*, (2) *gridInvoke* and (3) *gridDestroyResourceInvoke*. Processes modeled using these extensions are significantly shorter and more intuitive to model: The description of the activities used to create, invoke and destroy WSRF resources is reduced by a factor of approximately five with the extensions. Together with a further extension related to Grid security (see Section 3.3.3.5), it is possible to invoke any WSRF-based service, including important "standard" services of Grid middlewares, such as GT4's GRAM (Grid Resource Allocation Manager), which can be invoked to directly run applications (that are not wrapped as services) on Grid resources.

3.3.3.5 Security-related Extensions

Currently, the BPEL security concept is not equipped to deal with complex multi-protocol Grid environments and does not integrate with the Grid Security Infrastructure (GSI, details in Section 7.2.2). While BPEL is mainly focused on anonymous HTTPS-based TLS security or manual role-based authentication encoded in SOAP headers, Grid computing has a mandatory user-centric security approach using X.509 certificates which far exceeds the scope and capability of the BPEL security model.

To nullify this disadvantage of BPEL in Grid environments, a further extension to the aforementioned WSRF-related activities is proposed. It empowers BPEL to make use of the mechanisms provided by GSI by allowing the workflow developer to define the required security level (integrity or encryption), choose between different security protocols and so forth. Since GSI heavily makes use of certificates to perform authentication (and PKI-based message encryption and key exchange using the certificate's public key), the engine must be able to perform certificate management. In GSI, *delegation* (transfer of rights and privileges to another party) must also be supported in order to utilize Grid resources. This is why so-called *proxy certificates* (a certificate derived from the delegator's certificate, with a limited duration of validity) must be supported. The proposed system offers proxy management, including lifetime monitoring and refreshing of proxy certificates. Refreshing of proxy certificates is a key requirement, as workflow execution times can far exceed Grid proxy certificate lifetimes and an expired certificate would cause an abandonment of the workflow.

3.3.4 Development Environment

The development environment consists of several software tools for different purposes. First of all, a modeling tool named *Domain-Adaptable Visual Orchestrator (DAVO)*, which supports the entire BPEL standard, is proposed. Existing BPEL editors that have been developed in several research and commercial activities concentrate on the design and development of graphical BPEL editors focusing on a clear visualization and syntactically correct mapping of the graphical representation to BPEL code. Thus, the existing BPEL workflow editors are only suitable for Web service experts who are familiar with the details of Web services and BPEL. Non-Web service experts are normally overburdened by these editors. By contrast, DAVO provides abstractions for process modeling and is designed for non-Web service experts. DAVO is a domain-adaptable, graphical BPEL4WS workflow editor. The key benefits that distinguish DAVO from other graphical BPEL workflow editors are the *adaptable data model* and *user interface* which permit customization to specific domain needs. This increases usability for non-Web service experts.

To meet the specific requirements of Grid environments, the adaptability of DAVO is used to create a tool specifically for Grid-based workflows. The tool, ViGO (Visual Grid Orchestrator), offers – as its name suggests – extensions for service-oriented Grid computing based on WSRF [11] to permit easy handling of stateful Web services. Moreover, it features graphical dialogs to configure the security settings (for usage of Grid Security Infrastructure) and presents a visual feedback whether workflow operations use security or not.

The cooperation with researchers from other disciplines has shown that further simplifications in workflow modeling are desirable. As a consequence, it is proposed to separate workflow development into two distinct roles with clear areas of responsibility. Experienced users (BPEL experts) carry out the development of BPEL fragments for the needs of the given application domain. This task requires a standard BPEL modeling tool with the capability of storing these fragments. The second role is carried out by a domain expert who simply has to combine the fragments, as required for his/her application. Here, a tool is required that enables the domain expert to intuitively model his/her experiments, or his/her application in general. To achieve this goal, DAVO is extended to enable users to save BPEL fragments (called *SimpleBPEL fragments* or SBFs for short in the following) to a library. An end user may use another tool, *SimpleBPEL Composer*, to model a workflow from existing SBFs. Thus, no knowledge about BPEL or Web services is required.

3.4 Summary

The requirements that were deduced in Chapter 2 were used to construct the architecture of the proposed workflow system. The Business Process Execution Language (BPEL) was chosen as the basis for the workflow system to be developed. The architecture consists of two building blocks: execution environment and development environment. A stable, well-documented and industrial-proven implementation, ActiveBPEL, serves as foundation for the execution environment. It is extended using several components to fulfill the defined QoS-requirements. The extensions enable the system to (1) utilize distributed computing infrastructures, such as Grids and Clouds, (2) provide security mechanisms, (3) assure constant performance of the system, (4) improve reliability, and (5) control the cost of workflow execution. The development environment consists of several tools with graphical user interfaces that allow users to model workflows on different levels of abstraction, provide a monitoring feature and allow to manage Cloud resources.

Chapter 4
Automatic Infrastructure Scaling

Contents

4.1	Introduction	47
4.2	Technical Background	48
	4.2.1 Dynamic Resource Selection in BPEL	48
	4.2.2 Cloud Computing	50
4.3	Related Work	52
4.4	Cloud-enabled Auto-Scaling Architecture	53
	4.4.1 Extensions to the BPEL Engine	55
	4.4.2 Load Balancer	56
	4.4.3 Load Analyzer	58
4.5	Implementation	58
	4.5.1 Extensions to the BPEL Engine	59
	4.5.2 Load Balancer	60
	4.5.3 Load Analyzer	64
4.6	Experimental Results	64
4.7	Summary	68

4.1 Introduction

Scientific workflow systems and computing resources are typically shared by a number of researchers. When they access the system concurrently, situations might occur in which insufficient resources are available to efficiently execute all workflows. In the best case, this leads only to a prolonged execution time and thus a reduction in the perceived quality of service. The worst case would be that the execution of workflow steps takes so long that they are abandoned due to timeouts raised by the TCP stack of the underlying operating system. Ellison et al. conducted an in-depth discussion of the influence of simultaneous access to a static infrastructure in an excellent paper [59].

As already sketched in Section 2.3.2.1, the user should be guaranteed constant performance (ideally, he/she should have the illusion that he/she is using the workflow environment exclusively). Therefore, the system must be *scalable*, which implies the capability of increasing the system's computing capacity. Speaking of the workflow system developed in this thesis, the computing capacity can be increased by adding machines to the pool of available resources that offer the web services required by the workflows that are to be executed. Furthermore, the workflow system must be able to take advantage of an increased computing capacity; it must be able to *dynamically assign workflow steps to resources at workflow runtime*. While BPEL works well for modeling processes with target hosts for the execution of process steps that are known before runtime (see Section 3.3.2), it has some drawbacks when it comes to dynamically selecting target hosts at runtime. Details are given in Section 4.2.

This chapter presents an approach that allows the BPEL engine to dynamically schedule a workflow's service invocations at the time of workflow execution. As an example scheduling schema, load-based scheduling is discussed and implemented. Scalability of the underlying resource pool is achieved by integrating a provisioning component that dynamically launches virtual machines in on-demand infrastructures and deploys the required middleware components (Web/Grid service stack) on-the-fly.

What is more, the BPEL engine itself might be a bottleneck when many workflow instances are run in parallel. To solve this problem, a deployment scenario for the BPEL engine has been developed in which additional BPEL engines are automatically provisioned when the load increases. This procedure is transparent to workflow users, as the engines are placed behind a DNS-based load balancer. Details are described in Section 5.6.

This chapter is organized as follows: Section 4.2 details the underlying problem; in Section 4.3 related work is discussed. Based on these insights, Section 4.4 describes the proposed architecture as well as the design of the approach. Section 4.5 describes implementation details, while the implementation is evaluated in Section 4.6. The chapter is summarized in Section 4.7.

Parts of this chapter have been published in [53].

4.2 Technical Background

4.2.1 Dynamic Resource Selection in BPEL

BPEL offers a rich vocabulary and control mechanisms to model the control flow of workflows (like *receive*, *invoke* and *reply*, parallel execution, loops, error handling, and compensation-mechanisms to perform roll-back actions). For this chapter, the *invoke* activity is of particular interest. It is used to model the invocation of external services. The target service to be invoked is described via a partnerLink that – among others – contains two important elements: (1) *partnerLinkType* and (2) *EndpointReference* (EPR). (1) is static information that must be known at workflow design time. It refers to the WSDL description of a partner service's *portType*, while (2) refers to the concrete service to be invoked. An EPR contains a service's name, its port (and binding mechanism) and its address given by a URI. However, the language standard does not define any deployment-specific mechanisms like *Service Discovery* or *Resource Selection*.

Static definition of target hosts might be sufficient for typical business processes, such as the often quoted loan approval example, since these environments are quite static; services are offered continuously over the Internet and situations like peak loads are handled *internally* by the different providers (meaning that, if necessary, the provider's infrastructure handles load balancing internally using techniques like DNS load balancing, which makes it more complicated). When it comes to modeling computationally intensive workflows like scientific workflows with BPEL, the situation differs. Often, scientists would like to orchestrate a bunch of self-written services (which, in turn, encapsulate existing programs) to perform data analysis, simulations, and so forth. The services are typically installed on a number of workstations or a cluster within the researcher's department. The created workflows are accessed (concurrently) by a number of scientists. With such a setup, peak load situations might occur when many researchers access the workflows concurrently and/or the amount of available resources decreases due to hardware failure or other reasons. As a result, either the response times would increase or the invoked service might not react at all, causing the entire process to be abandoned. This may lead a decrease in the stability in the workflow system and and increase in cost due to wasted CPU hours as a result of lost intermediary results from preceding process steps. Therefore, it would be highly beneficial to have a BPEL implementation that automatically selects appropriate target hosts at runtime. Thereby, one must determine which machines offer the required service(s) and then apply some kind of load balancing to circumvent overloading machines.

While it is possible to achieve this with standard BPEL activities, such workflows are relatively complicated to model and clutter the workflow's logic with infrastructural concerns. Using standard BPEL activities, one would have to contact (*invoke*) a *Discovery* service (a UDDI registry, for instance) that returns the address of a matching target service. Internally, the service would have to select the machine (which hosts the required service) that matches best (for example, the machine with the lowest utilization). Then, within the BPEL workflow, one would have to assign the returned target address to the SOAP header of the corresponding *invoke* activity, as sketched in Listing 4.1. This is possible at runtime due to the two-part structure of the partnerLink definition, as explained above. The EPR is evaluated at runtime and may even be set at runtime (Listing 4.1). In total, this would lead to at least two additional *assign* operations (assign parameters to Discovery invoke operation, copy result from response to the actual invoke operation) and one additional invoke operation (invocation of Discovery Service) *per invoke operation of the workflow*.

```
 1  <assign>
      <copy>
 3      <from>
          <literal>
 5          <wsa:EndpointReference xmlns:ns="NSPACE">
              <wsa:Address>http://FQDN:PORT/SERVICE-ADDRESS</↵
                 wsa:Address>
 7            <wsa:ServiceName PortName="Port">ns:NAME</↵
                 wsa:ServiceName>
              <wsa:ReferenceParameters>
 9              <wsa:To>...</wsa:To>
                <wsa:Action>...</wsa:Action>
11            </wsa:ReferenceParameters>
            </wsa:EndpointReference>
13        </literal>
        </from>
15      <to variable="targetEPR"/>
      </copy>
17    <copy>
        <from variable="targetEPR" />
19      <to partnerLink="targetPL" />
      </copy>
21  </assign>
```

Listing 4.1: Manual runtime setting of an service endpoint in BPEL

4.2.2 Cloud Computing

The proposed system goes even further and introduces the feature of automatic scale out in peak load situations (and scale in when the utilization is low). Scale out means that the system scales horizontally by adding additional machines (running the required software) to the pool of available resources. Adding additional resources that can be used (almost) immediately stabilizes the workflow system when a peak load occurs; thus, response times can be decreased. Such resources may be acquired from on-demand infrastructures, which are typically referred to as Cloud computing infrastructures.

Cloud computing is concerned with offering and using abstracted IT infrastructures in networked environments, typically the Internet. It is commonly agreed that three layers of abstraction exist: Software as a Service (SaaS), Platform as a Service (PaaS) and Infrastructure as a Service (IaaS) [73]. While SaaS providers typically run Web-based applications that clients may access using their Web browser and pay for them via subscriptions, PaaS and IaaS are less focused on end-users. PaaS is tailored towards companies that want to offer services to customers, but do not want to host the services on their own. They can make use of PaaS offerings that allow them to deploy applications to hosting environments (such as .NET/Azure or Java/Google App Engine) installed on the PaaS provider's resources. For the given usage scenario, PaaS infrastructures are inadequate, as they typically do not allow users to execute "classic" binary applications ("native" code, such as .exe-programs on Windows, ELF binaries on Linux, etc.). Instead, they only allow users to deploy applications written specifically for the used platform, meaning that, for example, Google's App Engine only allows developers to run programs written in Java and Python. Windows Azure also clearly prefers so-called "managed code"[1] written in languages supported by the .NET runtime (such as C#, Visual Basic .NET, etc.). However, using so-called *VM roles*, it is also possible to run existing legacy applications. This is intended as a intermediate solution to help customers ease the migration of existing applications into Microsoft's Cloud offerings.

Especially IaaS-based Clouds are ideal environments for solving computationally demanding problems when no or insufficient local resources are available. IaaS-based Cloud computing delivers entire computing infrastructures (computing power, storage, etc.) based on a pay-per-use model. Users may access resources on-demand through simple interfaces such as Web services, without knowledge or control of the technology and the infrastructure used by the provider. For the implementation, many Cloud computing providers make use of virtualization. This allows providers to run more than one virtual machine on a dedicated host and offers user isolation, which enables the provider to give the customer full (root) access to the (virtual) machines. Root access is often necessary to install and configure software and to open the Cloud infrastructure for a broad variety of applications. Upon request, such a virtual machine is booted on a physical host in the infrastructure and it may be used like a dedicated physical host shortly after the request. The price varies depending on the requested configuration of the virtual machine (number of CPUs, amount of RAM, instance storage).

4.2.2.1 Amazon Web Services

One of the first actors on the Cloud market was Amazon, which founded a subsidiary company in 2002, Amazon Web Services (AWS). The first IaaS service, Amazon's Elastic Compute Cloud (EC2) [2], was introduced in August 2006. EC2 is a service that offers resizable computing capacity to customers. Using a Web service interface, customers may boot (and shut them down) new machines in minutes and use them to scale capacity of their infrastructure. The machines can be equipped with custom software (including the operating system). At present, AWS offers 9 different types of on-demand machines that vary in their hardware specifications and price (see Table 4.1 for details). AWS resources are paid per use on an hourly basis. In addition, one has to pay for traffic that enters and leaves Amazon's data centers. Amazon EC2 is currently available in five regions: US East (Virginia), US West (California), EU (Ireland), and Asia Pacific (Singapore and Tokyo). In addition, AWS offers several other services, such as Simple Storage Service (S3) [3], a highly redundant Cloud storage system, and Elastic Block Store (EBS). EBS provides storage volumes that can be attached to a running Amazon EC2 instance and exposed as a device within the instance. EBS and S3 are very helpful for running Cloud applications, since the data written to the

---

[1]"An application that is designed to be a hosted service in Windows Azure consists of discrete scalable components built with managed code [...].", http://msdn.microsoft.com/en-us/library/gg432976.aspx

Type	RAM	ECU	Storage	Arch	Price/hour
Standard					
Small (Default)	1.7 GB	1	160 GB	32 Bit	$0.095
Large	7.5 GB	4	850 GB	64 Bit	$0.38
Extra Large	15 GB	8	1690 GB	64 Bit	$0.76
Micro					
Micro	0.613 GB	1-2	EBS only	32+64 Bit	$0.025
High-Memory					
Extra Large	17.1 GB	6.5	420 GB	64 Bit	$0.57
Double Extra Large	34.2 GB	13	850 GB	64 Bit	$1.14
Quadruple Extra Large	68.4 GB	26	1690 GB	64 Bit	$2.28
High-CPU					
Medium	1.7 GB	5	350 GB	32 Bit	$0.19
Extra Large	7 GB	20	1690 GB	64 Bit	$0.76

Table 4.1: Amazon instance types and prices for region EU and Linux operating system (Windows instances cost more per hour due to license fees)

normal hard disk of an EC2 instance is lost when the machine is shut down. Therefore, data that needs to be maintained has to be stored, e.g. on S3, before a machine is shut down.

Other popular IaaS vendors are Rackspace[2], GoGrid[3] and Flexiant (the product is called FlexiScale)[4]. Using different brand names (e.g., Cloud Servers and Cloud Files for Rackspace), the vendors offer services comparable to the described services offered by Amazon. Resource usage is also paid per hour.

4.3 Related Work

Di Penta et al. [50] have presented a dynamic binding framework called WS Binder. It allows the (re-) binding of partnerLinks to services during the runtime of a process. For this aim, the authors use a proxy architecture. Based on a given policy, the framework is able to schedule an invoke operation to a specific service. This binding can either be done before or during the execution of the workflow. In addition, runtime recovery can be supported. However, the framework does not provide support to extend the pool of usable services, i.e. by booting a virtual machine.

TRAP/BPEL is another framework for dynamic adaptation of service compositions presented by Ezenwoye and Sajadi [60]. It makes use of a generic proxy pattern. The proxy is able to query a UDDI registry to find a suitable service. The binding is performed in an autonomic fashion, e.g., if a service call fails, a substitute is determined and the call is retried. Furthermore, the selection of a suitable service can depend on a policy. To make a BPEL process interact with the TRAP/BPEL framework, it has to be adapted. Although policies can be used for service selection, it is not possible to specify

---
[2] http://www.rackspace.com/cloud
[3] http://www.gogrid.com
[4] http://www.flexiant.com/products/flexiscale/

post-invocation policies, e.g. for fault handling. Furthermore, dynamic scaling of the infrastructure is not supported.

By introducing a new element (*find_bind*) into the BPEL language, Karastoyanova et al. have presented their approach for runtime adaptability [89]. The mechanism is able to find services, e.g. by querying a UDDI registry. Based on policies, it selects suitable services and binds them to process instances. If a service call fails, a process instance repair is guaranteed by rebinding to another port. Selection criteria can be modified at runtime. There is no support for dynamically providing additional target hosts.

Ma et al. [98] have presented a Grid-enabled workflow management system that is based on BPEL. The system allows interaction with stateful resources, dynamic service binding and scalability of workflow execution. In the scenario presented in the paper, the BPEL engine – and not the workflow's target hosts – is a bottleneck. Scalability is achieved by placing a load balancer in front of a cluster of BPEL engines. Calls to the workflow engine are then scheduled according to the engines' workload. Dynamic service binding at runtime is achieved in a manner similar to the approach presented below. At runtime, a provisioning service is contacted that searches for a host where the requested service is installed. However, the approach does not take the workload of target hosts into account. Furthermore, it does not provide any feature to dynamically provide additional target hosts.

Modafferi et al. present SH-BPEL [110], an approach to rebind services in the event of a failure. The authors describe a pre-processing-based recovery mechanism that makes use of standard activities and handlers of WS-BPEL. In order to do so, it is necessary to transform the BPEL process. Furthermore, so-called "extended recovery mechanisms" are available, allowing a dynamic rebinding. In addition, a "class level" recovery can be used. This allows users to exploit a recovery for all of a process' running instances as well as for all future instances of a specific process.

Mietzner and Leymann [109] have discussed the problem that no standard for a generic provisioning infrastructure exists. It is argued that an architecture is needed that allows developers to deploy applications in different environments independently of the actual provisioning engine. The authors introduce a set of services related to provisioning and BPEL-based workflows that make use of these services. Once widely accepted and implemented, the proposed architecture could be substituted for the provisioning component presented in this work. This would significantly reduce the implementation efforts.

4.4 Cloud-enabled Auto-Scaling Architecture

The presented solution combines the versatile and powerful composition and control mechanisms of BPEL with an adaptive runtime environment without breaking the compatibility with existing standards. The system seamlessly integrates dedicated and on-demand resources provided by IaaS-based Cloud infrastructures like Amazon EC2.

Figure 3.5 in Section 3.3.3.1 sketches the idea behind the approach. Simply put, the targets of a workflow's invoke operations are determined at runtime instead of being pre-defined at workflow design time. The system thereby monitors the utilization of already present machines; the invoke operation is then scheduled to the machine with the lowest load. If all machines are above a certain load threshold, the provisioning component scales out the machine pool by provisioning a machine from an IaaS infrastructure. The described procedure illustrates a very basic, load-based scheduling algorithm. However, the architecture is modularized and allows developers to replace the algorithm with more sophisticated ones.

The depicted architecture can even completely replace dedicated infrastructures, as the system could simply provision all required machines from Cloud infrastructures. In this scenario, resources would only have to be paid when they are actually used. Administration complexity would be reduced to a minimum.

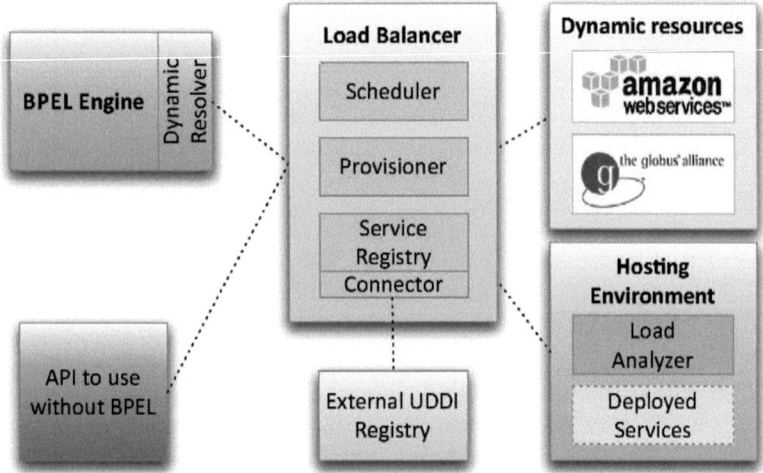

Figure 4.1: Components of the Load Balancing Architecture

The architecture has three components (see Figure 4.1):

1. The *Dynamic Resolver* extends the BPEL engine's invocation mechanism

2. The *Load Balancer* manages existing hosts, schedules service calls and provisions new hosts

3. The *Load Analyzer* collects information about the system load of hosts

The components interplay is as follows: Whenever, during the execution of a workflow, a service is to be invoked, the workflow system checks whether the target host has already been selected or not. In the latter case, the dynamic resolver tries to determine the best-matching target host. It contacts the load balancer and passes it the service description. The load balancer then queries an internal registry for hosts that have the requested service installed. The resulting list is filled with information concerning the performance and current load of the hosts. The list is then passed to a scheduling component that determines the best-matching host or provides a new host in the event that all hosts have a high load. Finally, the selected target host's address is passed back to the workflow system to execute the call.

Most importantly, all components have been designed with extensibility and exchangeability in mind. For instance, the scheduler allows developers to weave in different scheduling algorithms.

In the following, the design of the components and their interplay is discussed in detail.

4.4.1 Extensions to the BPEL Engine

The dynamic resolver is designed to avoid any changes to the BPEL engine's code, which eases portability to new versions. To achieve this goal, an extensibility mechanism of ActiveBPEL is used. Within the deployment descriptor of a workflow, the default invoke handler has to be replaced by a custom invoke handler, which allows developers to integrate the on-demand provisioning and load balancing mechanism. During the execution of a process, it is then invoked whenever a partnerLink is set to *dynamic* with the attribute *invokeHandler* pointing to the dynamic resolver's implementing class. An example is given in Listing 4.2 (Section 4.5.1).

The dynamic resolver/custom invoke handler then checks whether or not the corresponding BPEL *partnerLink* already has an endpoint address[5] set. In the latter case, it invokes the load balancer component to determine a concrete endpoint. In order to do so, the qualified name (*QName* for short)[6] of the *portType* and other parameters are passed to the load balancer component. The load balancer (see Section 4.4.2) in turn returns the endpoint address of the service that matches best. In this way, the dynamic resolver constitutes the interface between the BPEL engine and the load balancer component.

Since different scheduling strategies and infrastructural backends may be implemented, it is necessary to provide developers with the ability to define arbitrary parameters for dynamic endpoints. These parameters may be encoded into the string following the class name of the custom invoke handler. The syntax per parameter is as follows: *key=value*, whereby parameters are separated by colons. Any given parameter must be passed to the load balancer which then in turn passes the parameters to the scheduling and provisioning components. For instance, the workflow designer might want to

---

[5]Endpoint address is the technical correct term for an URL pointing to a Web service.

[6]The qualified name is the service's name plus a namespace definition in which the service is defined. The namespace typically refers to the domain name of the company which offers the service. Generally speaking, namespaces are used guarantee the global unambiguousness of an entity's name. In object-oriented programming languages, the concept also exists; in that context, namespaces are often referred to as packages.

define a minimum load threshold to start new virtual machines; authorization information for infrastructures like Amazon EC2 may be required.

4.4.2 Load Balancer

The load balancer is the architecture's main component. It consists of three sub-components: *scheduler*, *provisioner*, and *registry*. It manages on-premise hosts, continuously monitors their system load and makes scheduling decisions to avoid hosts from being overloaded. Whenever needed (the actual decision is made by the configured scheduling algorithm), it provisions new machines to keep the workflow system stable and reactive. To make the infrastructure as cost-efficient as possible, it releases Cloud resources (before expiration of an accounting period) when overall load drops. The system has to take into account that there must not be any running service calls on the machine to be shut down, which is not always easy to determine (details on this topic are given below).

The dynamic resolver contacts the load balancer whenever an endpoint for a target service needs to be resolved. Then, the registry is queried for hosts that have the requested service installed. Using the result list, the registry then collects the current system load on all qualified hosts. This information is then passed to the scheduler to make a scheduling decision according to the configured scheduling algorithm. This scheduling decision might involve starting new virtual machines by calling the provisioner. Eventually, the scheduler returns the target endpoint reference to the load balancer, which in turn replies to the dynamic resolver. The dynamic resolver then automatically invokes the target service on the chosen machine using the returned endpoint reference.

4.4.2.1 Registry

The registry manages all information about hosts and the services they offer. In particular, the endpoint of services must be accessible via their *portType*'s *QName*. Since starting and shutting down virtual machines are essential parts of the system, the registry must also be able to cope with the appearance and disappearance of hosts and services. Because a query may happen while a virtual machine is shutting down, it must be assured that the virtual machine must not appear in the result set of the query. To ensure that virtual machines are not shut down while they are in use, a construct that locks the shutdown procedure for virtual machines is required.

When virtual machines are started, information about them has to be saved persistently. Most important are the machine identifier (*id*) and the start time of the virtual machine, such that machines can still be managed (especially shut down) after the system is restarted. This improves the system's fault tolerance and ensures that running virtual machines may still be managed after the load balancer has been restarted.

Furthermore, the registry can query other (UDDI) registries, such as Grimoires [10], to extend its scope. Also, using a configuration file, a set of "static" hosts can be included in the registry, for instance, a company's dedicated/on-premise hosts. The acquisition of information regarding available services (i.e., service *QName*s, *portTypes*) is performed by parsing the WSDL documents of all offered services per host. Since the system is intended to integrate with the previously described WSRF services, it is important that the parser is able to parse the structure of WSRF-based services correctly.

To collect load values, the load analyzer is queried by the registry every time the registry is queried. To reduce communication costs, a cache holds the load information in memory; the cache is invalidated after a configurable interval. Thus, frequent queries do not affect the registry's performance.

4.4.2.2 Provisioner

The provisioner encapsulates interfaces to manage virtual machines in on-demand infrastructures like Amazon EC2 and Globus Virtual Workspaces [68]. It provides general abstractions, such as starting and stopping virtual machines, and methods for preparatory steps, such as starting middleware components.

With this abstraction, it is possible to develop drivers that interface with providers that use different implementation technologies and communication patterns for their management interfaces. These drivers may be plugged into the provisioner using a simple configuration file. Thus, the approach allows engineers to integrate new infrastructures without having to re-design the component itself. For example, Amazon EC2 provides Web service-based access to their management interface and does not deliver notifications when machines have finished booting, thus a polling-mechanism needs to be implemented in this case. On the other hand, Globus Virtual Workspaces makes use of WSRF-based services and implements WS-Notification, meaning that a caller is notified when certain events happen. The provisioner therefore needs to be generic and must hide implementation intrinsics.

The abstraction for this particular case is to provide a method `runInstanceBlocking`, which blocks until the virtual machine has booted. It is important to note that the method must not return before the service hosting environment (Web/Grid service stack) has been started. If it would do so, the services would not be available immediately, which would result in errors on the BPEL side when trying to invoke the services. While the signature of the method remains the same for each implementation that implements the `IProvisioner` interface, the implementations, of course, may heavily differ.

The provisioner registers and de-registers virtual machines in the registry after booting and shutdown. The registry then adds or removes all services installed on the virtual machine.

4.4.2.3 Scheduler

The scheduler gets information about the infrastructure, makes scheduling decisions and invokes the provisioner to start and stop on-demand resources. Since for different application scenarios different scheduling strategies are required, the scheduler allows developers to plug-in scheduling algorithms. A sample scheduling strategy and its implementation is described in Section 4.5.2.3.

The scheduler memorizes the starting time of virtual machines, since services like Amazon EC2 are billed per use, meaning that shutting down a virtual machine before expiration of an accounting period saves money. Therefore, it must tell the provisioner to shut down virtual machines in due time if the overall load is low. The system has to take into account that there must not be any running service calls on the machine to be shut down. While this may sound trivial, it is not straightforward to determine whether a service call (or the induced computation) has finished or not. This problem and a solution is discussed in depth in Section 4.5.

4.4.3 Load Analyzer

Many scheduling algorithms make scheduling decisions based on optimizing the throughput, meaning that it is favorable to schedule jobs or calls to hosts with low load, since assumingly these hosts finish the task faster than a host with higher utilization. Therefore, the system needs to collect load information for all target hosts to provide the scheduling algorithms with this information. The proposed solution employs a Web service, which is installed on every host, which determines data relevant to scheduling algorithms. This includes (but is not limited to) the machine's load, an approximate value of the system performance (by running a micro-benchmark) and the number of CPU cores. The service is queried by the registry in order to collect and update the machines's current performance values.

On systems where one (head) node represents a number of hosts (e.g. a cluster site in a Grid formation), the number of cores and the load are calculated using the following simple formula. Let n be the number of nodes in the system, $c(\cdot)$ a function that returns the number of CPU cores for a given node and $l(\cdot)$ a function that returns the load for a given CPU core. Then:

$$cores := \sum_{i=0}^{n} c(i) \qquad load := \frac{\sum_{i=0}^{n} \sum_{j=0}^{c(i)} l(j)}{cores}$$

If a cluster has heterogeneous nodes, the values above have to be calculated for each subgroup of homogeneous nodes.

Furthermore, the load analyzer provides a method to generate a list of all services being exposed by the application container to enable the load balancer to automatically determine the services' WSDL documents.

4.5 Implementation

The implementation is, as the Grid-related extensions, based on ActiveBPEL 2.0. However, the taken implementation approach does not require any changes to the source code of the BPEL engine. It makes use of its ability to substitute the standard invoke handler with a custom invoke handler. Since this concept exists in all versions of the BPEL engine, the solution is easily adaptable to newer versions of the engine; however, the invoke handler's interface (`IAeInvokeHandler`) has slightly changed from version to version.

4.5.1 Extensions to the BPEL Engine

To minimize the changes to the existing source code, the dynamic resolver is plugged into the engine using interfaces (`IAeInvokeHandler`) and observers provided by the engine. The dynamic resolver is used when a call is executed on a partnerLink marked with the `DynamicResolver` *invokeHandler* (see Listing 4)[7]. Due to this invokeHandler, the binding stays dynamic. Since the invokeHandler is specified via an URI, necessary arguments may be passed to the dynamic resolver via an URL encoding (lines 4 and 5 in Listing 4.2), as described above.

```
1 <partnerLink name="beatDetectionPL">
    <partnerRole endpointReference="dynamic"
3   invokeHandler="java:DynamicResolver
    ?threshold=1.0;accessID=***;secretKey=***;
5   imageID=ami-95cc28fc;availZone=us-east-1c"/>
```

Listing 4.2: Integration of a custom invoke handler (load balancer) into a workflow

When the dynamic resolver is executed, the partnerLink associated with the invoke activity is checked to determine whether or not its endpoint reference has already been set (Line 13 in Listing 4.3). In the latter case, the load balancer component is executed by calling the method `getEndpointForPortType(QName portType, Map queryMap)`. `queryMap` contains all parameters encoded in the URL in a key/value manner. The load balancer returns an endpoint reference (bean); its information is set as the partner reference of the used *partnerLink* before the call is executed.

```
1 public class DynamicResolver extends AeInvokeHandler {
    // ...
3 public IAeWebServiceResponse handleInvoke(IAeInvoke ↩
    invoke,
    String queryData) {
5   // Parse colon-separated parameter list and store the
    // key-value pairs in a hash map
7   Map<String, String> queryMap = buildQueryMap(↩
    queryData);

9   IAeWebServiceResponse response = new AeInvokeResponse↩
    ();
    QName portType = invoke.getPortType();
11
    IAeEndpointReference endpointReference = ((AeInvoke) ↩
    invoke).getPartnerReference();
13 // Check whether the target address is set or not
    if (AeUtil.isNullOrEmpty(endpointReference.↩
    getAddress())) {
```

---

[7]For the sake of simplicity, the package name of the custom invoke handler class has been omitted in the listing. It is `de.fb12.mage.bpel.lb.invokeHandler`

```
15    // Determine endpoint to be used by invoking the
      // load balancing framework.
17    erb = BpelLoadBalancer.getInstance().↵
          getEndpointForPortType(portType, queryMap);

19    // Fill the endpoint reference with the returned
      // address and service name
21    endpointReference.setAddress(erb.getAddress());
      endpointReference.setServiceName(erb.getServiceName↵
          ());
23    endpointReference.setServicePort(erb.getServicePort↵
          ());
      }
25    // Now, the target address is known and we can safely↵
          delegate
      // the work to the original invoke handler  ↵
          implementation
27    response = super.handleInvoke(invoke, null);

29    return response;
      }
```
Listing 4.3: Excerpt of the custom invoke handler (dynamic resolver)

4.5.2 Load Balancer

The load balancer is the only connection between the BPEL engine (i.e., the dynamic resolver) and the load balancing solution. No direct access to the scheduler, provisioner, or other components is necessary. This provides exchangeability and extensibility, since the components do not largely depend on each other. Furthermore, all described components implement interfaces (`IPerformanceMonitor`, `IProvisioner`, `IScheduler`) to ease exchangeability.

The load balancer is implemented as a singleton per BPEL engine; it is instantiated via a factory, and so are the other components like the registry and the provisioner. A configuration file is used to set the actual implementations, which are then loaded using Java reflection.

When the load balancer is invoked (Step 1 in Figure 4.2), it first queries the registry (2) for services matching the given port type, represented as a `QName`. A list of endpoints, encapsulated in `EndpointReference-Beans` (ERBs), is returned (3) and passed to the registry's performance monitor (4). It hands back a list of `double` values representing the target hosts' load (5). The load balancer then passes the two lists and parameters, such as the mentioned threshold, to the scheduler (6); the configured scheduling algorithm is employed, and the endpoint of the computed target host is returned to the dynamic resolver (7, 8). If the scheduler decides to start additional virtual machines, the provisioner is invoked (6a). After starting a new virtual machine, it is registered (6b, 6c) and the corresponding endpoint is returned (6d).

To assure cost-effectiveness, the scheduler monitors virtual machines and, if the overall load is low, tells the provisioner to shut them down before expiration of an accounting period. The system has to take into account that

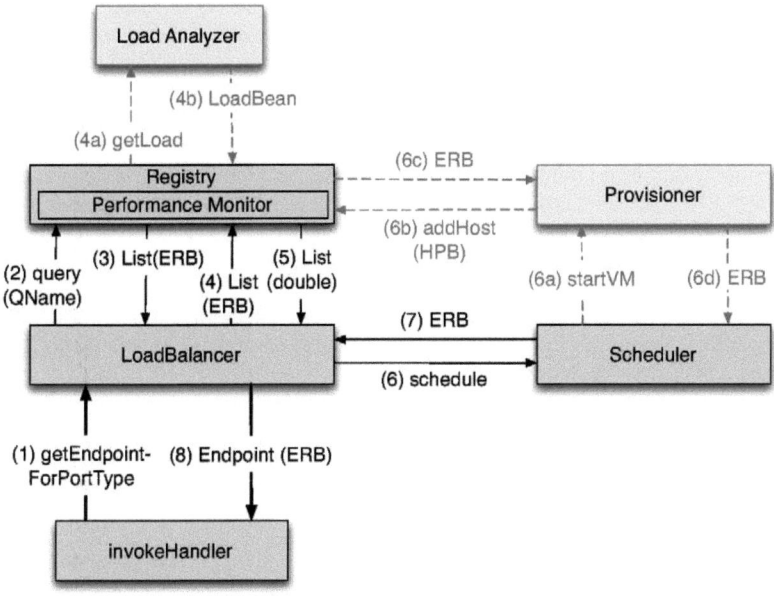

Figure 4.2: Sequence of calls to determine a dynamic endpoint

there must not be any running service calls on the machine to be shut down, which is not trivial to determine. For example, consider an asynchronous call to a service that results in an asynchronous callback when the service has finished the computation. To solve this problem, the dynamic resolver increments a counter for each host in the registry that represents the number of active calls to services on that host. When a process finishes, the process graph is examined for invoke operations. For every invoke operation, the target host is determined and the counter value is decremented. The scheduling algorithms simply have to check whether the counter for the virtual machine to be shut down is zero, before telling the provisioner to shut it down. Therefore, the implementation needs to be notified about the termination of processes to decrement the per-host counter that prevents the virtual machines from being shut down. For this purpose, the load balancer registers itself as an event-listener in the BPEL engine (`IAeEngineListener`). Upon process termination, `handleEngineEvent` is invoked; the host names of the finished process' invocation targets are extracted and the registry is invoked to decrement the lock counter.

4.5.2.1 Registry

The registry manages available information on hosts and services and stores them on disk, such that the data is still available after a restart. It is configurable via an XML document that is used to set up a set of permanently available hosts. Hosts are managed by so-called `HostPropertyBeans` containing information about the startup time (relevant for virtual machines), the virtual machine type, the type of middleware (*serverType*) and so on.

When a host is added – either by loading the static hosts or by the provisioner – the load analyzer is queried to acquire a list of all services exposed by this host. Depending on the type of middleware (*serverType*) on the target host, different clients are used to query the service list and system load. Currently, two clients for plain Web services and WSRF-based services exist.

The retrieved services' WSDL descriptions are then parsed to extract the services' *QName*s and binding addresses. This information is stored in `EndpointReferenceBeans`.

When the registry is queried for a specific *portType*, the list of available services is scanned. Furthermore, external registries are queried, if configured. They can be accessed by an interface `IRegistryConnector`. A list of all services matching the given *QName* is returned.

The Registry has a subcomponent called *PerformanceMonitor* which interacts with the Hosting Environment. The PerformanceMonitor is responsible for determining the load on the target machines. In order to keep the communication costs as small as possible, a cache stores this information for a configurable time in memory.

4.5.2.2 Provisioner

Since the provisioner has been designed to support several backends, it is organized into two parts: (1) an abstract class provides two methods `start` and `stop` that handle tasks that are independent of the backend, like registering and deregistering hosts. Before that, they call `_startVM` and `_stopVM` in the implementing sub-class (2) whereby the start operation returns an ERB with information needed to register the machine. In addition, the abstract class is responsible for the persistence of running virtual machines to avoid information loss due to restarting of the load balancer component.

The `_startVM` method must not return before the virtual machine and the middleware have booted. Otherwise, the workflow engine might try to invoke a service on the new virtual machine prior to its availability. The implementation therefore periodically tries to invoke the "Version" service, which is part of Apache Axis and therefore guaranteed to be present. It returns as soon as the service can be successfully invoked or aborts after several retries.

As an implementation example, the prototype implements a backend for Amazon EC2 [2]. It makes use of "Typica" [14], a Java-based open source library developed at Xerox. The implementation is able to start and stop virtual machines, configure the virtual machines' firewalls (some ports need to be open for SOAP communication and all other ports should be closed) and execute user scripts after booting a virtual machine. Since Amazon Machine Images (AMI) cannot be altered after creation, a script that downloads the middleware from an Amazon Simple Storage Service Bucket (S3, [3]) has been developed. This assures that the middleware can easily be upgraded (or new services may be installed) without needing to create a new AMI. The middleware is downloaded from S3, since external traffic (like a *wget* from an external server) is billed and Amazon-internal traffic is not billed.

4.5.2.3 Scheduler

In the following, the implementation of a simple scheduling strategy is discussed as an example. An excerpt of the source code is listed in Listing 4.4.

The input values for the scheduler are the names of matching hosts (M), load values (load) and a threshold value (t). The scheduler first computes all qualified hosts M_q, where $M_q := \{m \in M |\, \text{load}_m < t\}$. If M_q is non-empty, for all hosts in M_q, the free capacity

$$c_m = \frac{WIPS_m}{max(\text{load}_m, 0.01)}$$

is computed. *WIPS* stands for Whetstone Instructions Per Second and is computed using the Whetstone benchmark that performs integer, floating point and array operations to determine the performance of a host. The value of 0.01 is required if a host has a load of 0. Then, the host with the highest value for c_m is chosen, meaning that the host with the lowest utilization is selected (Line 38). Otherwise (Line 25), if M_q is empty, the scheduler requests a new host from the provisioner. After the startup of the new virtual machine, the waiting call is immediately scheduled to the host.

```
   public IEndpointReferenceBean scheduleRequest(
2      QName portTypeQName,
       Collection<IEndpointReferenceBean> endpoints,
4      Vector<LoadBean> loadVector, double threshold,
       Map<String, String> parameters) throws Exception {
6
       TreeSet<SimpleSchedulerBean> candidates = new
8      TreeSet<SimpleSchedulerBean>();

10     int machineNo = 0;
       for (IEndpointReferenceBean eprBean : endpoints) {
12         LoadBean loadBean = loadVector.get(machineNo);
           double loadPerCPU = loadBean.getLoad() / loadBean.↵
              getCores();
14
           if (loadPerCPU < threshold) {
16             double availBogo = loadBean.getBogomips() /
                  (loadPerCPU > 0 ? loadPerCPU : 0.01 );
18             SimpleSchedulerBean schedulerBean = new ↵
                  SimpleSchedulerBean(eprBean, loadBean, ↵
                  availBogo);
               candidates.add(schedulerBean);
20         }
           machineNo++;
22     }

24     // No nodes with value < threshold found
       if(candidates.size() == 0) {
26         IProvisioner provisioner = LoadBalancerFactory.↵
```

```
             getInstance().getProvisioner();
             IEndpointReferenceBean erb = provisioner.startVM(↵
                portTypeQName, parameters);
28           SimpleSchedulerBean ssb = new SimpleSchedulerBean↵
                (erb, null, Double.NaN);
             candidates.add(ssb);
30       }

32       // Throw an exception if no target host could be ↵
            determined
         if (candidates.last().getEndpointReferenceBean() == ↵
            null) {
34          throw new SchedulerException("Unable to schedule to↵
                exisiting machine.");
         }
36       // Return the EPR of the node with the highest ↵
            available BogoMIPS
         // last() returns the entry with the highest value
38       return candidates.last().getEndpointReferenceBean();
     }
```

Listing 4.4: Source code excerpt of the load-based scheduling algorithm

4.5.3 Load Analyzer

The load analyzer in the prototype has been realized for Linux. It inspects `/proc/loadavg` and `/proc/cpuinfo` to determine the *Load Average* and the core count. In virtualized environments, the computed percentage of CPU usage cannot be used as an indicator for CPU load, in contrast to *Load Average*. The machine may only have been assigned a part of the physical computing power; in this case, the percentage of CPU usage would always be below 100%. The *WIPS* benchmark is executed in order to approximate the system's performance. For cluster environments, only a prototypical implementation is currently available. It queries the Monitoring and Discovery System of the GT4 to acquire information about available and used cores.

4.6 Experimental Results

To evaluate the approach, the medical use case (see Section 2.2.2) is used. To recall the technical implementation of the application, it is briefly described again below.

As input, the workflow receives real patient data that is continuously measured and recorded using sensors attached to the patient's body. Since the data format (European Data Format, EDF) of the recorded vital signs is different from the format required by the Physio Toolkit (WaveForm DataBase, WFDB), a data conversion is needed (*InvokeEDF*). Afterwards, Q-S peaks are detected within the ECG signal (*InvokeWQRS*). The results are passed to the annotation reader service (*InvokeAnnotationReader*), which in turn decodes the input and passes the results to the beat detection service *InvokeBeatDetection*, which detects R waves within the signal. In parallel, the output of *InvokeWQRS* is passed to the apnoea detection service (*InvokeApnoea*) that analyzes the input signal and detects respiration dropouts (to diagnose the sleep apnea syndrome). The total data amount to be transferred within the workflow is approx. 258 MB (plus 118 MB for data transfer from the client to the first service when the workflow is started). The net runtime of the services (without network overhead) on modern hardware (see below) is 140 seconds for the longest path and 65 seconds for the other path (which is executed in parallel, see Figure 2.1). Therefore, the minimum execution time including data transfers (using a 100 MBit/sec network and idle resources) is around 180 seconds. While the per-instance runtime is quite short, it should be noted that the presented application is instance-intensive, meaning that the physicians often perform many analyses in parallel.

The workflow engine and all virtual machines are hosted with Amazon's EC2 infrastructure. The region US-east was chosen since it offers the lowest prices among all available regions. Placing the BPEL engine in the Cloud has the advantage that it, at least partially, eliminates network latency between Germany and the USA in the measurements. While this is true for data transfers between the BPEL engine and virtual machines running in the same region, it does not apply to data transfers between the BPEL engine and static resources. Since data transfers to Amazon's EU-west (Ireland) region are not notably speedier than those to the US, this does not help to solve the problem. However, the general problem cannot be circumvented when using *task-based* scheduling, since the scheduling algorithm cannot take (data) dependencies into consideration. The scheduling approach presented in Chapter 6 operates on the whole workflow graph instead of only looking at one particular task per scheduling decision.

The evaluation was performed with different setups. In each of them, on-premises and/or Cloud resources were used. The static/on-premises resources are two Core2Duo E6850 machines with 2 GB RAM running Fedora 11 Linux hosted at our faculty. The used resource type at Amazon was "High-CPU Medium Instance" with 1.7 GB of memory and 5 EC2 Compute Units (split on two cores, meaning that the systems have 2×2.5 ECU) hosting an Ubuntu Linux. Details concerning the instance types and corresponding prices can be found in Table 4.1.

The framework was tested using the following three scenarios: scenario (1) simulates increasing load by starting a new workflow every 30 seconds. In scenario (2), at an interval of 90 seconds, two workflows are started simultaneously to simulate an abrupt increase of resource demand. The scenarios were run until eight workflows had been started. Finally, to test the system in peak load situations, in scenario (3) four workflows are started concurrently.

All measurements represent the mean value of 20 runs of each scenario, resulting in more than 400 workflow runs in total.

Figure 4.3 allows for comparison the execution times for all scenarios in two different environments: the first one does not allow additional virtual machines to be provided, while in the second setup, additional (Cloud) resources can be used.

The numbers indicate that the load-based scheduling approach outperforms static resource allocation. In scenario 1, using static allocation to

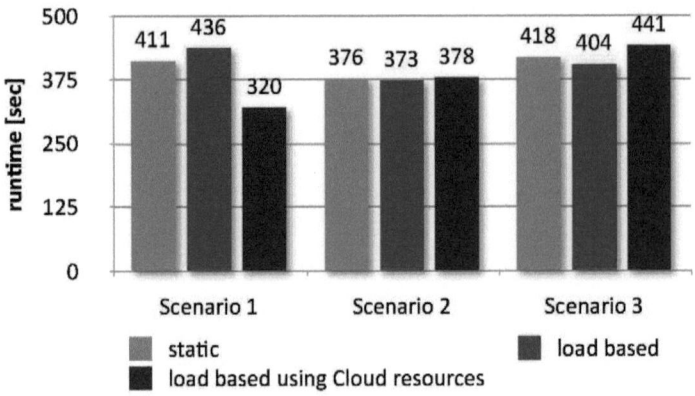

Figure 4.3: Workflow runtimes for all scenarios using static and load based allocation

physical resources (that are clearly faster than the virtual machines used), workflow execution takes 411 seconds in average. Load-based allocation (only to physical resources) takes marginally longer (436 seconds, a plus of 6% in runtime). This is due to the fact that in static (manual) allocation, all invoke operations that depend on the output of predecessors were clustered to the same machine, which avoids data transfers. However, the load-based allocation mechanism schedules the invoke operations to the machines with the lowest load, which leads to unnecessary data transfers in some cases. When the system was allowed to provision additional Cloud resources, the average runtime significantly reduced (to 320 seconds, a decrease of 28%). The runtime reduction results from making heavy use of on-demand resource provisioning: on average (over all 20 runs of the scenario), the scheduler requested 5.1 additional virtual machines. The high number results from the short time (30 seconds) between the starts of the workflow instances. Due to the short pause between workflow starts, the virtual machines that have been started in previous workflow run i, are still occupied in run $i + 1$, $i + 2$ and so on. This pattern is visible in Figure 4.4, which displays the workflow execution and start times for one of the 20 scenario runs. In the workflow runs with net runtimes about 290 seconds (run 1, 4, 5, 7), no additional resources were provisioned.

The fact that the runtimes are equal to static allocation or even slightly *slower* in Scenarios 2 & 3 when Cloud resources are used is due to the startup delay of virtual machines (typically between 60 and 90 sec, see Figure 4.5). The current implementation does not provide virtual machines in advance, meaning that whenever the system decides to set up a new virtual machine, the startup delay prolongs the execution of the initiating workflow. The overhead must be put into perspective, since subsequently executed workflows could use the additional resources without any delay (as it happens in Sce-

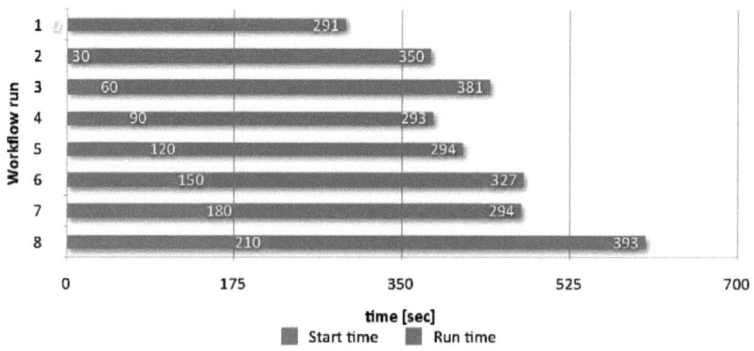

Figure 4.4: Runtimes of (one out of 20 runs of) workflow instances for scenario 1

nario 1). Furthermore, for longer-running and/or instance-intensive workflows, the provisioning overhead does not carry weight.

The overhead could be circumvented, if the decision to provision virtual machines were to be decoupled from the actual (task-based) scheduling. For instance, the provisioner could periodically (and independently from the scheduler) monitor the load of virtual machines. If the average load over all machines were above a certain threshold, it would add additional resources. The scheduling algorithm would then automatically make use of the increased resource pool. This would decouple the provisioning process (and induced startup overhead) from actual workflow execution.

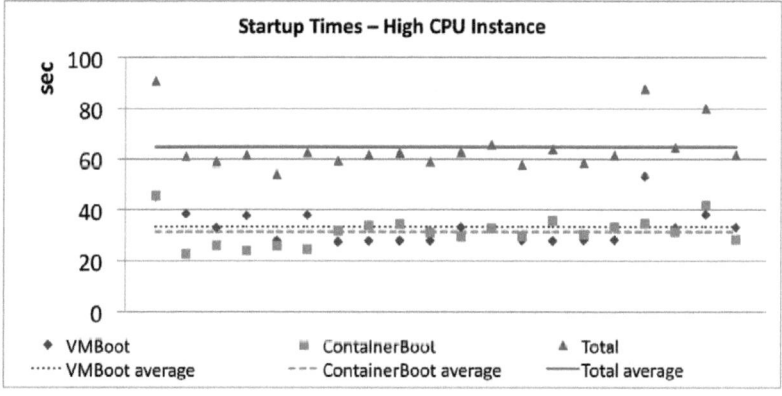

Figure 4.5: Virtual machine and middleware boot times using Amazon's instance type High-CPU Medium

In addition, the runtimes of the different components have been analyzed separately. A registry query takes around 2.5 msec; determining the load takes around 100 msec per host. If the load is cached, the time is reduced to about 1 msec, which is negligible. Making the scheduling decision takes about 1 msec, except when a new virtual machine has to be booted.

To sum up, the approach provides efficient load balancing capabilities. If, without the solution, multiple workflow instances are run in parallel, the runtime increases linearly with the number of instances. Using the solution, the runtime remains almost constant.

4.7 Summary

In this chapter, the need for automatic infrastructure scaling has been discussed. Building on that motivation, shortcomings of current BPEL implementations with respect to dynamic service selection and resource provisioning have been discussed.

The presented solution was first discussed on an architectural level. It allows the BPEL engine to dynamically schedule a workflow's service invocations at workflow execution time. As an example scheduling schema, load-based scheduling has been discussed and implemented. Scalability of the underlying resource pool is achieved by integrating a provisioning component that dynamically launches virtual machines in on-demand infrastructures and deploys the required middleware components (Web/Grid service stack) on-the-fly. The approach was quantitatively analyzed using the medical workflow presented above. The results indicate that the system fulfills the requirements: it does scale and provides almost constant performance with a growing number of running workflow instances. However, the result from the evaluation also motivates further research concerning more sophisticated workflow scheduling strategies that take (data) dependencies between workflow steps into consideration.

Chapter 5
Improved Fault Handling in BPEL

Contents

5.1	Introduction	70
5.2	Fault Handling in BPEL	71
	5.2.1 Status Quo	71
	5.2.2 Improvements to the Handling of Infrastructural Errors	72
	5.2.3 Using Replication	73
5.3	Related Work	73
5.4	Design	74
	5.4.1 Fault Tolerance Module	75
	5.4.2 Dynamic Resolver	78
5.5	Implementation	79
	5.5.1 Fault Tolerance Module	79
	5.5.2 Dynamic Resolver	83
5.6	Fault-Tolerant and Auto-Scaling Deployment of the BPEL engine	83
	5.6.1 Relevant Services of Amazon Web Services	84
	5.6.2 Scenario Architecture	86
	5.6.3 Configuration of the Required Services	86
5.7	Experimental Results	90
5.8	Summary	95

5.1 Introduction

The development of distributed applications induces problems that simply do not exist in non-distributed environments. Instead of tying application components together via (local) method or function calls in a programming language like Java or C, the different parts of an distributed application often reside on different resources. Then, the components communicate over networks via remote procedure call (RPC) mechanisms. When BPEL is used to develop distributed applications, the application's components are loosely-coupled via message exchanges controlled by the execution engine. The components are typically not installed on the same machine and may only be reached via the Internet. Due to this fact and the highly distributed nature of these composed applications, the occurrence of failures (e.g. network failures, software failure on remote hosts) is quite likely.

In particular, when long-running or computationally intensive workflows are to be executed, fault handling is very important, since the failure of a single component might lead to an abandonment of the entire workflow. This may lead to a decrease in stability within the execution system or an increase in cost due to wasted CPU hours as a result of losing intermediary results of preceding workflow steps. This would be perceived as a low quality of service of workflow execution by the concerned user. While the BPEL standard already defines fault handling mechanisms, *infrastructural failures*, like network timeouts and server outages, should not be handled using the language mechanisms, as this would clutter the composition logic with non-functional aspects.

Consequently, this chapter introduces an advanced fault handling mechanism that improves and eases fault handling without needing to alter existing BPEL workflows. The mechanism identifies classes of faults that can be handled automatically. Using a policy language, the workflow developer can configure automatic recovery behavior without the need for adding explicit fault handling mechanisms to the BPEL process. The approach makes use of the provisioning component presented in Chapter 4 and provides automatic Cloud-based redundancy of services to allow substitution of defective services.

What is more, the BPEL engine itself presents a single point of failure. To solve this problem, a deployment scenario for the BPEL engine has been developed in which additional BPEL engines are automatically provisioned when an engine is determined to be unhealthy. This procedure is transparent to workflow users, as the engines are placed behind a DNS-based load balancer.

This chapter is organized as follows. Section 5.2 states the problems to be solved. Section 5.3 discusses related work. In Section 5.4, the conceptual design and the proposed architecture of the solution are presented. Section 5.5 describes implementation details. A fault-tolerant and auto-scaling deployment scenario for the BPEL engine is described in Section 5.6. Section 5.7 discusses experimental results using a sample workflow. Section 5.8 summarizes the chapter.

Parts of this chapter have already been published [84, 86].

5.2 Fault Handling in BPEL

5.2.1 Status Quo

The BPEL standard is, as briefly described in Section 3.3.2, equipped with a fault handling mechanism. The mechanism, however, heavily clutters a workflow's description with the non-functional aspect of fault handling. It is clearly necessary to catch and handle faults related to the *logic* of a workflow, like in the example in Listing 5.1. The listing displays a small portion of a workflow that intends to invoice a certain amount of money from a customer. When the credit card cannot be approved (Line 2), the corresponding error message is simply sent back to the client. This kind of fault should and must be handled explicitly within a workflow's logic since it is directly related to the (business) logic.

Technically speaking, fault handlers may be described either on the process level or for each scope (scopes are hierarchically organized parts in which a process can be divided). The *faultHandlers* element contains an arbitrary number of *catch* (and optionally one *catchAll*) elements that define fault types to which to react (comparable to a *switch-case* construct with *default* case in other programming languages). Listing 5.1 illustrates a simple example of fault handling. One fault (*buy:CreditCardNotApproved*) is explicitly handled by simply returning the fault message to the client that started the process (Lines 5–8). All other faults (*catchAll*) are handled by setting "Other fault" as the fault message (Lines 12–17) and returning the fault message to the client (Lines 18-21).

```
   <faultHandlers>
2   <catch faultName="buy:CreditCardNotApproved"
            faultVariable="Fault">
4    <!-- Make a callback to the client -->
     <invoke partnerLink="Client"
6              portType="buy:ClientCallbackPT"
               operation="ClientCallbackFault"
8              inputVariable="Fault"/>
    </catch>
10  <catchAll>
     <sequence>
12    <assign>
       <copy><!-- Create the Fault variable -->
14      <from expression="string('Other fault')"/>
        <to variable="Fault" part="error"/>
16     </copy>
      </assign>
18     <invoke partnerLink="Client"
               portType="buy:ClientCallbackPT"
20             operation="ClientCallbackFault"
               inputVariable="Fault"/>
22   </sequence>
    </catchAll>
24 </faultHandlers>
```
Listing 5.1: Manual fault handling in BPEL

Even this very simple example illustrates that the process logic is heavily bloated by fault handling. While this cannot be avoided for business faults (because) they clearly influence the logic of the process, it should be avoided for faults related to the underlying infrastructure. Chan et al. provide a more thorough discussion [37] on this topic. In a nutshell, they state that it is not reasonable to try to recover all kinds of failures. They exemplify that recovery mechanisms should interfere, if, for instance, a network timeout or a socket reset occurs.

5.2.2 Improvements to the Handling of Infrastructural Errors

It should be possible to handle faults related to *infrastructural* errors (like network timeouts and software faults in invoked services) without further interfering with the BPEL process. Despite bloating workflows with lots of fault handling code, explicit and recurring fault handling for infrastructural errors would increase the time required to develop workflows (and thus cost).

Especially when processes with many invoke operations are executed, it is quite likely that at least one service malfunctions or is not available. Without fault handling for every single invoke operation, the entire process would fail if one or more services fail (since the faults would be propagated to the BPEL engine, which in turn would propagate them to the client). Assume a (simple) process with $n = 10$ services and a likelihood l of 0.01 (1%) for each service to fail. Then, the likelihood that the process finishes successfully is only:

$$(1 - l)^n = 0.99^{10} \approx 0.904 \approx 90\%$$

For many of these infrastructural faults, there is a straightforward strategy for recovery. For example, if a network timeout occurs, the invocation could be retried several times (with a maximum number of attempts). If this does not solve the problem, the service could be substituted by an equivalent service on another machine (typically referred to as *failover*). This failover operation could also be retried several times, leading to a failure of the process if none of the attempts is successful. To make the solution as flexible as possible, the recovery behavior must be configurable. There might be, for instance, cases in which a retry does not make sense or the maximal number of attempts for substitution needs to be set to a specific value.

A substitution can either be performed using equivalent components that are already running somewhere or by deploying and starting the required components on demand. The first case implies that for each service at least one fallback service runs on a different machine. On-demand provisioning is especially useful to avoid the need for additional spare hardware (see Section 5.2.3). Cloud computing infrastructures like Amazon's EC2 (see Section 4.2.2.1) can be used to host the required software; a user would only pay for the additional resources when they are actually used (pay-as-you-go pricing).

5.2.3 Using Replication

Another way to achieve improved fault tolerance with respect to infrastructure induced errors is to make use of *replication*. In this case, one would, using active replication as an example, schedule every invoke operation to more than one machine in parallel, which would increase the likelihood of an successful completion. The result of the operation would be the first non-erroneous response. However, this solution has a major drawback: It dramatically increases the total amount of work to be done, meaning that the machines that execute the invoke operations will have a higher utilization. Details concerning the use and an sample implementation of active replication in Web service environments have been published by Salas et al. [120]. Therefore, given the opportunity of on-demand resource provisioning (within 30 to 90 seconds, see Figure 4.5), traditional replication is ruled out as a potential solution.

5.3 Related Work

Di Penta et al. [50] have presented a dynamic binding framework called WS Binder. It allows the (re-) binding of partnerLinks to services while a workflow is running. For this aim, the authors use a proxy architecture. PartnerLinks are bound to proxy services instead of the original target services, meaning that the workflows need to be adapted to run in the environment. If a failure occurs at runtime, the proxy services are rebound to target services determined by the framework's discovery and selection component. Target services are determined using a given policy that may contain QoS parameters. By introducing a proxy service for every possible target service of a workflow, the complexity of the whole environment is increased. Furthermore, the framework does not provide support for extending the pool of usable services, i.e. by booting a virtual machine.

TRAP/BPEL is another framework for dynamic adaptation of service compositions presented by Ezenwoye and Sajadi [60]. It makes use of a generic proxy pattern. The proxy can query a UDDI registry to find a suitable service. The binding is performed in an autonomic fashion, e.g., if a service call fails, a substitute is determined and the call is retried. Furthermore, the selection of a suitable service can depend on a policy. To make a BPEL process interact with the TRAP/BPEL framework, it has to be adapted (all invoke operations must call the generic proxy rather than the actual service). Information about the actual target service has to be encoded in the input variable of the invoke activity for the proxy. This implies that the modeling of processes becomes much more complicated, and common workflow modeling tools do not provide graphical assistants for this. Furthermore, this is a source of errors. During deployment, workflow engines normally validate whether the input variables of invoke activities match the schema definition of the target services. If not, process deployment fails. In this case, the engine can only validate whether the input variables match the proxy's schema. It cannot validate whether the encoded input parameters of the actual target service are compliant with the actual target service's schema. Although policies can be used for service selection, it is not possible to specify post-invocation policies, e.g. for fault handling. Furthermore, the framework does not offer the possibility to dynamically provide new machines that host a service equivalent to the failed service to recover from errors and prevent the entire workflow from failing.

By introducing a new element (*find_bind*) into the BPEL language, Karastoyanova et al. [89] have presented their approach for runtime adaptability. The mechanism is able to find services, e.g. by querying a UDDI registry. Based on policies, it selects suitable services and binds them to process instances. If a service call fails, a process instance repair is guaranteed by rebinding to another port. Selection criteria can be modified at runtime. It does not support dynamically providing additional target hosts, and it is not possible to define different recovery strategies for different types of errors.

A self-healing approach has been pursued by Subramanian et al. [126]. The authors distinguish between different kinds of failures, e.g. functional, operational or semantic failures. Depending on the kind of failure, different solutions are proposed. These cover data mediation, substitution or process reorganization. The self-healing behavior is controlled by certain policies. The authors provide a minimal prototype, SelfHeal-BPEL, that allows developers to simulate failure situations. The system then suspends the running process, applies the solution that has been retrieved from the failure database before, and finally resumes the corrected processes.

5.4 Design

In this section, the design of the solution that meets the requirements stated above is presented. Implementation details will be described in Section 5.5.

The proposed solution adds a policy-based fault handling mechanism to BPEL without making any changes to the language standard. Using policies, it allows workflow developers to enable and disable both retry and substitute actions. To reduce the number of required policies, a *Fault Classifier* clusters faults into groups. Instead of defining a policy for every type of fault, policies can be specified for each group of faults. Besides, the policies permit users to set parameters such as the maximum number of retries, what kind of resources (dedicated hosts, Cloud resources, etc.) may be used for substitution, and so on. The overall architecture is sketched in Figure 5.1; the components are described below.

The solution substitutes the default invocation mechanism of the BPEL engine with the *Fault Tolerant Invoke Handler* that executes and monitors every invoke operation. After an invocation (Step 1 in Figure 5.2), the answer is analyzed (Step 3) and classified by the Fault Classifier. If a fault has occurred, the *Policy Processor* applies all policies that have been defined for the classified fault (Step 4) to determine the next action to be taken. Depending on the applied policy (Step 5), the call may (6a) be retried or (6b) the service may be substituted by an existing service or by starting a machine in the Cloud. Substitution of services is carried out using the on-demand pro-

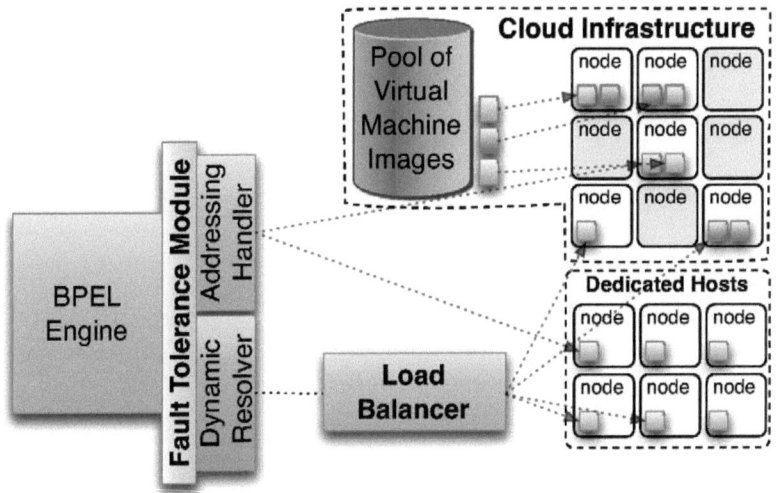

Figure 5.1: Bird's-eye view on the proposed fault handling architecture

visioning approach (dynamic resolver, and load balancer with provisioner from Chapter 4). If both recovery strategies (*Retry* and *Substitution*) have been disabled in the applied policies, the process would fail since the error would be propagated to the BPEL engine.

This procedure is illustrated in Figure 5.2. The components and their interaction, as well as the policy schema, are discussed in detail in the following sections.

5.4.1 Fault Tolerance Module

The Fault Tolerance Module encapsulates the whole functionality sketched above. The different functions (fault classification, processing of policies, service invocation) form sub-components.

5.4.1.1 Fault Tolerant Invoke Handler

The Fault Tolerant Invoke Handler is the only component that interacts with the workflow engine. As before, a major design goal is to realize this interaction without modifying the engine's source code in order to facilitate portability to new versions. Basically, the invoke handler is woven into a process using the process' deployment descriptor. The engine then executes the custom invoke handler instead of the default one.

BPEL allows two different addressing mechanisms for target services: *static* or *dynamic* addressing. In the first case, the fault tolerant invoke handler simply delegates the invocation to the standard BPEL *Addressing Handler* (Step 1a in Figure 5.2) to execute the call. In the latter case of dynamic

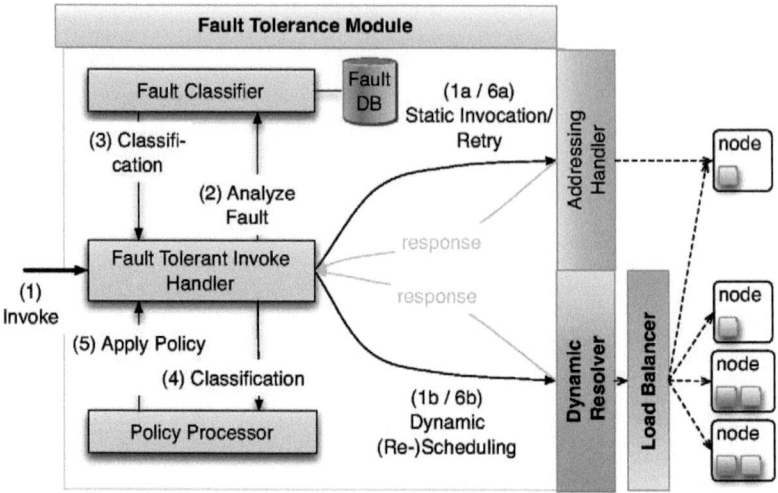

Figure 5.2: Interaction of the sub-components of the Fault Tolerance Module

addressing, the actual target address must be resolved before the invoke operation can be executed (Step 1b in Figure 5.2). This is done using the dynamic resolver that has been described in detail in Chapter 4. By using the second approach, the dynamic resolver's load balancing and scaling capabilities are automatically used in combination with the improved fault handling.

When the response from the invoked service arrives, the mechanism checks whether it contains a fault message or not. In the first case (Step 2), the message is passed to the Fault Classifier (see Section 5.4.1.2). The classifier's result is then passed to the policy processor that applies all configured policies. The result contains zero or more recovery strategies with priorities. When a policy with the *Retry* strategy exists, it is to be performed before policies using the *Substitution* strategy. No recovery strategy is available when retry and substitution have been explicitly disabled or the number of retries has exceeded the configured value. If a recovery strategy is available, it is used to repeat the invocation. A counter value representing the number of retries in the strategy is then incremented.

If the retry strategy is applied, the previously invoked service is invoked again (Step 6a in Figure 5.2). Otherwise, the dynamic resolver is executed (Step 6b) to perform a dynamic scheduling on those resources declared in the substitution strategy.

5.4.1.2 Fault Classifier

Basically, the fault classifier categorizes specific exceptions and invocation faults into general fault categories. This reduces the number of polices that need to be defined, since policies are applied to those categories (of group faults) instead of individual faults. The mapping from individual faults to the corresponding group is adjustable, as described in the implementation section. Some sample mappings are given in Table 5.1. It is noteworthy that the fault classifier must be able to classify two types of faults: (1) invocation faults that may occur during service operations and (2) faults that are induced by the fault handling framework itself (*VMFault* and *SchedulerFault* classes in Table 5.1). For the second kind of fault, special handling policies need to be defined, for instance, if the startup of virtual machines (i.e. Cloud resources) fails, the substitution strategy should be adapted, so that the framework does not further try to acquire virtual machines.

5.4.1.3 Policy Processor

When the policy processor is invoked, a fault category that is previously determined by the Fault Classifier is used as input instead of individual faults. The policy processor uses a map-like structure to search for a policy for a given fault.

In general, policies are attached to individual target services using the BPEL partnerLinks. However, for certain cases it is favorable to be able to define global policies that are automatically applied to all partnerLinks. One such case is the aforementioned VMFault. For instance, the occurrence of such a fault should disable the provisioning of Cloud resources (at least until the cause of the error has been resolved). Therefore, the architecture allows users to define global and local policies. In general, local policies should be able to overwrite the behavior defined in global policies. However, to obviate overwriting of "special" rules (like the example), policies can be declared as *final*.

The schema-like definition of a policy is described in Listing 5.2. A policy container can contain one or more *Fault* elements. The global and local policies have to be kept in separate containers and files. Those files can be stored in the process deployment archive used by the engine itself. To identify the scope of attached policies, the invoke handler accepts two parameters: *GlobalPolicy* and *LocalPolicy* which both point to the XML files containing the definitions. Listing 5.4 gives an example.

```
  <Faults>
2   <Fault name="NCName" final="true | false">
    <byCause name="FaultCategory"/>
4   <OriginHost retry="true | false">
      <MaxTries value="int"/>
6   </OriginHost>?
    <Substitute resources="NONE | PHYSICAL_ONLY | ↩
      EXISTING |
8                          NEW | DIFFERENT | ALL">
      <MaxTries value="int"/>
10  </Substitute>?
    </Fault>+
12 <Faults>
```

Listing 5.2: Schema-like Definition of a Policy

Each policy specifies a behavior for a certain fault category. The fault category itself is specified by the *byCause* element. A *OriginHost* (Retry) or

Substitute strategy (or both) must be specified that influences the behavior of the fault tolerant invoke handler.

In Listing 5.3, a reasonable example of a global policy is given. For instance, for the category VMFault (error during the provisioning of a virtual machine) it is defined that a substitution may only be done by using machines that are already running (*resources="existing"* in Line 4). This rule is declared as final, meaning that user-defined local policies may not overwrite it. The other two rules define reasonable default values for workflows, but may be changed via overwriting by local policies. For example, all faults classified as Service Faults (type *ServiceFault*, Lines 19–27) should not be handled at all (maxTries set to zero for retry and substitution), since service faults are typically related to incorrect input data or internal service errors that depend on the given input parameters; thus, retrying (on another host) does not help to recover from the fault.

```
   <faults>
2    <Fault name="VM Boot Fault (global)" final="true">
       <byCause value="VMFault" />
4      <Substitution resources="existing">
         <MaxTries value="2" />
6      </Substitution>
     </Fault>
8
     <Fault name="Middleware Fault (global)">
10     <byCause value="MidlewareFault"/>
       <OriginHost retry="false">
12       <MaxTries value="0" />
       </OriginHost>
14     <Substitution resources="different">
         <MaxTries value="5" />
16     </Substitution>
     </Fault>
18
     <Fault name="Service Fault (global)">
20     <byCause value="ServiceFault"/>
       <OriginHost retry="false">
22       <MaxTries value="0" />
       </OriginHost>
24     <Substitution resources="none">
         <MaxTries value="0" />
26     </Substitution>
     </Fault>
28 </faults>
```

Listing 5.3: Example of global policy rules

5.4.2 Dynamic Resolver

The dynamic resolver has been discussed in Chapter 4. It is employed by the fault handling approach to provide "on-demand redundancy," meaning that the spare machines (to replace faulty ones) do not run all the time, but are provisioning when required. Moreover, its load balancing and scaling capabilities are automatically used by the fault handling approach when dynamic addressing is configured in the workflow's partnerLinks. The integration of fault handling requires the component to be extended, so that it can cope with restrictions set by policies. For instance, the scheduler must now be able to reschedule calls only to existing machines in the event of a *VMFault*, instead of providing a new Cloud resource. In addition, the scheduler must now be able to make a distinction between the resource types mentioned in Listing 5.2. For example, on-premises (physical) resources and on-demand (virtual) resources must be distinguished to support the *PHYSICAL_ONLY* mode of the substitution strategy.

5.5 Implementation

As before, it was a major design goal to avoid changes to the source code of the BPEL engine. The exchangeability mechanism of invoke handlers is once again used to embed the fault tolerance mechanism into the BPEL engine. Since the fault tolerance mechanism operates per service, it is a natural choice to use the *partnerLink* definitions within the process deployment descriptor to integrate the framework into process descriptions. Listing 4 demonstrates the integration of the fault tolerance mechanism, as well as the URL-encoded definition of policies. It defines both a global and a local policy.

```
  <partnerLink name="ecgAnalyzerPL">
2   <partnerRole
      endpointReference="dynamic"
4   invokeHandler="java:FaultTolerantInvokeHandler?
                   GlobalPolicy="global.xml"
6                  LocalPolicy="local.xml" /> />
```

Listing 5.4: Integration of a the fault tolerant invoke handler and two policies into ActiveBPEL engine

5.5.1 Fault Tolerance Module

The fault tolerance module encapsulates the entire functionality described in Section 5.4. The different functions (fault classification, processing of policies, service invocation) form sub-components that are described in the following.

5.5.1.1 Fault Tolerant Invoke Handler

The fault tolerant invoke handler is embedded into workflows using the custom invoke handler technique described before. When the target endpoint of an invoke operation is already set (static addressing), it carries out the operation using the standard invoke handler AeInvokeHandler of the ActiveBPEL engine. If the address of the target service has not been resolved yet (endpointReference="dynamic"), it first contacts the Dynamic Resolver to determine the address of an appropriate target service. In both cases, the response of the Web service call is examined once the call has finished. If it contains a fault, the code in Lines 16–23 of Listing 5.5 is invoked. The code performs a fault classification, applies matching policies, increments the fault counter (needed to check whether the maximum number of retries has exceeded) and repeats the invocation (note the `while`-loop in Line 13). It repeats as long as `state.getActualStrategy` is not `null`. The `state` object automatically returns the appropriate strategy that matches the applied policy (Line 8), if any. If the number of retries is exceeded, it returns `null`, such that the while loop is exited. If Substitution is performed, restrictions concerning the target system's type, such as `PHYSICAL_ONLY`, are passed on to the Dynamic Resolver.

```java
   public class FaultTolerantLoadBalancer extends ↵
       AeInvokeHandler {
2  // ...
     public IAeWebServiceResponse handleInvoke(IAeInvoke ↵
        invoke, String queryData) {
4     // ...
      // ...
6     ILoadBalancerState state = new FTState();
      PolicySet pS = new PolicySet();
8     // load policies configured in invoke handler
      pS.load(queryMap, invoke.getProcessName());
10    // ...

12    // Repeat
      while(state.getActualStrategy() != null) {
14     // perform invoke ...
       IAeWebServiceResponse response = super.handleInvoke↵
          (...);
16     if (response.isFaultResponse()) {
        // ... fault occurred
18      FaultClassifier fc = getFaultClassifier();
        IFault fault = fc.classify(response);
20      APolicy policy = pS.getPolicy(fault);
        policy.apply(state);
22      state.incrementFaultCounter();
       }
24   }
```

Listing 5.5: Excerpt of the fault handling mechanism in Fault Tolerant Invoke Handler

5.5.1.2 Fault Classifier

The classifier has to handle two kinds of exceptions: (1) local exceptions that arise within the framework itself (for instance, exceptions during scheduling) and (2) remote exceptions that occur when *invoke* operations fail. In the first case, plain Java exceptions have to be analyzed, whereas in the latter case, SOAP fault messages that contain the error must be analyzed.

Therefore, the Fault Classifier defines two entry points:

1. `IFault classify(Throwable)` for local exceptions and

2. `IFault classify(IAeWebServiceResponse)` for remote exceptions

The classification of Java `Exceptions` or `Throwables` is performed by establishing a map-like structure that contains the mapping between the `Exception` and the defined `IFault` implementations. Mapping a SOAP fault to an `IFault` is more difficult, because the actual structure of a SOAP fault varies depending on the framework used for the implementation of the service (e.g. Apache Axis[1], gSOAP[2] or the Microsoft Internet Information Service[3]). Each individual framework generates different error messages. For this reason, the classifier first tries to identify the framework before introspecting any error details. The available error information is then mapped to an `IFault` implementation (see Table 5.1 for some examples).

So far, the following `IFaults` (categories) have been implemented:

VMFault faults thrown in the context of on-demand provisioning.

SchedulerFault faults caused by the scheduling framework.

PermanentTransportLayerFault permanent faults related to the communication subsystem. Example: Target host unknown – the (operating) system is unable to resolve the hostname to an IP address. Such faults are assumed to be uncorrectable by retrying, e.g., if a `NoRouteToHostException` is caught, it is very likely that the same exception is thrown when a retry is performed.

TransportLayerFault non-permanent faults related to the communication subsystem. Example: Connection refused by target host. Such faults can typically be overcome by a retry.

MiddlewareFault subsumes all faults related to the middleware, such as exceptions thrown directly by the Java Virtual Machine. In most cases, a substitution is more plausible than a retry on the same machine.

ServiceFault comprises all faults explicitly thrown by the target service. By default, such faults are not handled by policies, since they are very likely to be business logic faults that should be handled at the process level and therefore need to be propagated to the engine.

GeneralFault faults that are not otherwise categorized.

5.5.1.3 Policy Processor

The policy processor takes care of loading and managing policies. Both loading and parsing of the policies is lazily executed when the Policy Processor is invoked. During parsing of the XML file that describes the policies, the actual classes that implement the policies' behaviors are instantiated using Java's class loading mechanism (`Class.forName, newInstance`) as

---
[1] http://ws.apache.org/axis/
[2] http://www.cs.fsu.edu/~engelen/soap.html
[3] http://www.iis.net/

Exception	Fault Category
VMException.class	VMFault
SchedulerException.class	SchedulerFault
HeapException.class	MiddlewareFault
ConnectException.class	TransportLayerFault
SocketException.class	TransportLayerFault
SocketTimeoutException.class	TransportLayerFault
MalformedURLException.class	PermanentTransportLayerFault
NoRouteToHostException.class	PermanentTransportLayerFault
UnknownHostException.class	PermanentTransportLayerFault
UnknownServiceException.class	PermanentTransportLayerFault

Table 5.1: Sample mappings of individual faults to groups

listed in Lines 17–27) of Listing 5.6. After the instantiation of the policies, the precedences and immutableness (attribute *final*) are considered (see Lines 31–41).

All policy classes implement a `void apply(...)` method that is applied on the `state` object in the invoke handler (see Line 17 in Listing 5.5). This step applies the settings that have been parsed from the policy XML file to the actual fault tolerance strategy.

```
   private void loadPolicies(String filename) {
 2   // ...
     Document policyDoc = loadDocument(filename);
 4
     NodeList faults = policyDoc.getElementsByTagName("↵
         Fault");
 6   // faults contains a list of all XML elements <Fault>
     // Iterate and parse them
 8   for (int i = 0; i < faults.getLength(); i++) {
       Node faultElement = faults.item(i);
10     // ...
       // Iterate over child elements (byCause, ... , ↵
           Substitution)
12     NodeList children = faultElement.getChildNodes();
       for (int j = 0; j < children.getLength(); j++) {
14       Node child = children.item(j);
         // ...
16       APolicy policy = null;
         try { // Instantiate policy
18         String pBaseName = child.getNodeName();
           String pPkg = SystemPolicy.class.getPackage().↵
               getName();
20         String pClassName = pPkg + "." + pBaseName + "↵
               Policy";

22         Class<? extends APolicy> aPolicyClass = (Class<? ↵
               extends APolicy>) Class.forName(pClassName);
           policy = aPolicyClass.newInstance();
24       } catch (Exception e) {
           logger.error("Unable to create policy for " + ↵
               child.getNodeName(), e);
26         continue;
```

```
28      }
        // load method of policy class parses policy-↵
            specific attributes
30      policy.load((Element) faultElement);

        if (policies.containsKey(policy.getCause())) {
32        // a policy for that cause is already loaded.
          // check whether it is final or not
34        APolicy ap = policies.get(policy.getCause());
          if (!ap.isFinal())
36          policies.put(policy.getCause(), policy);
          else
38          logger.warn("Unable to load '" +
                  policy.getName() + "' policy. "+
40                "Trying to overwrite a final policy.");
        } // End policy for catetory already loaded
42        else // New policy, register in classif. map
              policies.put(policy.getCause(), policy);
44      } // <byCause>, <OriginHost>, <Substitution> loop
     } // <Fault> loop
46   // ...
     }
```
Listing 5.6: Parsing and instantition of fault handling policies in class de.fb12.mage.bpel.recovery.policies.PolicySet

5.5.2 Dynamic Resolver

The dynamic resolver is only briefly discussed here, as the implementation has already been discussed in Chapter 4. It had to be extended to allow the passing of policies to the load balancer. The load balancing component was enhanced to be able to handle restrictions induced by policies. For instance, the scheduling algorithms must now respect that even in situations with high load, it may not be allowed to provide new Cloud resources (`Substitute resources="PHYSICAL_ONLY"`).

The Load Balancer is based on the chain-of-responsibility design pattern. A new processing element has been added to that chain in order to apply the restrictions. The new processing element (called *Filter* in Figure 5.3) checks restriction type setting. If necessary, it removes faulty (e.g. for the setting `resources="DIFFERENT"`) and inappropriate machines (`PHYSICAL_ONLY`), or biases the scheduling and provisioning component (`EXISTING`, `NEW`).

5.6 Fault-Tolerant and Auto-Scaling Deployment of the BPEL engine

Using the presented automatic infrastructure scaling (Chapter 4) and the improved fault tolerance mechanism described in this chapter, the engine is capable of reacting to increasing and decreasing demand and recovering from faults. However, one performance bottleneck and single point of failure still

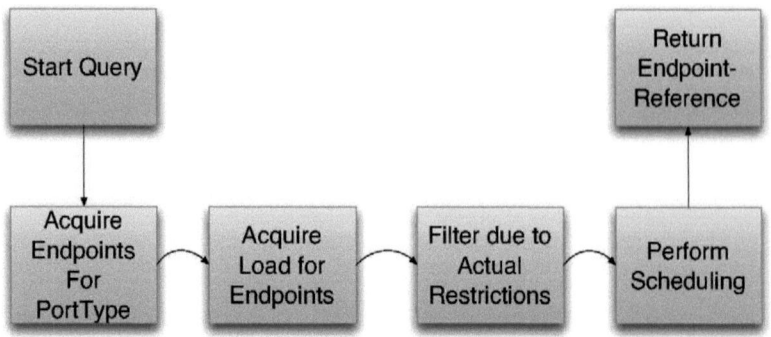

Figure 5.3: Chain of responsibility of the Load Balancer

remains. In case of high demand, the BPEL engine itself may be overburdened by managing and executing the workflows running in parallel. At best, this causes the system simply to slow down. In the worst case, workflow instances could be abandoned or, if the engine runs out of memory, the system could break down completely. A hardware or software fault on the machine running the BPEL engine would lead to a complete stagnation of the workflow system.

To circumvent these possible causes of error, a deployment scenario for the BPEL engine is presented. It utilizes several services provided by Amazon's Cloud infrastructure. The services used are described briefly below. Afterwards, their interplay to achieve both scalability and fault-tolerance is described.

5.6.1 Relevant Services of Amazon Web Services

5.6.1.1 Elastic Load Balancer

Amazon Elastic Load Balancer (ELB) is a service that automatically distributes incoming traffic across a group of EC2 instances. From a user's perspective, the mechanism is invisible. Instead of connecting directly to a specific instance, one uses the load balancer's DNS name. The load balancer then redirects the traffic to the actual instances.

The service has the capability of monitoring the health of the managed EC2 instances. If unhealthy instances are found, traffic is rerouted to other instances. The service can be configured using a command line interface or graphically with Amazon's Management Console. In Figure 5.4, the health check configuration dialog is shown. One has to define the protocol to be used to perform the health check (either TCP or HTTP), the target port, the path (local part of the URL), timeout values, the check interval and two threshold values (unhealthy and healthy).

The service may be used in combination with Amazon Auto Scaling which allows users to configure automatic scaling (in and out) operations, as de-

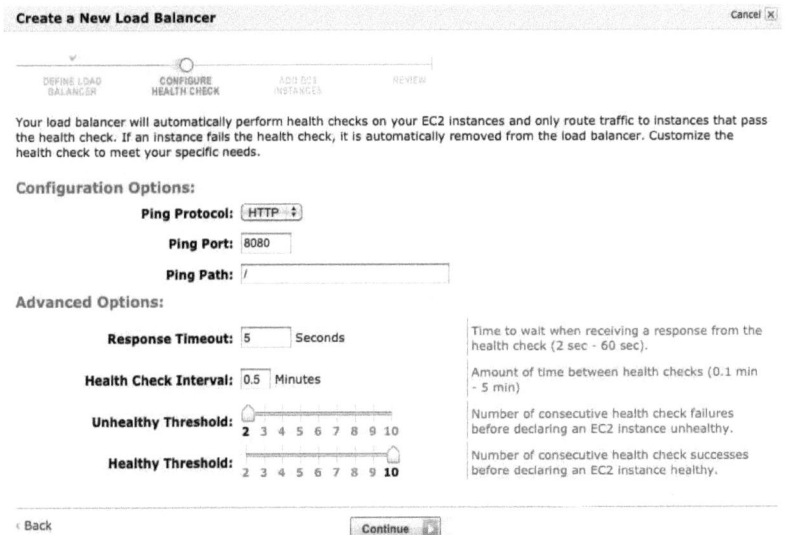

Figure 5.4: Graphical configuration (Amazon Management Console) of ELB health check

scribed in Section 5.6.1.2.

5.6.1.2 Auto-Scaling

Amazon EC2 Auto Scaling (AS) is a service which, in combination with Amazon CloudWatch, features automatic scaling in and out of EC2 instances based on user-defined conditions. The conditions are based on a variety of metrics, such as CPU utilization, network traffic, and disk I/O. To use the service, one has to define an *auto scale launch configuration*, in which it is defined which machine type (and image) should be used to scale out. In the definition of the *auto scaling group*, it is defined how many machines the group should contain at minimum, at optimum and at maximum. Furthermore, one can define over which availability zones the machines should be distributed to increase failure resistance. *Auto scale policies* define the actions to be performed when events (generated by CloudWatch) occur. In those policies, it is defined how many machines should be added or removed during scaling procedures.

The service is free, meaning that no additional charges apply (despite the hourly charges for running EC2 instances).

5.6.1.3 CloudWatch

CloudWatch is a service that monitors running EC2 instances and performs actions when certain conditions are met. Such metrics range from resource utilization (CPU) to disk I/O and network utilization. One can define the monitoring granularity (with 1 minute as the shortest interval) and threshold values (per metric) that trigger alarms. Alarms may in turn either simply lead to a notification of the resource administrator (using Amazon Simple Notification Service, SNS) or the execution of the previously-described auto-scaling policies.

The basic service is free, however, detailed monitoring (1 minute granularity) costs $ 0.015 per monitored machine and hour.

5.6.2 Scenario Architecture

The combination of the described Amazon services allows users to deploy a BPEL engine in a way that enables auto-scaling and fault tolerance. The basic idea is to prepare an Amazon Machine Image (AMI) that contains the BPEL engine and software packages required to run it. The image is then used to build an auto-scaling group. The group is monitored by Amazon CloudWatch to guarantee availability and responsiveness. When the engine achieves certain threshold values (defined in CloudWatch *alarms*) or falls short of them, CloudWatch executes auto-scaling policies to increase or decrease the number of machines within the group. The increase operation starts machines using the (custom) AMI defined in the auto-scaling group's launch configuration.

Elastic Load Balancing is used to make the group configuration transparent to workflow users and let the group appear as one machine. The auto-scaling group, which might contain more than one BPEL engine when demand is high, is thereby reachable via a unified DNS name. ELB distributes the client requests (for instance, to start workflows) among all running machines within the auto-scaling group. Whenever a machine is declared as "unhealthy" (based on user-defined threshold values defined in the corresponding CloudWatch alarm), it is automatically removed from the ELB, such that it no longer receives requests. Since CloudWatch is able to monitor how many healthy instances exist in a configured ELB, one can trigger the provisioning of a new instance to assure that the number of healthy instances does not drop below a certain minimum value.

The architecture, including relevant actions, is depicted in Figure 5.5.

5.6.3 Configuration of the Required Services

There are two ways to prepare the required Amazon Machine Image and user software. The first one is to create an custom AMI, place the required software in it and store it to Amazon S3. Then, one can use the AMI by specifying the AMIs *id* in the virtual machine's launch configuration and does not have to perform any further steps. This procedure is quite simple, but it does have two downsides: (1) storing an AMI on S3 costs money (approximately $0.15 per GB and month), (2) it is not possible to alter an AMI once it has been created. Therefore, whenever a change in the deployed software is required, one must derive a new AMI and store it to S3.

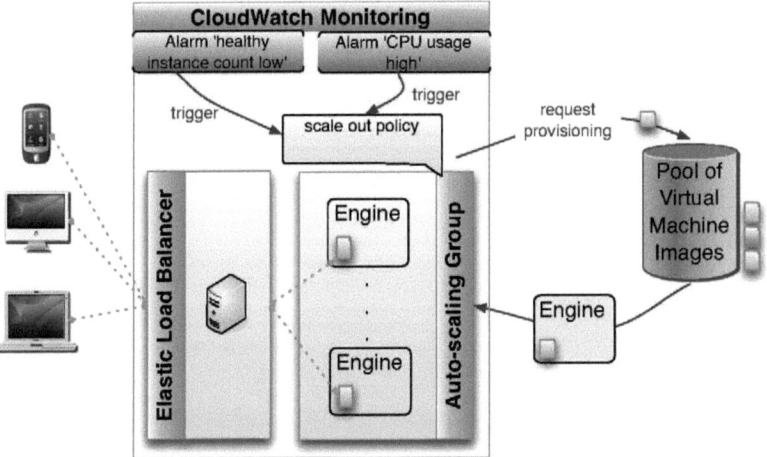

Figure 5.5: Deployment scenario for the BPEL engine

The second way is to use a standard AMI provided by Amazon or other EC2 users and configure the required software just after the virtual machine has finished booting. This is possible since Amazon offers a way to pass *user data* to the launch configuration. This user data (typically a shell script) is then executed by the virtual machine after the boot process has finished. Within such a script, one can download software, unpack and configure it, run it and much more. The advantages are clear: (1) there is no additional cost for S3, since no (custom) image needs to be stored, and (2) the procedure is flexible since the user software is stored externally and may be changed. However, this procedure is impossible for complicated setups.

For the described deployment scenario, the second approach is employed. The user data script (see Listing 5.7) downloads Java 1.6 and an archive containing a pre-configured Apache Tomcat Server with the ActiveBPEL engine installed. It then unpacks both archives, configures the environment (*PATH* and *JAVA_HOME* variables) and launches the BPEL engine, which already contains the workflows to be deployed. The software packages are stored in Amazon S3 and are made accessible via Amazon CloudFront, a content distribution network offered by Amazon.[4]

```
1 #!/bin/bash
  cd /tmp
3 #Java 1.6 is required and not installed in the AMI -> ↩
      download
  wget http://d14ajiii2136h1.cloudfront.net/jre-1.6.tgz
5
```

---

[4]While it would be possible to download directly from S3, CloudFront has the advantage that it replicates the data to different geographical locations. Therefore, the download speed should be relatively independent of the placement of the virtual machine. In contrast, S3 places the data in the region of the enclosing *bucket* (comparable to a directory). The user has to define the bucket location at the time of creation.

```
  #Unzip and configure Java Runtime
7 tar xfz jre-1.6.tgz
  export JAVA_HOME=`pwd`/jre1.6.0_07/
9 export PATH=$JAVA_HOME/bin:$PATH

11 #Download the archive containing the BPEL engine and ↩
   unpack
   wget http://d14ajiii2l36h1.cloudfront.net/as_ab_tomcat.↩
   tgz
13 tar xfz as_ab_tomcat.tgz

15 #Start the engine
   cd ab_tomcat/
17 bin/startup.sh
```

Listing 5.7: Configuration steps (bundled in bash script startAS.sh) required to run the BPEL engine on an Amazon-provided AMI

The first step in setting up the described deployment scenario is the configuration of the Elastic Load Balancer service. The configuration steps using Amazon's Command Line Interface (CLI) are delineated in Listing 5.8. A Load Balancer named *ASBPELEngine* is set up in availability zone *us-east-1d*. It forwards all HTTP traffic incoming on port 8080 (standard port for Web application containers like Apache Tomcat) to port 8080 on the instances (in the auto-scaling group). The health check uses HTTP and tries to contact all servers at port 8080 every ten seconds. If a health check fails twice in succession, the instance is declared as unhealthy and removed from the load balancing group. If an unhealthy machine successfully completes the health check ten times in succession, it is declared healthy again.

```
1 $ elb-create-lb ASBPELEngine
    --availability-zones us-east-1d \
3   --listener "protocol=http,lb-port=8080,instance-port↩
    =8080"
  > DNS_NAME BPELEngine-839625028.us-east-1.elb.↩
    amazonaws.com
5
  $ elb-configure-healthcheck ASBPELEngine
7   --healthy-threshold 10 \
    --interval 10 --unhealthy-threshold 2
9   --target HTTP:8080/ \
    --timeout 5
11 > HEALTH_CHECK  HTTP:8080/  10  5  10  2
```

Listing 5.8: Configuration of Amazon's Elastic Load Balancer service

The configuration process to set up an auto-scaling group that automatically scales out (scale in is not described here) consists of three steps. First, a launch configuration has to be set up, specifying which image, machine type and key (for ssh login) to use. The launch configuration *ASBPELEngineConfig* uses the AMI *ami-8c1fece5* (featuring Ubuntu Linux provided by Amazon) and uses the machine type "Standard Small" (confirm Table 4.1). On startup, it executes the script described in Listing 5.7 (-user-data-file startAS.sh).

Afterwards, the auto-scaling group (*ASBPELEngineGroup*) is configured; it should contain at least one machine and five machines at most. It uses the just described launch configuration and is placed in the same availability zone (*us-east-1d*) as the load balancer. The last setting (*–load-balancers ASBPELEngine*) is of high importance: it links the auto-scaling group to the load balancer, meaning that the load balancer is thereby configured to distribute traffic over all machines in the group.

Lastly, an auto-scaling policy is defined that scales out the pool of existing machines by one machine (*ASBPELEngineScaleOutPolicy*). By using the option -g ASBPELEngineGroup, one can define that the newly provisioned machine should be added to the auto-scaling group *ASBPELEngine-Group*. The policy itself does not define when it is to be executed, this is done by defining alarms in CloudWatch (see below).

```
1  $ as-create-launch-config ASBPELEngineConfig \
     --image-id ami-8c1fece5 --instance-type m1.small \
3    --key doernemt --user-data-file startAS.sh
   > OK-Created launch config
5
   $ as-create-auto-scaling-group ASBPELEngineGroup
7    --grace-period 90\
     --min-size 1 --desired-capacity 1 --max-size 5 \
9    --launch-configuration ASBPELEngineConfig \
     --availability-zones us-east-1d \
11   --load-balancers ASBPELEngine
   > OK-Created AutoScalingGroup
13
   $ scaleOutARN=`as-put-scaling-policy ↩
     ASBPELEngineScaleOutPolicy \
15   --adjustment=1 -g ASBPELEngineGroup
     -t ChangeInCapacity`
17 $ echo $scaleOutARN
   > arn:aws:autoscaling:us-east-1:458761905469:↩
     scalingPolicy:0d7a7fe6-bd27-4c10-a310-dbeacfdf7438:↩
     autoScalingGroupName/ASBPELEngineGroup:policyName/↩
     ASBPELEngineScaleOutPolicy
```

Listing 5.9: Configuration steps to set up Amazon EC2 auto-scaling service

To actually enable the auto-scaling group to react to changes regarding the demand and failure of resources, the definition of CloudWatch alarms is required. In the given case, at least two alarms are required. One has to assure that at least one machine is running to which the load balancer can forward incoming request. The second one needs to monitor the utilization of the resources in the auto-scaling group and trigger provisioning if the utilization crosses a certain threshold.

The first alarm, *HealthyCount*, monitors the Load Balancer using the metric *HealthyHostCount* (Lines 2–3 in Listing 5.10) and executes the policy *ASBPELEngineScaleOutPolicy* (Line 7), if less than one healthy machine is found (Lines 4–6).

The second alarm, *CPUHigh*, monitors the auto-scaling group using metric *CPUUtilization* and executes the same scale-out policy if the average load over all machines (-statistic Average) is above 70 % (-threshold 70, -unit Percent) for more than 60 seconds (-period 60).

```
   $ mon-put-metric-alarm --alarm-name HealthyCount \
2    --dimensions LoadBalancerName=ASBPELEngine \
```

```
    --metric-name HealthyHostCount --namespace AWS/ELB
4   --statistic Minimum --period 60 --threshold 1 \
    --comparison-operator LessThanThreshold \
6   --evaluation-periods 1 --unit Count   \
    --alarm-actions $scaleOutARN
8
  $ mon-put-metric-alarm --alarm-name CPUHigh \
10   --dimensions AutoScalingGroupName=ASBPELEngineGroup \
    --metric-name CPUUtilization --namespace AWS/EC2
12   --statistic Average --period 60 --threshold 70 --unit↵
        Percent \
    --comparison-operator GreaterThanThreshold \
14   --evaluation-periods 2 --alarm-actions $scaleOutARN
  > OK-Created Alarm
16

18 > OK-Created Alarm
```
Listing 5.10: Amazon CloudWatch configuration for auto-scaling and fault tolerance

Practical experience has shown that the described approach works as desired. CloudWatch is able to hold the required monitoring intervals exactly and reliably triggers the execution of the scale-out policy. Since EC2 provisions virtual machines within 30–90 seconds (including the execution of *startAS.sh*), the configured environment quickly reacts to failure and peak loads on the machines hosting the BPEL engine.

5.7 Experimental Results

To evaluate the fault tolerance approach, the medical workflow is used to perform runtime measurements and evaluate whether or not the developed approach is able to recover from faults. Since the same workflow is used as for the evaluation of the on-demand provisioning approach, the performance overhead induced by the fault tolerance approach can be classified.

To enforce service faults during the measurements, the Web services were modified to throw different SOAP faults with a certain probability. This probability was set to 30%; thus, the workflow shown in Figure 5.6 has a probability of successful execution of about $0.7^5 = 0.16807$. In a first scenario, the workflows were executed 200 times on a pool of dedicated machines. Then, Cloud resources were added to provide spare hardware in case of substitution.

The dedicated machines used were Core 2 Duo E6850 with 2 GB RAM, and as Cloud resources of Amazon EC2's "small instances" (1.7 GB RAM, 160 GB hard disk, 32 Bit Linux, 1 ECU, $0.095 per hour, see Table 4.1) were used.

The policies for all fault categories were set to perform the same number of retries. If q is the fault ratio of each service and r the number of retries

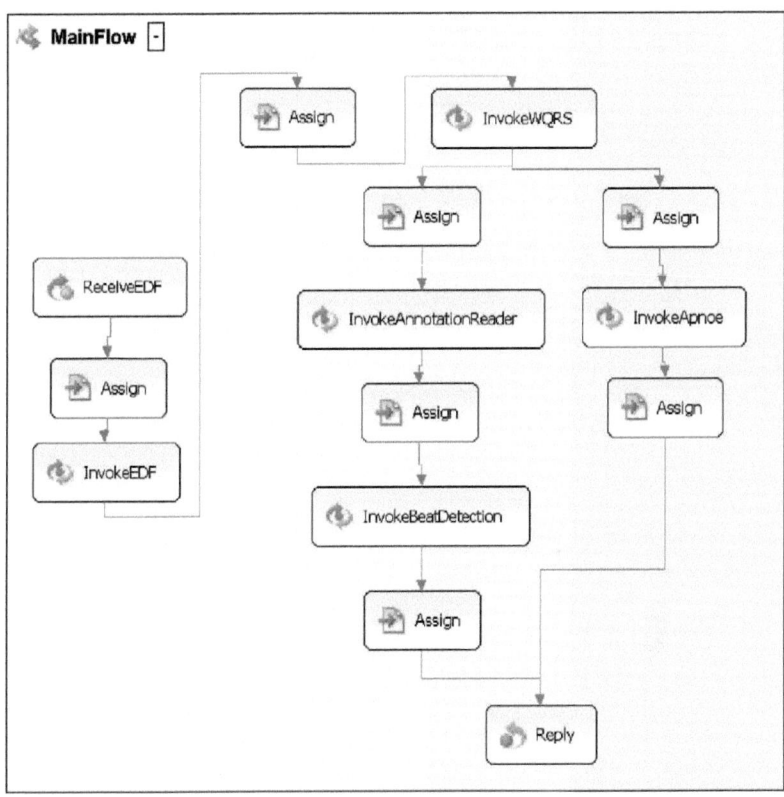

Figure 5.6: Medical workflow. Screenshot taken from DAVO, the visual modeling tool

Number of Retries	Theoretical Fail Ratio	Empirical Fail Ratio
0	0.83193	0.85258
1	0.37597	0.35856
2	0.12790	0.11155
3	0.039849	0.0398
4	0.012091	0.0159
5	0.0036397	0.0159

Table 5.2: Theoretical and empirical workflow fail ratios

and substitutions specified in the policies, then

$$\sum_{i=0}^{\#Services-1} q^{r+1} \cdot (1 - q^{r+1})^i$$

quantifies the probability for an unsuccessful workflow run. In Table 5.2, the theoretical and empirical values are shown.

In Figures 5.7–5.9, the workflow runtimes for the non-Cloud scenario with different settings of the parameter r are shown: $r = 0$ means that no recovery is allowed, $r = 1$ means that only *one* retry or *one* substitution is performed. For $r = 0$ it is evident that the majority of workflows fail early (after approximately 15 seconds). The initial data transfer always succeeded; then, the invocation of the first service frequently failed. In some cases, the workflows were abandoned later due to faults in subsequent service invocations. These later failures can be observed in the other cluster points: one at approx. 35 seconds, one at ca. 50 seconds and another close to 65 seconds.

The figures for $r = 1$ and $r = 3$ also contain cluster areas in the data for successful workflow runs. They correlate with the different number of retry and substitution that needed to be performed. For instance, for $r = 1$, many successful workflow executions are clustered at around 130 seconds runtime (which is comparable to the runtime of the successful runs for $r = 0$), such workflow runs obviously finished without a retry operation. The second clustering area is around 140–150 seconds, such successful runs used on retry operation. The picture is not as clear for $r = 3$, but one still can sea a clustering area at 130 seconds (0 retries), a (fuzzy) clustering area at 140–150 seconds and some successful runs that took up to 170 seconds (3 retries).

In some cases, the number of retries exceeded the configured r, meaning that the workflow terminated with failure. For $r = 3$, only 10 of 250 workflow runs failed (4%). This value is quite close to the theoretical value of 3, 98%. It is obvious that the majority of workflows runs longer than the raw execution time (approx. 120 seconds, see successful runs for $r = 0$). This is, among others, due to the fact that input data has to be transferred to the surrogate machine. As a rule, one can say that with increasing r, the average runtime increases while at the same time the failure ratio decreases. For $r = 4$, four of the workflows failed in 250 runs – 1.59 % (the theoretical fail ratio is 1,2%). The empirical value for $r = 5$ is exactly the same as for $r = 4$

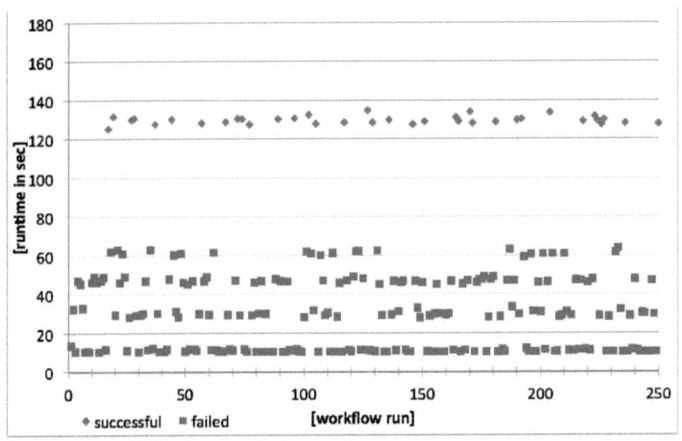

Figure 5.7: Runtimes of the workflow for $r = 0$

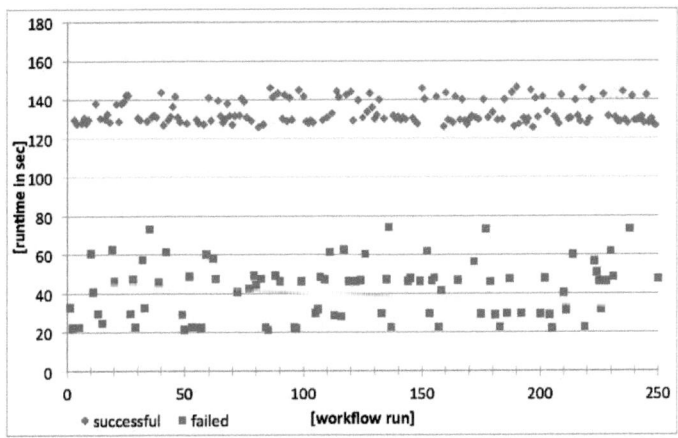

Figure 5.8: Runtimes of the workflow for $r = 1$

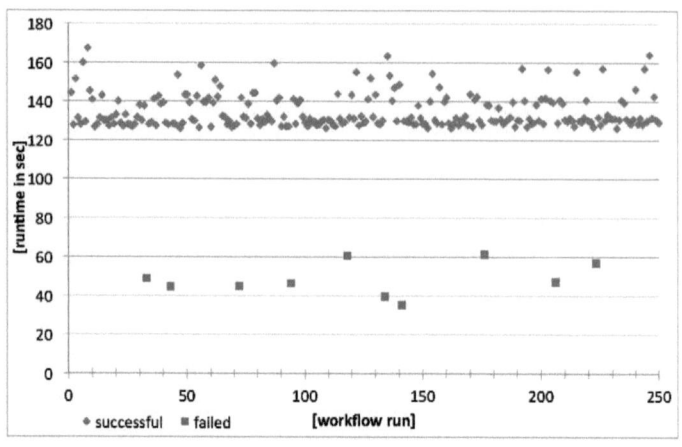

Figure 5.9: Runtimes of the workflow for $r = 3$

– theoretically, it should be 0,3 %. This minor blemish is explainable: the sample (250 values) is relatively small.

In Figure 5.10, the runtime of workflows in a pure Cloud-based setup with $r = 3$ and substitution is illustrated. The average runtime (122.57 sec) is below the average runtime of workflows on dedicated resources (134.64 seconds for $r = 3$). While this might be surprising (because of the lower computational power of the virtual machine), this is due to the higher network bandwidth available at Amazon's EC2. The virtual machines within the EC2 are (guaranteed to be) connected via a 250 MBit/s network, but the dedicated machines were connected by a 100 MBit/s network.

The provisioning of Cloud resources (including the startup of middleware components) takes approx. 60 seconds (see Figure 4.5). Internal monitoring showed that eleven additional Cloud resources[5] were started. With one exception (run 154)[6], the average runtime for the corresponding runs (196, 69 seconds) is much higher than the workflow runs without provisioning procedures. This is due to the fact that the provisioning procedure interrupts the workflow execution for ca. 60 seconds. Roughly calculated, the average runtime of workflows using this setup (122, 57 seconds) plus the provisioning overhead (60 seconds) sums up to the measured average runtime for work-

---

[5]Additional resources were provisioned in workflow runs 2, 18, 65, 71, 84, 92, 108, 143, 154, 192, and 208.

[6]The runtime for run 154 is about 89 seconds. This is due to the fact that the workflow failed after three substitutions with no avail. Therefore, it did not execute all workflow steps, but was prolonged by 60 seconds due to the provisioning process.

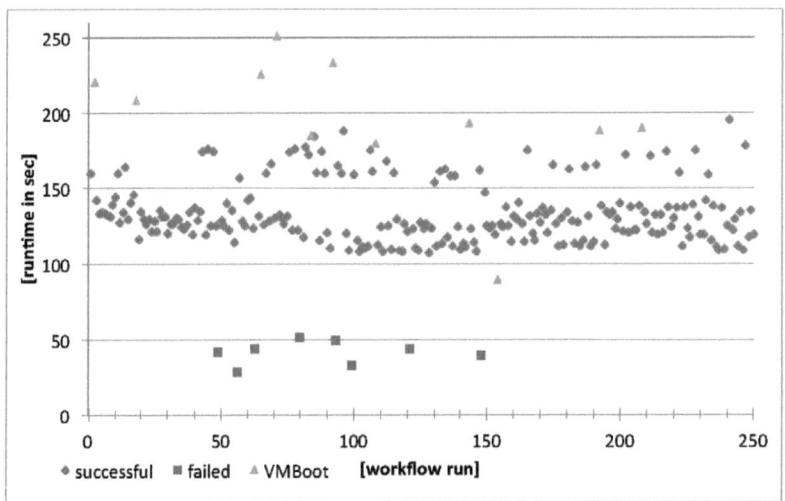

Figure 5.10: Runtimes of the workflow for $r = 3$ with Cloud-backed redundancy

flows with provisioning.

5.8 Summary

The approach developed in this chapter has been motivated by the need for an approach to transparently handle infrastructural faults when BPEL is used to execute computationally-intensive workflows in distributed computing.

Classes of faults that can be automatically handled have been defined. The approach is based on policies used to configure automatic behaviors without needing to add explicit fault handling mechanisms to a BPEL process. It provides automatic redundancy of services using a IaaS-based Cloud computing infrastructure to allow substitution of defective services without requiring sparse hardware running in the background.

An implementation based on Amazon's Elastic Compute Cloud has been presented. The approach has been evaluated in terms of reliability and performance using the medical use case presented in Chapter 2. It has been shown that the approach works reliably and the overhead is acceptable, even when Cloud resources are provided at runtime.

Furthermore, the BPEL engine itself has been identified as a single point of failure and potential performance bottleneck. To circumvent these shortcomings, a deployment scenario that makes use of services offered by Amazon's Cloud infrastructure has been developed. The approach utilized Elastic Load Balancing to make a group of resources available via *one* unique address and distribute the load over all available machines. Auto-scaling and CloudWatch are used in conjunction to monitor the health and load of the machines. Policies have been defined to automatically scale out the system in cases of failure or high utilization.

Chapter 6
Cost and Data Flow Aware Scheduling

Contents

6.1	Introduction	97
6.2	The Influence of Data Transfer on Workflow Runtime ...	98
6.3	Related Work	101
6.4	Design of CaDaS	103
	6.4.1 Framework Components	104
	6.4.2 Multi-Objective Scheduling Algorithm	107
6.5	Implementation	109
	6.5.1 Workflow Annotations	109
	6.5.2 Workflow Execution	110
6.6	Experimental Results	117
6.7	Summary	121

6.1 Introduction

One of the main reasons for spreading tasks through resources in distributed systems is to reduce the total runtime of dependent tasks. If two tasks A and B do not directly depend on each other (meaning that, for instance, B does not need the output produced by A as input), it is possible to execute both tasks in parallel on different resources, which reduces the execution time. If A and B depend on each other, speeding up the execution of A and B is still possible by placing the tasks on an underutilized machine (such that the tasks do not have to share the CPU with other tasks) or, generally, by placing the tasks on the most powerful machine. For both described cases, a common question arises regarding how to handle data dependencies between dependent tasks. The runtime reduction gained by parallelization might be used up by the time it takes to transfer input data to a resource. Therefore, the task placement algorithm should take data dependencies between tasks into account.

In order to apply this to the workflow system presented here, other aspects also need to be considered. Most notably, despite workflow runtime, cost becomes an important factor for scheduling decisions. In Cloud environments, data transfer between resources and resource usage itself cost money. The services consumed by a workflow might be distributed in different ways: (1) some may run on resources in Cloud A, some in Cloud B; (2) some may run on locally available resources, some on on-demand resources (hybrid Cloud); (3) they might be distributed among different geographical regions/data centers of the same Cloud provider. To circumvent the disadvantages induced by distribution, an adequate scheduling algorithm should schedule workflow steps to Cloud resources such that both data transmission time (or makespan in general) and cost are optimized.

To address the sketched problems, this chapter presents a multi-objective scheduling algorithm that takes data dependencies between BPEL workflow steps into account. It takes both workflow execution time (consisting of computational time and data transmission time) and cost induced by the resource selection into account. Since multi-objective approaches produce *Pareto optimal* solutions, the workflow user can define weights for both criteria that lead to an unique solution. Moreover, the algorithm determines whether the provisioning of additional resources (from an IaaS infrastructure) would lead to a better result.

This chapter is organized as follows: Section 6.2 further describes the problem and introduces some boundary conditions induced by peculiarities of Cloud infrastructures. Section 6.4 presents both the scheduling algorithm and the design of required extensions to the workflow environment. Section 6.5 describes details of the implementation which again uses Amazon EC2 as am IaaS infrastructure. Section 6.6 presents experimental results that demonstrate the feasibility of the approach using the medical workflow. Section 6.3 discusses related work and Section 6.7 summarizes the chapter.

Parts of this chapter have already been published. In a first paper, the general idea of data flow-based scheduling of BPEL workflows has been presented [54]. The approach used workflow runtime as the only objective. Therefore, the approach was further refined and extended such that cost may be considered as a criteria for resource selection [83].

6.2 The Influence of Data Transfer on Workflow Runtime

As described in detail before, the BPEL standard does not describe deployment details, especially not how target addresses for the services used by invoke operations are resolved. There are two possibilities: (1) static definition at the time they are developed and (2) dynamic lookup of target machines at runtime. Possibility (1) allows developers to explicitly take data dependencies between invoke steps into account, meaning that one could manually define that Service B is executed on the same machine as Service A if B depends on data produced by A. However, if the workflow is run in parallel several times, the machine hosting A and B could be overloaded and the workflow's runtime would increase (or the workflow might even fail due to timeouts). On the other hand, possibility (2) allows the system to dynamically select the target machines right before the execution of the invoke operation, as described in Chapter 4. If the target machine selection does not consider data dependencies (which was one of the main disadvantages of the presented sample task-based scheduling algorithm in Chapter 4), workflow runtime might actually *increase* compared to a sequential execution on a single resource.

Figure 6.1 sketches a very basic example where the runtime is *decreased* due to opportune resource selection. It is assumed that a resource cannot execute more than one task simultaneously. The runtime decreases (right side of the figure) because workflow Steps A and B (that both depend on data produced by Step P(redecessor)) may be executed in parallel *and* the amount of data to be transferred is minimal. Therefore, the parallelization does not introduce a high data transfer overhead.

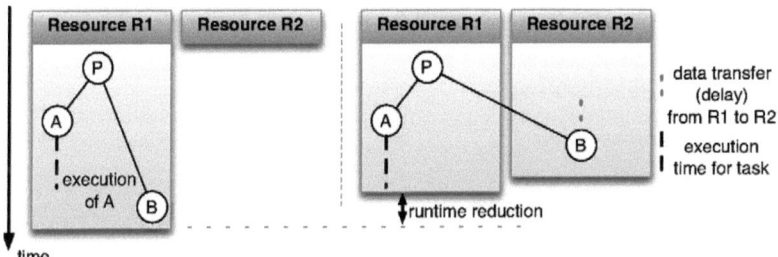

Figure 6.1: Runtime decrease induced by opportune resource selection. On the left side, the non-parallelized version is shown, while the right side displays a distributed version

A counter example is given in Figure 6.2. In the example, Task A and B also depend on P, but the amount of data to be transferred from P to B is much larger than in the previous example. In this case, it would be favorable to place Task B on Resource $R1$ (no data transfer required) and place Task A on Resource $R2$.

Such matchmaking is further complicated by the fact that resources typically have to be shared between workflow instances. This means that the scheduler has to take into account that a resource (in particular its CPU) has to be shared, which prolongates a service's execution time, which, in turn, could make transferring data to an underutilized remote resource a favorable decision. To avoid sharing resources, one could introduce a reservation sys-

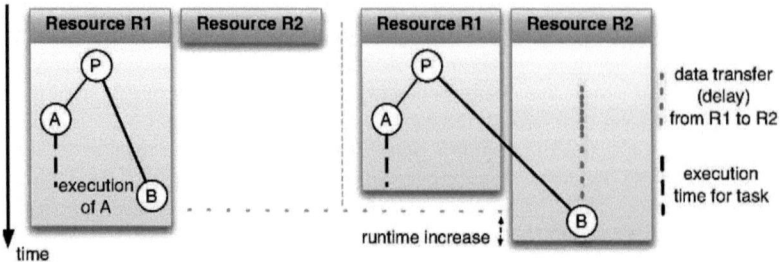

Figure 6.2: Runtime increase induced by unfavorable resource selection

tem which would assign resources exclusively to *one* service at a time. This would introduce another form of delay: wait time for the resource to become available, which the scheduler would have to respect as well.

It is noteworthy that the delay induced by data transfers is not independent of the actual resource selection. On the one hand, the connection speed ("bandwidth") is not equal for all resource pairs (R_x, R_y). This is especially important when the system is used in a hybrid Cloud infrastructure or in a federation of Clouds. In this case, one has to deal with fast (local-area/Intranet) connections within the resource pools (nowadays between 100 MBit/sec and 10 GBit/sec) and a potentially much slower wide-area/Internet connection *between* the pools. On the other hand, the *available* connection speed may differ (heavily) from the *theoretical/physical* connection speed. That is because the network load varies, particularly in public networks (i.e., the Internet), where one has to share the media with many other users.

Practical experiments with Amazon's Cloud infrastructure in the last three years have shown that the connection speed *within* Amazon's data centers at any given time has met the promised 250 MBit/sec. However, the connection speed from our institution (connected to the Internet at 400 MBit/sec) *to and between* Amazon's data centers/regions varies heavily. We have not yet found an explanation for this trend, though time of day seems to play a role. This fact necessitates an infrastructure that monitors the available bandwidths continuously and makes the measurement results available to the scheduler immediately. Sample measurements of the actual connection speeds between Amazon's worldwide data centers are sketched in Figure 6.3. The measurements present a snapshot (median of measurements taken within 24 hours in the Spring 2011); there is no claim regarding the universal validity of the sample values.

The data flow within a BPEL workflow is not explicitly modeled. Instead, it is implicitly given by the *assign* operations between *invoke* activities. Assign operations copy data from a source variable (typically the preceding invoke's output variable) to a destination variable (typically the succeeding invoke's input variable). Input and output data of invoke operations are modeled using the attributes *inputVariable* and *outputVariable* that both map to *messageTypes* in the corresponding service's WSDL description.

Therefore, it is necessary to analyze the workflow's assign operations and

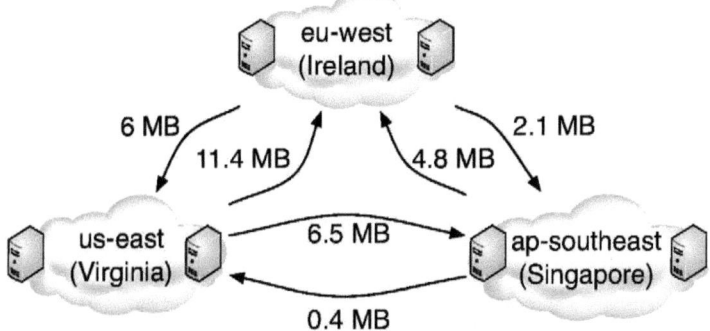

Figure 6.3: Real-life measurements of data transfer speeds between different data centers of the Cloud provider Amazon. The values have a high degree of fluctuation, especially connections to and from the data center in Asia. Therefore, continuous monitoring of connection speeds is mandatory

construct a data flow graph before any algorithmic processing can be done. In addition to the automatic analysis, some user interaction is required. The user has to annotate a rough estimation of expected data volumes for each edge in the data flow graph, because this information is completely independent from the workflow logic and cannot be guessed. The development tools presented in Chapter 8 provide a special "data flow view" that is automatically derived from an analysis of the assign operations and allows users to annotate required data. In Figure 6.4, both the control and data flow of the medical workflow are illustrated.

Once the data flow graph has been generated and filled with information on the expected service runtimes and data transfer times, the workflow steps can be assigned to resources. Since it has to be performed at workflow runtime (as explained above), the runtime of the scheduling algorithm itself is crucial because it directly influences workflow runtime. Therefore, the algorithm must not be computationally intensive, while still taking several parameters into account: current load of all possible target machines, current link speed between the machines, the amount of data to be transferred between the machines, and cost induced by resource selection and data transfers.

6.3 Related Work

Scheduling, and workflow scheduling in particular, is a very well researched area. On that score, a variety of related work exists. Hence, the discussion of related work focusses on papers recently published with the application domains Grid and Cloud computing.

Wang et al. [136] have presented a so-called look-ahead genetic algorithm (LAGA). LAGA operates on a DAG and optimizes both the makespan (defined by the execution time) and the reliability (defined by a failure factor).

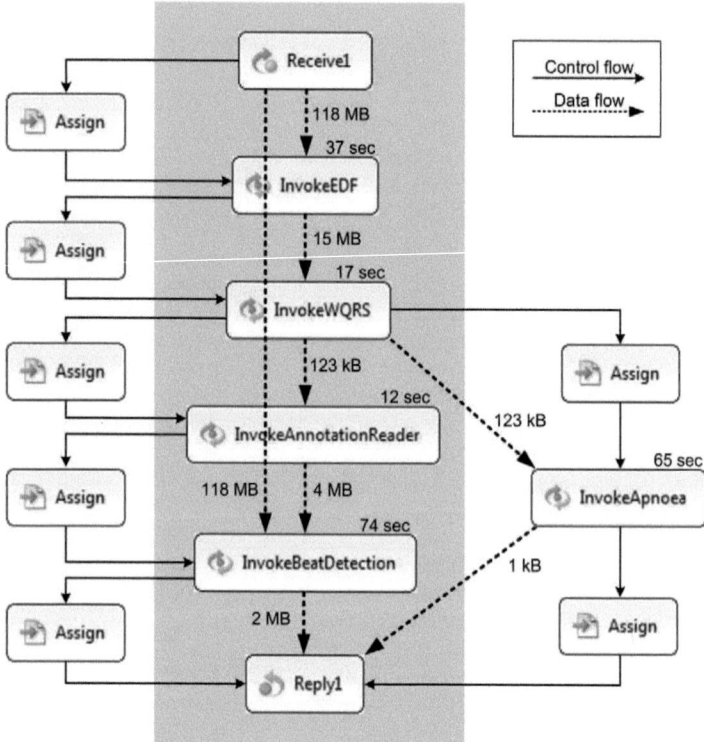

Figure 6.4: Control and data flow of the medical workflow. The data flow has been derived by analyzing the assign operations

For this aim, three different heuristics are employed, one with resource priority and two with task priority. Furthermore, the look-ahead mechanism enables the GA to avoid invalid solutions. The algorithm achieves a better solution than other list heuristics.

Yu et al. [145] have proposed a workflow execution planning approach that makes use of a multi-objective evolutionary algorithm. The authors focus on Quality of Service metrics, namely the trade-off between execution time and cost, while meeting deadline(s) and budget requirements. The planner generates a set of alternative solutions if optimization criteria are in conflict with each other. Furthermore, corresponding fitness functions that account for the minimization of the objectives and penalty functions of constraints have been developed.

Both approaches have the common drawback that they only operate on DAG structures and, in their presented form, do not deal with dynamic infrastructures. For this reason, they cannot be used for Web service orchestration with BPEL.

A load balancing approach for BPEL workflows is presented by Ferber et al. [62]. They introduce three scheduling algorithms (round robin, lowest counter first, and weighted random) in order to dynamically invoke Web services from a BPEL workflow. Therefore, they wrap each invoke activity within the process in a pre- and processing step, i.e., they need to modify the process itself and thereby mix up the levels of infrastructural and business logic. However, they do not take data dependencies between different invoke activities into account or consider the follow-up costs of their scheduling decision. Furthermore, their system is not designed to dynamically provision new machines in case of peak-load situations.

Lee et al. [94] also identified the need to become aware of the underlying network infrastructure/topology in IaaS environments when it comes to data intensive workloads. They developed a simulation-based algorithm to estimate the performance of resource allocations for Hadoop MapReduce jobs. Therefore, detailed resource allocation policies are provided that allocate virtual machines on hosts within specific racks inside the provider's data center. While such a detailed scheduling is certainly helpful for applications that heavily make use of communication, like MapReduce or MPI jobs, Web services are typically not that interlocked. Furthermore, IaaS providers do not enable customers to specify on which specific node a virtual machine should be provisioned; only more coarse-grained possibilities like availability zones are provided.

6.4 Design of CaDaS

Based on the problem described above, this section presents the design of the CaDaS (Cost and Data Flow-Aware Scheduler) framework that uses a multi-objective heuristic algorithm to determine scheduling decisions of invoke activities of BPEL workflows. The framework basically consists of two logical units: one represents the infrastructure and provides functionality to manage virtual machines, while the other represents the algorithm itself (see

Figure 6.5). The infrastructural model provides information about network and (virtual) machine characteristics that the algorithm can take into account.

6.4.1 Framework Components

CaDaS contains three main building blocks: (1) scheduler, (2) provisioner, and (3) service registry. The scheduler determines mappings between workflow tasks and resources (see Figure 6.5). It creates an internal representation of the workflow that is used by the multi-objective *Genetic Algorithm* on which the scheduler is based (detailed in Section 6.4.2). The provisioner has already been presented in the context of Chapter 4. It is responsible for managing Cloud resources, i.e., provisioning new resources when needed and de-provisioning unused resources.

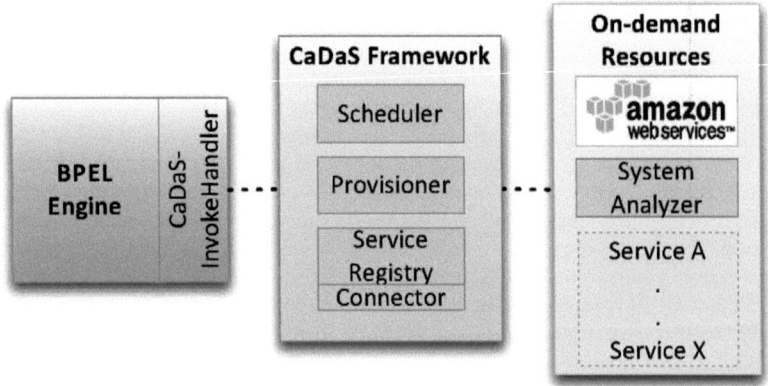

Figure 6.5: Architectural components of CaDaS from a birds-eye view

The registry contains all infrastructural data, such as locally available resources, running virtual machines, connection speeds between resources, and resource reservations that result from computed mappings. The model that the registry uses as the basic representation is hierarchical. Cloud providers typically have different data centers located within different countries or regions. These geographically distributed data centers are represented by *zone*s. Each of these data centers might offer different virtual machine types that a user can start. These different machine types are represented by *vm-Type* elements. Furthermore, one specific virtual machine is able to boot different images, i.e., different operating systems, which are represented by *image* elements in the model; see Figure 6.6 for a simplified representation.

Based on this general model, several other attributes are needed. First, each zone must be annotated with cost attributes (*feeIn*[1] and *feeOut* in Figure

---
[1] As a side note, it should be remarked that Amazon changed the pricing model as of July,

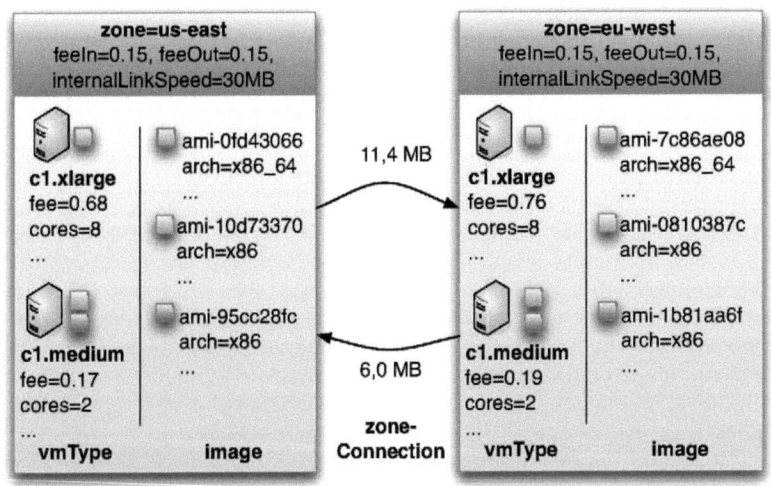

Figure 6.6: Internal representation of a Cloud topology and resources

6.6) that model data transfer costs. A distinction between internal transfers within a zone and external transfers has to be made. The internal connection speed is represented by the attribute *internalLinkSpeed*, whereby the connections to other zones are modeled using separate objects. *zoneConnections* store information about connections between zones and corresponding link speeds – the latter must be updated continuously to reflect the current network load. The information available in zoneConnections enables the algorithm to take communication speeds (and the induced cost) into account. Using this information and the user's preference values, the algorithm can determine whether it is better to wait for a local resource to become available or to move the data to a different zone and execute the task there (which may induce cost and an execution delay).

To prevent a network overload only by monitoring it, the monitoring is performed passively by the *SystemAnalyzer*, i.e., no packets are transmitted to measure the transfer rate, but the data transfers performed between different zones are used to determine the connection speeds. Furthermore, this information (obtained from distinct machines in zones) is used representatively for all machines in a zone – thereby, a newly provisioned machine is equipped with the measured value, rather than a pre-set theoretical value. Without this mechanism, the machine would have the (possibly highly inaccurate) value until it transmitted some data. An inaccurate value in turn might have the effect that the machine is never used – resulting in a never-updated zoneConnection. Since measurement values only represent a particular moment of time, exponential smoothing is used to profile the connection speed

---

1st, 2011: incoming data transfer is now free of charge. See http://aws.amazon.com/pricing_effective_july_2011/?ref_=pe_12300_20380280 for details.

over time.

Each image must contain information about in which zone it is available and which virtual machine types are compatible with this specific image (e.g., a 64-bit Debian Linux can not be booted by a 32-bit virtual machine). Each vmType must have annotations with the computing costs per hour and some hardware related attributes, such as the number of (virtual) CPU cores, each core's speed (measured in EC2 Compute Units, ECU).

The model described above considers static structures like data centers and machine types, but to operate efficiently, the scheduler also needs to model runtime information to coordinate the invoke activities on different machines. Hence, a reservation system is designed to support this. This reservation system operates on the granularity of a CPU core and prevents peak-load situations (per host) by exclusively assigning the core to an invoke operation. Reservations have a specific period of validity that is derived from service runtimes and necessary data transfers. The beginning of a Web service invocation (t_{data}) and the start of the reservation's period of validity (t_{start}) are not the same since the data transfer has to take place first, and it does not consume mentionable computational resources. The offset between the two is automatically determined by the estimated data transfer time, which is computed as $min(kbpsOut_{src}, kbpsIn_{dest})$. As depicted in Figure 6.7, the system calculates reservations such that no resource usage overlap occurs. This includes that the stage out of a preceding workflow step $i-1$ does not interfere with the stage in of the succeeding workflow step i, if executed on the same machine.

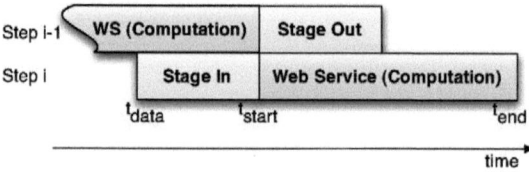

Figure 6.7: Reservations for a single CPU core and data transfers (stage in and stage out)

Despite the fact that virtualization provides a homogeneous environment to host the middleware, it does not abstract from all the characteristics of the underlying machine. Since Amazon uses different host machines with different CPUs inside (e.g., Intel Xeon and AMD Opteron), virtual machines differ in their performance, although they might be in the same instance type group. Among other aspects, such as changing network connection speeds, these performance deviations have a considerable impact on service runtimes [121]. Therefore, it is not expected that these reservations can be kept precisely and their duration limits are interpreted with +10% of the reservation's period of validity before a reservation becomes invalid. If the service finishes earlier than expected, a *backfilling* of subsequent invoke activities should be attempted by utilizing gaps between existing reservations. Otherwise, a rescheduling and therefore a recomputation of existing reservations is triggered.

6.4.2 Multi-Objective Scheduling Algorithm

Since BPEL is a non-DAG and Turing-complete language, it is not possible to directly apply any of the existing workflow-based scheduling algorithms without any constraints. Some algorithms transform the cyclic structure of a BPEL process into a DAG. To achieve this, they either make use of an upper barrier for the iteration of *while* loops, or they defer this decision to the runtime of the process [58, 119]. Even if a BPEL workflow can be transformed into a DAG structure, scheduling in DAG structures is still NP-complete and only computable in polynomial time for some simple cases [92]. The number of tasks of a workflow as well as number of available resources can grow very quickly, especially when virtual resources may be allocated. The time necessary to compute a schedule should ideally not significantly increase the workflow runtime, meaning that calculating all possible task-resource mappings – and selecting the best – is not feasible, since the complexity would grow exponentially with the number of tasks and resources.

The usage of a heuristic algorithm ensures an acceptable runtime of the scheduling algorithm itself since it reduces the complexity of the search space significantly. This provides a compromise between scheduling runtime and optimality of the assignment. Within heuristic approaches, a genetic algorithm provides a good trade-off between runtime and quality of the result. A genetic algorithm adopts the principles of evolution to find a solution to an optimization problem. Therefore, it uses operations such as mutation, selection and elitism to calculate the mapping between workflow tasks and resources [33, 63].

Because resources are billed in a pay-per-use manner in Cloud environments, the algorithm's objective function differs from those of typical scheduling algorithms in that it is multi-dimensional. In addition to workflow runtime, workflow execution cost has to be considered. Hence, the solution candidates are not totally, but partially, ordered and a selection function that computes a single solution based on the two objectives is required. The following types of genetic algorithms are capable of dealing with multi-objective optimization problems: Non-dominated Sorting Genetic Algorithm (NSGA II) [45], Strength Pareto Evolutionary Algorithm (SPEA2) [147, 148] and Pareto Archived Evolution Strategy (PAES) [91]. Yu et al. argue [145] that SPEA2 has good convergence properties (much better than PEAS) and, due to the high degree of parametrization, is adaptable to different application areas. Therefore, SPEA2 is used as the basis for this work. The pseudo-code in Listing 6.1 illustrates the order of operations.

```
1 generateInitialPopulation();

3 while ( !abortCriteria ) {
    doSelection();
5   doCrossOver();
```

```
     doMutation();
   7 paretoSet = calcParetoSet();
     }
   9 return paretoSet;
```
Listing 6.1: Pseudo-code for a multi-objective genetic scheduling algorithm

A scheduling algorithm can operate on the entire workflow graph (*workflow-based*) or on just a single task (*task-based*) of the workflow. The latter does not take (data) dependencies between steps into account and is therefore not feasible here. Hence, the presented algorithm operates on an entire workflow and calculates the task-resource mapping.

At first, the algorithm generates an initial population (a set containing so-called *individuals*), see Line 1 in Listing 6.1. An individual in turn represents a *complete* (randomly chosen) mapping between all workflow tasks and resources. Thereby, candidate resources are resources that are ealready running or virtual machines (to be provisioned). Since Cloud providers offer different virtual machine types and operate data centers at different geographical locations, representatives for all of these combinations are added to individuals of the initial population. Adding those "placeholder" virtual machines offers a major benefit: it implicitly includes the possibility of starting additional virtual machines into the scheduling scheme without introducing further complexity – the scheduling algorithm handles those machines identically to machines that are already running. The only difference is such a placeholder machine would have to be provisioned when the scheduler decides to include it into the resource pool. The size of the population depends on the number of existing resources (both physical and virtual), virtual machine types per zone, and workflow graph size.

After that, the algorithm iterates to improve the fitness of the individuals in the population (Line 3). Fitness means the quality of mapping with respect to cost and runtime. Thereby, both runtime and cost are aggregated over all workflow steps. The cost and runtime of a each step in turn depends on the underlying resource (since resource prices vary between different zones) and the geographical location of the resource from which the required input data is staged. To calculate both values, the system uses the values from zones and zoneConnections (see above).

Within *doSelection*, the algorithm selects the fittest candidates (those who dominate others according to the objective function, Line 4). Afterwards, using *doCrossOver* (Line 5) and *doMutation* (Line 6), new individuals are generated. In contrast to the generation of the initial population, the new individuals are based on properties of the fittest existing ones.

calcParetoSet (Line 7) collects the set of individuals that dominate others. An example is given in Figure 6.8 in which the fitness value of one individual is determined by the number of individuals by which it is dominated. Thus, a fitness of 0 means that no other individual dominates this specific one.

When the algorithm terminates (abort criteria are detailed below), a single individual is determined based on the calculated Pareto front and a user-supplied weighting function (which defines the relevance of the two dimensions to the user). The solution represents the best mapping given the user's preferences. Based on this mapping, reservations for the selected candidates are made.

It is obvious that the quality of the algorithm's interim results cannot decrease while iterating, as the worst results are removed in every step; in the worst case, the results would simply not improve between iteration steps. If the Pareto set does not change in a number of subsequent iterations, the algorithm terminates. Furthermore, to provide an upper bound for the scheduler's runtime, there is a hard limit of iterations, which depends on the population size.

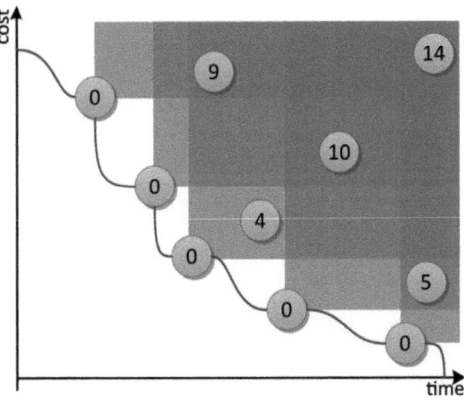

Figure 6.8: Fitness values of individuals and dominating ones (Pareto front).

6.5 Implementation

As for the previously introduced features, a main requirement for the implementation is their non-invasive realization. This means that neither existing standards nor implementations should be changed but rather be extended by the use of available extension mechanisms. Therefore, the custom invoke handler mechanism is used as a hook to integrate the scheduler's implementation into the BPEL engine.

6.5.1 Workflow Annotations

The data flow of a BPEL workflow is not explicitly modeled, but implicitly given by the *copy* statements within *assign* activities. However, the amount of data within the flow is not given, since this information is completely independent of the workflow logic. This necessitates user interaction: the estimated data amounts to be transferred between services need to be annotated. While putting this information into the BPEL process itself would break compatibility with the standard, putting it into the process deployment descriptor, as mentioned earlier, does not.

```
1  myself = m₁ : m₂ : ... : mₙ;
   src : 1 = s₁,₁ : ... : s₁,ₗ₁; dest : m₁ = d₁,₁ : ... : d₁,ₖ₁;
3  ⋮
   src : n = sₙ,₁ : ... : s₂,ₗₙ; dest : mₙ = dₙ,₁ : ... : d₂,ₖₙ;
```
Listing 6.2: Format of Data Flow Invoke Handler String

In Listing 6.2, m_i refers to the *bpelLocations* (XPath) of *invoke* operations. $s_{i,j}$ is formatted as follows:

$$s_{i,j} = \text{bpelLocation}[\text{dataAmount} = x_{i,j}, \text{compTime} = y_{i,j}].$$

where $x_{i,j}$ is the amount of data transferred between $s_{i,j}$ and m_i ($y_{i,j}$ is the execution time of service $s_{i,j}$). $d_{i,j}$ is defined analogously, but refers to the outgoing edge of the data flow graph.

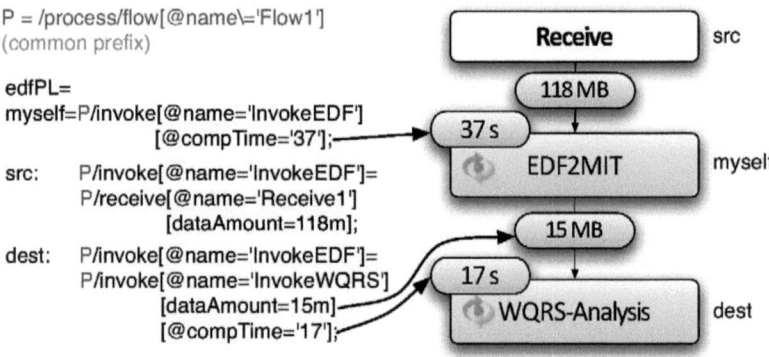

Figure 6.9: Example of a Data Flow Invoke Handler String

To preserve compatibility with the BPEL standard, data flow annotations are stored within a workflow's deployment descriptor. An example for the encoding of annotations is given in Figure 6.9. It exemplifies the annotations for the partnerLink of the EDF service. The information is passed from the custom invoke handler (*CaDaS-InvokeHandler*, see Figure 6.5) to the ModelGenerator that in turn generates a graph representation that can be processed by the scheduler.

6.5.2 Workflow Execution

To realize the main goal of minimizing changes to the workflow engine, interfaces and observers provided by the workflow engine are used. The

CaDaS-InvokeHandler (IH) implements the `IAeInvokeHandler` interface provided by the workflow engine. The invoke handler is embedded into workflows using the aforementioned deployment descriptor and uses the format described above to encode annotated data. It is therefore used by the BPEL engine instead of the standard invoke handler.

The sequence of calls starting from the invocation of a workflow to the execution using a computed invoke-to-resource mapping is as follows:

Generation of Graph Representation The execution of a workflow's first invoke operations triggers the creation of the data flow model that is then used by the scheduler. Obviously, this step does not have to be carried out repeatedly for the same workflow instance. *CaDaS-InvokeHandler* calls the method `getProcessInfo` of class `ProcessManager`[2]. ProcessManager maintains one `ProcessInformation` instance for every running workflow instance. ProcessInformation instances in turn contain all information that are relevant for the schedule of the given workflow instance: the data flow graph, reservations for resources, and virtual machines used by the instance. The data flow graph is generated by class `ModelGenerator`[3]. The class parses the invoke handler strings and constructs a model representation (constituted by `Graph`, `Node`, and `Edge` objects). Node objects store information concerning the required computational time for the workflow step, while Edges store the data amount to be transferred from Node to Node. Listing 6.3 shows an excerpt of the generation of the data flow graph. Note that the parsing of the invoke handler strings is omitted.

```
1  private Graph generateDataflowGraph() {
     Graph graph = new Graph();
3    for(InvokeHandlerParameters ih : invokeHandlers) {
       // ...
5      for(String myselfStr : getMyselfs(ih.getDfgFragment↵
           ())) {
         Node myself = graph.getNodeByBpelLocation(↵
             myselfStr);
7
         if (myself == null) {
9          myself = new Node(myselfStr, ih.getPortType());
           graph.addNode(myself);
11       } else if(myself.getPortType()==null){
           myself.setPortType(ih.getPortType());
13       }
         addSrcNodes(myself,
15         getSources(ih.getDfgFragment(), myselfStr),
             graph);
17
         addDestNodes(myself,
19         getDestinations(ih.getDfgFragment(), myselfStr)↵
             ,
             graph);
21     }
     }
```

[2]Package de.fb12.mage.bpel.cadas.processManagement
[3]Package de.fb12.mage.bpel.cadas.dataflowgraph

```
23      return graph;
     }
25
     private void addSrcNodes(Node myself, List<String> ↵
         bpelLocations, Graph graph) {
27      for (String srcStr : bpelLocations) {
          DataAmount dataAmount = extractDataAmount(srcStr)↵
              ;
29        srcString = extractBpelLocaton(srcStr);

31        Node srcNode = graph.getNodeByBpelLocation(srcStr↵
              );

33        if (srcNode == null) {
            srcNode = new Node(srcStr);
35          graph.addNode(srcNode);
          }
37
          Edge edge = new Edge(dataAmount);
39        edge.src=srcNode;
          edge.target=myself;
41
          if(!srcNode.getOutEdges().contains(edge)){
43          srcNode.addOutEdge(edge);
            myself.addInEdge(edge);
45        }
        }
47    }
```

Listing 6.3: Excerpt of the generation of the data flow graph model from invoke handler annotations

Check for Existing Mapping and Reservations The next step checks if a task-resource mapping already exists, i.e. the scheduler has already run. If so, it determines if a *valid* reservation for the current invoke operation exists. It is not expected that reservations can be kept precisely and their duration limits are interpreted with +10% of the reservation's period of validity before a reservation becomes invalid. As an example, if a reservation has a duration of two minutes (120 seconds), it is still considered valid if the execution of the reservation is delayed up to 12 seconds after the calculated start (of the reservation). However, if the reservation start were more than 12 seconds before the current time (stamp), the reservation (and thus *all following reservations* for the very resource) would be declared as invalid (see Line 25 in Listing 6.4); a rescheduling of the affected workflow steps would be triggered. The step furthermore checks if *backfilling* is possible (Lines 13–24). Whenever a workflow step completes (much) earlier than expected (say, at point in time t_e), subsequent workflow steps would be unnecessarily delayed, because they would have to wait $t_r - t_e$ seconds (t_r is the start time of the next step's reservation). In such a case, the ReservationAgent would try to find a gap in the selected resource's schedule in which the reservation fits. In the worst case, exactly the same reservations would be placed again if no resources are available earlier; therefore, the backfilling mechanism can only improve the result.

```
1  private boolean hasValidReservation(String bpelLoc, ↩
       ProcessInformation pi) {
     Reservation res = pi.getReservationByBpelLoc(bpelLoc)↩
       ;
3    if (res == null) {
       return false;
5    }
     final long NOW = System.currentTimeMillis();
7    // Validity period (10 percent goodwill), at least 1 ↩
       sec
     final long VALID_INT = Math.max(RESERVATION_MIN_INT,
9          (int)((res.getDuration()) * RES_INT_PERCENT));
     final long TRANSFER_START =   res.getStart() - res.↩
       getDataTransferTime();
11
     // Backfilling for very early task
13   if(NOW < (TRANSFER_START - VALID_INT)){
         IHostPropertiesBean hpb = pi.↩
           getResourceByBpelLocation(bpelLoc);
15       pi.removeReservationMappingByBpelLocation(bpelLoc);
         // Insert reservation finds earliest gap in the ↩
           schedule
17       Reservation newRes =  hpb.getReservationAgent().
           insertReservation(NOW, res.getDuration(),
19         res.getDataTransferTime(),
         "Process (Backfilling)" + pi.getProcessID(), ↩
           bpelLoc);
21       pi.putReservationMapping(bpelLoc, newRes);

23       return true;
     }
25   // invoke too late -> reservation invalid
     else if(NOW > (TRANSFER_START + VALID_INT))
27       return false;

29   // invoke within tolerance, go on
     else return true;
31 }
```
Listing 6.4: Check for the validity of resource reservations and backfilling mechanism

Execution of the Genetic Algorithm The Genetic Algorithm (GA) is executed whenever an invoke operation without a valid resource reservation is to be executed. Reasons for not having a (valid) reservation are: (1) the Genetic Algorithm has not been executed yet (i.e. the workflow execution just started), (2) a workflow step has exceeded its reservation; therefore, the reservation system declared succeeding reservations invalid, or (3) the workflow contains a *while* loop, in which case reservations are placed per loop iteration, meaning that the GA has to be executed (for the subgraph represented by the loop) at the beginning of every iteration.

Regardless of the reason for executing the GA, the procedure is as follows. At first, it is determined if the workflow contains a loop. If not, the GA can operate on the entire workflow. Otherwise, a pre-processing of the graph structure is required: cycles (loops) are removed and nodes "behind" the cycle are completely ignored, because one does not know how many iterations the loop contains, no schedule can be computed. Those nodes would be scheduled later because the preceding step in the scheduling procedure (see Paragraph *Check for Existing Mapping and Reservations*) would then detect that no mapping exists and would trigger the scheduling of the subgraph. Then, the algorithm (as described in Section 6.4.2) is executed. First, it creates an randomly chosen initial population (which is managed by the workflow's ProcessInformation instance). To be able to profit from the provisioning of additional (Cloud) resources, those resource candidates must be added to the initial population. To do so, the total number of workflow steps in the graph is calculated and a candidate resource for each machine type in each geographical region of the Cloud provider's infrastructure is added. This step is carried out by the `ResourceManager`[4]. An excerpt of the corresponding source code is given in Listing 6.5.

```
1  public void addCandidateResources(ProcessInformation pi↩
       , Graph g,
       Map<String, String> queryMap) {
3      // Get virtual machine classes
       Map<String, TreeSet<IVMType>> vms = getVMClasses(pi);
5
       // Iterate over all VM classes
7      cands = new ArrayList<IHostPropertiesBean>();
       for (String ec2cu : vms.keySet()) {
9          // Add VM with most cores in VM class
           IVMType vmType = getVMClasses(pi).get(ec2cu).last↩
               ();
11         int cores = vmType.getCores();
           int tasks = g.getNodes().size();
13         // total number of VM cores needed to compute all ↩
               tasks
           int toAdd = Math.max(Math.round(((float) tasks) / ↩
               cores), 1);
15
           // Get all zones that allow to provision VMs
17         ConfigurationReader conf = ConfigurationReader.↩
               getInstance();
           for (Map<String, String> zone : conf.getElements("↩
               zone")) {
19             Map<String, String> vmTypeMap = conf.getElement(
                   "vmType", "zone", zone.get("name"));
21             // No VMTypes for the zone found -> zone does not↩
                   allow to provision
               if (vmTypeMap.isEmpty() == true)
23                 continue;

25             // add one or more machines PER zone
               for (int i = 0; i < toAdd; i++) {
27                 // Avoid adding more machines than allowed per ↩
                       zone
                   if (vmsPerZone.get(zone.get("name")) >= ↩
                       MAX_VM_PER_ZONE) {
```

---

[4]Package `de.fb12.mage.bpel.cadas.resourceManagement`.

```
29              continue;
                }
31              Map<String, String> parameter = new HashMap<↩
                    String, String>();
                parameter.putAll(queryMap);
33              parameter.put("region", zone.get("name"));
                // ..
35              IHostPropertiesBean candHPB = new ↩
                    HostPropertiesBean(
                    parameter,
37                  // ..
                );
39              candHPB.setBogomips(vmType.getBoGoMips());
                cands.add(candHPB);
41          }
        }
43  }
    }
```
Listing 6.5: Addition of candidate resources to the initial population

After that, the algorithm iterates to improve the fitness of the individuals in the population. Thereby, both runtime and cost are aggregated over all workflow steps. The cost and runtime of a each step in turn depends on the underlying resource and the geographical location of the resource from which the required input data is staged. To calculate both values, the system uses the values from zones and zoneConnections. As an example, the calculation of the data transfer delay between two workflow steps for a given resource selection is shown in Listing 6.6.

```
    private long calcTimeForDataTransferInMSec(
2   IHostPropertiesBean hostSrc,
    IHostPropertiesBean hostTarget, DataAmount dataAmount){
4
      if(hostSrc.equals(hostTarget)){
6       return 0;
      }
8
      IZone srcZone = hostSrc.getZone();
10    IZone destZone = hostTarget.getZone();
      double minimumConnectionSpeed = 0;
12
      // We need to distinguish if both machines are in the
14    // same zone or not. If not, we have to calculate the
      // minimal transfer speed between the zones using
16    // zone connections. Otherwise, we use the internal
      // speed as basis
18
      if(srcZone.equals(destZone) == false) {
20    ZoneConnection zc = Registry.getInstance().
            getZoneConnection(srcZone.getZoneName(),
22                            destZone.getZoneName());
      minimumConnectionSpeed = Math.min(
24        zc.getKbpsOut(), zc.getKbpsIn());
      } else {
26    minConnSpeed = srcZone.getkbpsIntern();
      }
28
```

```
           return (long)(((double) dataAmount.getValueInKB()
30                        / minConnSpeed) * 1000);
         }
```
Listing 6.6: Calculation of the data transfer delay between two workflow steps

The algorithm terminates after the execution of the method *calcParetoSet* which collects the *set* of individuals that dominate others. A single individual is determined based on the calculated Pareto front and user-supplied weights for both criteria.

Reservations and Resource Provisioning Once the schedule has been computed, resource reservations are made according to the schedule. When virtual machines that have not been provisioned in preceding workflow executions are to be used, the system must provision them. One important detail of the provisioner's implementation is its tight integration with the reservation mechanism. It takes into account that virtual machines have a startup delay (boot time, installation of required Web service stack). Assume that a reservation for a (not yet provisioned) virtual machine for time t exists. Then, the provisioner would begin the provisioning at $t-d$, where d is a configurable delay (`BOOT_DELAY` is set to 90 seconds in the actual implementation). The implementation is done using the helper class `Scheduler-Timer` that is implemented as a thread. Machines that are to be provisioned are added to a queue by invoking `scheduleProvisioning` (see Line 1 in Listing 6.7). The method checks if the machine has to be booted immediately (Line 8). Otherwise, it is added to the queue. SchedulerTimer periodically examines the queue (method `provisionScheduledMachines`) and starts machines, if required.

Furthermore, SchedulerTimer keeps track of virtual machines that are already running and de-provisions them shortly before an accounting period (one hour for EC2) expires if there are no pending reservations or currently running computations.

```
1   public void scheduleProvisioning(IHostPropertiesBean ↩
        hpb, long availabilityTime) {
      synchronized (provisionSchedule) {
3       ProvisionSchedule schedule = new ProvisionSchedule(↩
            hpb, availabilityTime);

5       // If current time + time of next thread activity ↩
            is
        // after the, requested availability, immediately
7       // provision machine
        if(System.currentTimeMillis() + BOOT_DELAY_MS + ↩
            TIMER_DELAY_MS >= availabilityTime) {
9         logger.info("Immediate scheduled provisioning");
          provisionMachine(schedule);
11      } else{
          // Add machine to schedule
13        provisionSchedule.put(hpb.getId(), schedule);
        }
15  }
```

```
}
// ...
private void provisionScheduledMachines() {
    synchronized (provisionSchedule) {
        for(ProvisionSchedule schedule : ↩
            provisionSchedule.values()) {
            if(System.currentTimeMillis() + BOOT_DELAY + ↩
                TIMER_DELAY >= schedule.getAvailabilityTime↩
                ()) {
                provisionMachine(schedule);
            }
        }
    }
}
```

Listing 6.7: Excerpt of class SchedulerTimer. De-provisioning of unused machines is not shown.

One interesting implementation detail concerning the *doSelection* step in the scheduler is that random selection is not based on a uniform distribution, but rather uses a weighted distribution that favors individuals with better fitness (Roulette Wheel Selection Scheme [135]). By favoring fitter individuals, the population's quality quickly increases, which in turn results in a faster convergence towards the optimal solution and shorter runtime of the algorithm. While the mutation operation randomly exchanges single candidates, a special variant of the crossover operation is used. Normally, the crossover does not consider topological information of the underlying problem (workflow graph) and simply exchanges two randomly chosen mappings of individuals. The implemented variant, *Branch Crossover*, uses topological information and exchanges whole branches (more accurately, mappings for a complete branch) between individuals. The underlying assumption is that, due to the preceding selection operation, the individuals quite likely contain good mappings for subgraphs, i.e., branches. Like the optimizations in the selection operation, the branch crossover reduces the number of required iterations of the algorithm.

6.6 Experimental Results

This section presents and evaluates experimental results of CaDaS. To demonstrate the advantages induced by data flow aware scheduling, the experimental results are compared to the load-based algorithm, which has been presented as an example for task-based scheduling algorithms in Chapter 4.

The evaluation was performed within different scenarios, which simulate different patterns of utilization. In each of them, four Cloud resources (EC2 small instances) were used as static/on-premises hosts located in Amazon's *eu-west-1* and *us-east-1* regions[5]. The scheduler was allowed to provision

---
[5]This is due to the fact that there seems to be a peering problem between the University of Marburg and the carrier(s) of Amazon's data centers. The throughput between our institution and Amazon EC2 instances fluctuates between 10 kB/sec and 1000 kB/sec, while at the

on-demand resources in the following regions: *us-east-1*, *eu-west-1*, and *ap-southeast-1*. The values depicted in Figure 6.3 were taken as the initial connection speeds between the regions. In all regions, the virtual machine types Standard Small (*m1.small*), High-CPU Medium (*c1.medium*), and High-CPU Extra Large (*c1.xlarge*) were allowed (see Table 4.1 for details); all machines used Debian Linux images in which the provisioner deployed the required Web service stack during startup.

The framework was tested using the following three scenarios: Scenario 1 simulates increasing load by starting a new workflow every 15 seconds. In Scenario 2, at an interval of 15 seconds, two workflows are started simultaneously to simulate an abrupt increase of resource demand. The scenarios are run until 50 workflows have been started. Finally, to test the system in peak load situations, in Scenario 3, 10 workflows are started concurrently (repeated five times with 15-minute pauses in between).

To classify the overall runtime of a scheduled workflow, the three scenarios were performed in different setups. The first setup is static scheduling, i.e., two resources are allocated manually within the BPEL process. The second setup uses the existing load-based scheduler and the third setup is based on CaDaS. All measurements represent the mean value of 20 runs.

Scenarios 1 and 2 deliver similar results: the load-based approach (BPEL-LoadBalancer, BLB) was unable to complete the scenarios, as it clustered too many tasks per machine, which led to an dramatic increase in workflow completion time (and, thus, TCP timeouts). The reason is that the load value increases slowly (due to the initial data transfer that does not cause a high load) while many workflows are started in quick succession, and are therefore scheduled to the same machine.

user weights (perf:cost)	VMs used: us, eu, ap; small/medium	cost in USD per scenario	runtime in sec
10:1	0/0, 3/7, 0/0	1.615	124
1:1	0/0, 2/6, 0/0	1.33	187
1:10	0/0, 0/0, 0/0	0	1,224

Table 6.1: Results for Scenario 1 (50 x 1 workflow)

The numbers in Table 6.1 clarify that the user-defined weights have an impact on workflow runtime and cost: when performance is prioritized (setting 10:1), the average workflow runtime is 124 seconds, and the cost is 1.615 USD for the whole scenario. If performance and cost are equally important (setting 1:1), the runtime increases to 187 seconds (am increase of about 50%), while the cost is reduced by approximately 28 cents or 21 %. When

---

same time the data transfer rates between between Amazon's data centers range from 5 and 20 MB/sec. Therefore, using static resources that are located at our university would only have one effect: CaDaS would not schedule tasks to them, as the low transfer rates would lead to a low rating ("unfit") of the corresponding individual.

cost is prioritized (setting 1:10), no virtual machines are started at all, resulting in a runtime increase of about 1000 %.

user weights (perf:cost)	Additional VMs used: us, eu, ap; small/medium	cost in USD for scenario	runtime in sec
10:1	0/0, 3/14, 0/0	2.945	157
1:1	0/0, 1/12, 0/0	2.375	249
1:10	0/0, 0/0, 0/0	0	1,531

Table 6.2: Results for scenario 2 (25 x 2 workflows in parallel)

Scenario 2 delivers similar results as Scenario 1 (see Table 6.2), but with higher absolute values. The graphical representation of the measurement results (Figure 6.10) clearly demonstrates that the use of virtual machines (and provisioning just-in-time) leads to almost constant runtimes despite increasing load.

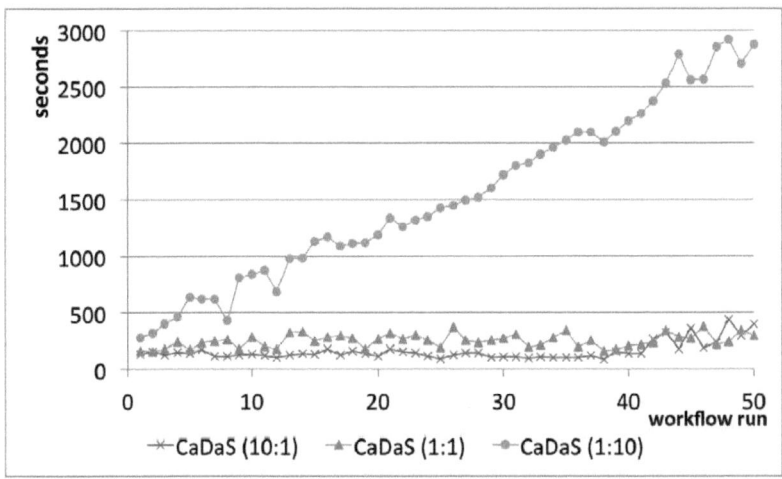

Figure 6.10: Workflow runtimes for Scenario 2 with different user weights. The results clearly demonstrate that the use of virtual machines (and provisioning just-in-time) leads to almost constant runtimes in spite of increasing load.

Scenario 3 (Figure 6.11) simulates peak-load situations by starting 10 workflows in parallel (repeated 5 times with 15-minute pauses in between).

This scenario could be completed by all schedulers. However, when using static resource allocation, one can see a clear pattern: the workflow runtime dramatically increases (from about 600 seconds to more than 1,000 seconds) until the 10th workflow has finished. The same pattern can be recognized when CaDaS is used with a weighting of 1:10, meaning that cost is dominant. Then, no virtual machines are provisioned, which leads to increasing runtimes. The absolute values are below those of the static approach, since four instead of two machines can be utilized.

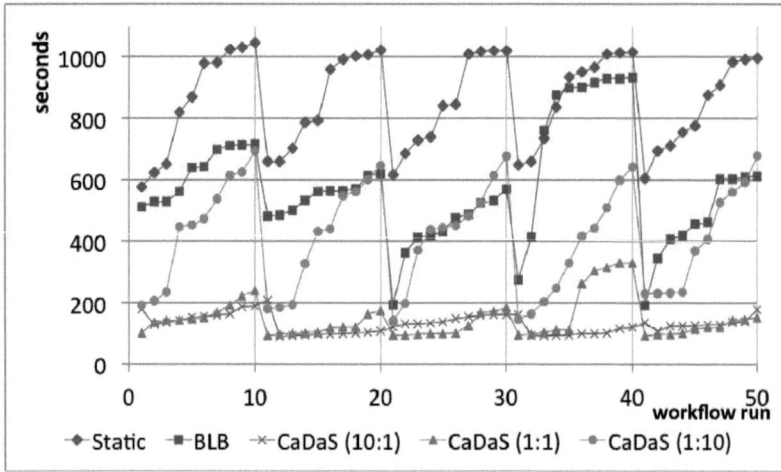

Figure 6.11: Workflow runtimes for scenario 3 (ten workflows in parallel, repeated five times with 15 minutes pause)

When virtual machines may be provisioned (BLB, CaDaS 10:1, CaDaS 1:1), two effects occur: First, BLB shows an increase in runtime within each iteration, while the absolute runtime values decrease from iteration 1 to 3. In iteration 4 (workflow run 31 to 40), new virtual machines had to be provisioned since the machines used previously were de-provisioned (expiration of accounting period, no usage of machines during pause). The second effect is that the runtimes using CaDaS only slightly increase within the iterations. The reservation system first performs reservations on the four existing machines. Then, the algorithm calculates that is more beneficial to provision additional machines than waiting for the existing machines to become available again. At this point, several virtual machines (0/0, 3/9, 0/0 for 10:1; 0/0, 0/9, 0/0 1:1) are started in parallel. To summarize, the proposed scheduling algorithm performs well and computes results in a timely manner (typical runtimes of CaDaS are about 17 ms for the given workflow). It satisfies the defined requirements, i.e., it computes more sophisticated schedules than the compared algorithms while respecting user-defined preferences.

6.7 Summary

In this chapter, a novel multi-objective workflow scheduling algorithm as well as its implementation and integration in the ActiveBPEL engine has been presented. It is tailored towards the needs of Cloud-based workflow applications: in particular, if the workflow tasks are geographically distributed, data transmission can be the main bottleneck. The algorithm therefore takes data dependencies between workflow steps into account and schedules them to Cloud resources based on the two conflicting objectives of cost and execution time according to the preferences of the user. Some implementation details have been described. The implementation is based on, but not limited to, the ActiveBPEL engine and Amazon's Elastic Compute Cloud. Experimental results indicate that both the workflow execution times and the corresponding costs can be reduced significantly.

Chapter 7
WSRF- and Grid-Related Extensions

Contents
7.1	Introduction		123
7.2	Technical Background		124
	7.2.1	Web Services Resource Framework	124
	7.2.2	Grid Security Infrastructure	126
7.3	Related Work		127
7.4	WSRF Extensions		129
	7.4.1	Manual Invocation of WSRF Services	129
	7.4.2	BPEL Extension: GridInvoke	131
7.5	Support for Grid Security Infrastructure		133
	7.5.1	Status Quo and Requirements	133
	7.5.2	Security Extensions to BPEL	133
	7.5.3	Automatic Security Configuration	137
7.6	Implementation		139
	7.6.1	WSRF Extensions	139
	7.6.2	Support for Grid Security Infrastructure	141
	7.6.3	Automatic Security Configuration	145
7.7	Evaluation		147
7.8	Summary		151

7.1 Introduction

The Grid computing paradigm [69] has become a well established method for high performance computing. The initial vision of the Grid encompasses a collection of different computer clusters under a common infrastructure that allows uniform access to those heterogeneous systems. Many traditional cluster applications have been wrapped and can now be executed on a number of different clusters via Grid computing technology.

While the first generation of Grid computing solutions implemented their own proprietary interfaces, the introduction of the service-oriented computing paradigm and the corresponding Web service standards such as WSDL [39] and SOAP [132] in the field of Grid computing through the Open Grid Services Architecture (OGSA) [67, 70] opens up the Grid to the wider world of interoperability in the business sector. While OGSA describes the higher-level architectural aspects of service-oriented Grid computing, the Web Services Resource Framework (WSRF, see Section 7.2) [112] is a fine-grained description of the infrastructure required to implement the OGSA model. The transition from traditional Grid systems to the service-oriented WSRF-Grid creates the opportunity for more complex and versatile Grid applications which can be integrated into existing business applications using workflow languages like BPEL.

BPEL works well for traditional Web services, but has a number of drawbacks with respect to the more complex world of WSRF-based Grid computing, especially where security is concerned. Moreover, it is a tedious task to manually deal with the (factory) pattern introduced by the underlying WSRF standard. Currently, the BPEL security concept is not equipped to deal with complex multi-protocol Grid environments and does not integrate with the Grid Security Infrastructure (GSI). While BPEL is mainly focused on anonymous HTTPS-based TLS security or manual role-based authentication encoded in SOAP headers, Grid computing has a mandatory user-centric security approach using X.509 certificates which far exceeds the scope and capability of the BPEL security model.

To nullify these disadvantages of BPEL in Grid environments, extensions to the BPEL standard are proposed and implemented. The first extension eases the integration of WSRF-based services in BPEL processes, while the second empowers BPEL to make use of the mechanisms provided by GSI.

The rest of this chapter is organized as follows: Section 7.2 briefly introduces the technical backgrounds of both WSRF and GSI. Equipped with this knowledge, the approaches to integrate both technologies into BPEL are explained in Section 7.4 and Section 7.5.

Parts of this chapter have been published in [51], [52], [56], and [123].

7.2 Technical Background

7.2.1 Web Services Resource Framework

The Web Services Resource Framework (WSRF) [11] has been proposed due to some shortcomings of normal, stateless Web services when used in distributed computing. In many cases, Web services must provide the user with the ability to query and manipulate the state of the service. While it is also possible with "normal" Web services to implement some notion of state,

the WSRF specification defines a consistent and interoperable way to do so.
The WS-Resource Framework builds on the work of the Global Grid Forum's (GGF) Open Grid Services Infrastructure (OGSI) Working Group. It is basically a refactoring of the ideas and interfaces developed in the OGSI V1.0 specification with adaptions concerning recent developments in Web services architecture (such as WS-Addressing [32]).

Web services are described by messages that flow to and from them. The format of those messages is described by the service's WSDL document. Any manipulation to a service's resources (i.e., any state change) must in some way be represented in the exchanged messages. WSRF introduces the idea of a standardized XML document description, the so-called *Resource Properties* document, which is referenced by the service's WSDL description. It explicitly describes a view on the service's resources (called *WS-Resource*). By using the Resource Properties document schema, WSRF allows the definition of simple, generic messages which interact with the WS-Resource.

To identify a *WS-Resource*, WSRF includes the identifier as part of the *EndpointReference* (defined by the WS-Addressing specification) in exchanged messages (see Figure 7.1). Since *EndpointReference*s are part of the SOAP

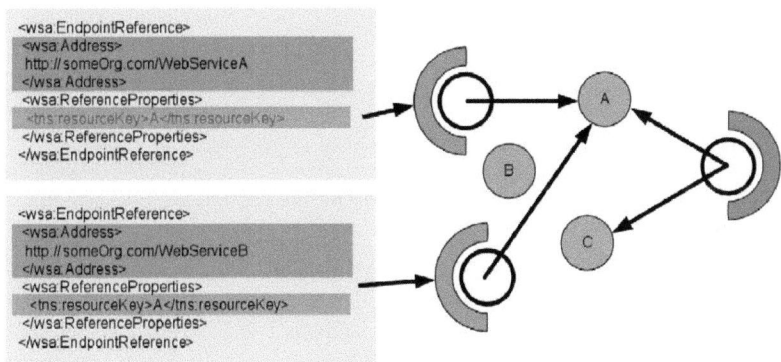

Figure 7.1: WSRF resource pattern

header, WSRF simplifies the form of the WSDL document that describes the service. The WSDL for a "stateful" operation only contains parameters relevant for the service's logic, not elements of the SOAP header. To identify a concrete *Resource Document* (often referred to as an "instance" of the corresponding service), the identifier must be passed with every SOAP call to and from the service. The identifier (and corresponding *Resource Document*) is created when the service's "create" operation is invoked. The response of this operation contains the created identifier (see Listing 7.1).

```
1 <ns:createDocumentResponse>
```

```
  <wsa:Address>http://www.example.com/SampleService</↵
    wsa:Address>
3 <wsa:ReferenceParameters>
  <rpimpl:DocumentId>id1</rpimpl:DocumentId>
5 <wsa:ReferenceParameters>
  </ns:createDocumentResponse>
```
Listing 7.1: Example response containg a resource identifier

WSRF furthermore contains sub-specifications, like WS-Resource Lifetime (WSRF-RL), WS-ServiceGroup (WSRF-SG) and WSRF-BaseFaults (WSRF-BF) which are irrelevant for this work and are therefore not discussed in any further detail.

7.2.2 Grid Security Infrastructure

The Grid Security Infrastructure (GSI) is the part of the Globus Toolkit [8, 66] that provides security features. It is based on public key cryptography and uses X.509 certificates to identify users and hosts. It relies on a third party, i.e., certificate authorities (CA), to certify the link between a public key and a certificate's subject. GSI offers four distinct functions:

1. message protection (signing or encrypting messages)

2. authentication (identifying the caller/sender)

3. authorization (checking of access rights)

4. delegation (performing tasks on behalf of a delegator)

GSI provides these functions by implementing several security specifications:

1. Transport Level Security (TLS) and Message Level Security (*WS-Security* and *WS-SecureConversation*) as protection mechanisms for messages in combination with SOAP. Both mechanisms use XML-Encryption and XML-Signature for message protection.

2. X.509 certificates or username/password tokens for authentication.

3. Security Assertion Markup Language (SAML) assertions for authorization.

4. X.509 proxy certificates and WS-Trust for delegation.

TLS entails SOAP messages conveyed over a network connection protected at the transport level (often HTTPS is used) and provides both message integrity (by signing) and privacy (via encryption). Message Level Security specified by the *WS-Security* standard in combination with the SOAP specification allows developers to add a security related payload (e.g. integrity protection, or encryption) to each message.

The Globus Toolkit 4 (GT4) provides two mechanisms, GSISecureMessage (based on WS-Security) and GSISecureConversation (based on WS-SecureConversation) for authentication and secure communication on the message level. In GSISecureConversation, the client establishes a context with the server with the initial message. This context has the purpose of authenticating the client identity to the server and of establishing a shared secret key using a collocated GSISecureConversation service. As soon as the context is established, messages can be secured (signed or encrypted) using the shared secret key from the context.

The GSISecureMessage approach is simpler, since the client does not establish a context before sending data (i.e. invoking operations) to the server. The client uses existing keys, such as the server's public key from its X.509 certificate.

The difference between GSISecureMessage and GSI-SecureConversation is that the latter produces less overhead if several messages are exchanged. Establishing a secure context requires some time, but symmetric encryption is much faster than using public key cryptography. Experimental results concerning the overhead of the different security methods are presented in Section 7.7. Furthermore, GSI-SecureConversation does not require the destination host's public key to be present on the client side, and GSI-SecureConversation features credential delegation. Both provide integrity protection, encryption and replay attack protection.

GSI supports authentication through X.509 certificates or user name/password and delegation through X.509 proxy certificates and the WS-Trust standard. Delegation allows a client to delegate a X.509 proxy certificate to a service. The target service can then perform tasks on behalf of the user who owns the certificate. Globus uses WS-GRAM (Grid Resource Allocation Manager) to interact with local scheduling systems on clusters and requires delegation to execute tasks as the user given in the proxy certificate.

A proxy certificate is derived from the user's certificate and consists of a new certificate and a private key. The new certificate contains the owner's identity, modified slightly to indicate that it is a proxy. It is signed by the owner, rather than a CA. Proxies have limited lifetimes, i.e. the proxy should no longer be accepted by others after the lifetime has expired.

7.3 Related Work

Several papers address the applicability of BPEL in service-oriented Grid environments. For example, Leymann [96] extensively illustrates the advantages of using workflow systems with a focus on Grid environments. It is argued that some extensions to the BPEL standard may be needed to fully integrate BPEL workflows into Grid environments. The author states that monitoring capabilities in particular are missing and a separate standardization effort is required. Therefore, he concludes that Grid-specific extensions of BPEL should be specified instead of defining new Grid-specific standards.

Slomiski [122] discusses the benefits and challenges of using BPEL in Grid environments. The author compares both Open Grid Services Infrastructure (OGSI) [67] and WSRF-based Grid middlewares and concludes, that WSRF is much easier to use with BPEL than OGSI since WSRF defines extensions to WS technology instead of redefining it. Furthermore, questions regarding supporting large data transfers, long running workflows and monitoring are briefly discussed. However, the paper does not address the particular question regarding invoking stateful services from BPEL.

Tan and Turner [127] describe their experience on orchestrating WSRF-based Grid services (Globus Toolkit 4) using BPEL. They identify two main problems: (1) security mechanisms cannot be used due to technical problems like incompatible Axis [25] versions, and (2) it is not possible to easily address WS-resources. The authors' solution to the addressing problem is to pass the endpoint reference identifying the created resource as an operation parameter to the Grid service. The service then has to identify the resources using the reference received in the SOAP call. This approach is not feasible since it requires handling code in every Grid service that is to be orchestrated. Hence, it is impossible to invoke existing standard services like WS-GRAM (Web Service Grid Resource Allocation and Management).

Chao et al. [38] propose an architecture to enable Grid service composition based on OGSI and BPEL. To hide complexity, their approach wraps Grid service clients as Web services called Proxy Web Services. These Proxy Web Services are orchestrated in workflows using standard BPEL. All operations performed on the Proxy Web Services will be delegated to the actual Grid service. The approach seams feasible for OGSI which is, as already mentioned, much more difficult to use with BPEL than WSRF. However, it adds complexity to the Grid environment by creating a Proxy Service for every single Grid service. For this reason, the solution is not feasible for real-life WSRF-based Grids.

Amnuaykanjanasin and Nupairoj [23] present a BPEL-based approach for orchestrating OGSI-based Globus Toolkit 3 Grid services using proxy services. Proxy services are facade services which hide the Grid service's complexity and are invoked by the workflow engine instead of the original service. The call is then delegated to the Grid service. This introduces an indirection and increases the infrastructure's complexity, since the number of running services is doubled. The approach supports security mechanisms of Globus Toolkit 3 security based on WS-Security [113]. Despite the fact that the complexity of Grid environments is increased by this approach, the solution is interesting, since it allows the usage of security and notification features. However, lifetime management of proxy certificates is not addressed at all.

GridAssist [131] is another approach that allows the invocation of secured Grid services from workflows. It is divided into a client and a server application. The client is responsible for workflow modeling and acts as a client to run workflows. The GridAssist Controller is the corresponding server application which executes workflows. It makes use of the Globus CoG Kit (Commodity Grids Kit) to interact with Globus Toolkit 2 and 3 services (especially GridFTP and the Grid Resource Allocation Manager). Workflows consist of a XML workflow description as well as the proxy certificate to be used for execution. Proxy lifetime is not managed by the execution environment. Workflows are not exposed as Web services and can only be invoked using the client application. This prohibits the integration of GridAssist workflows as applications in Grid environments.

7.4 WSRF Extensions

The use of factory patterns to instantiate resources (see Figure 7.2) is very common in WSRF-based frameworks. A factory is a Web service exposing an operation (typically named `createResource` in GT4 services) to create resources. Invoking this operation creates a new resource, generates an unique ID to identify the resource in later service calls and associates the resource with a Web service. Thus, to invoke a stateful Web service, the invoking client needs to know the ID of the resource(s) to be used. Since BPEL was designed to operate on non-stateful Web services, there is no standard way to store the unique identifier returned by the factory service and automatically use it in invoke operations on the service to which the resource was assigned. Consequently, the identifier must be copied manually to the `ReferenceProperties` [32] element of the SOAP [132] message, which adds additional complexity to the process definition and requires detailed knowledge of the specification of WSRF.

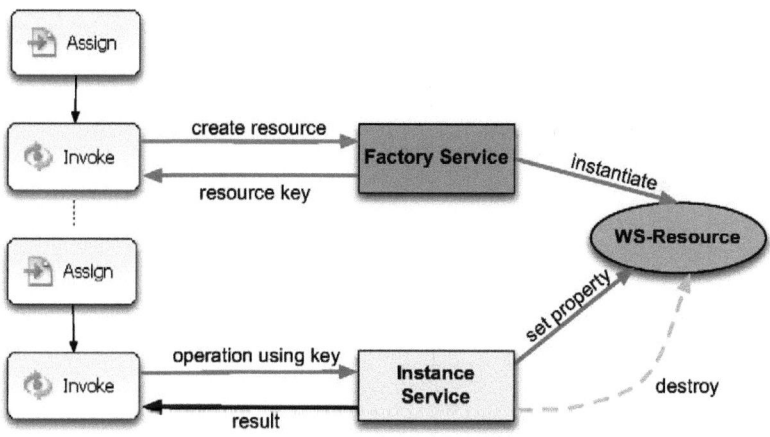

Figure 7.2: Invocation of WSRF service using standard BPEL operations

7.4.1 Manual Invocation of WSRF Services

A solution to this problem using standard BPEL activities has been presented by Zager [146] who proposed to store the ID retrieved by the factory call, manually extract it using BPEL's assign operations, and copy it to the `referenceProperty` element of the WS-Addressing field to be used in the invocation of the service to which the resource is assigned (see Figure 7.2). This solution is not very intuitive, requires a great deal of additional code writing as well as changes to the WSDL description of the WSRF service (it must make SOAP header elements visible in the WSDL). Furthermore, it makes use of a proprietary extension (*inputHeaderVariable*) to the BPEL standard which has been implemented in Oracle Process Manager [115]. The author therefore concludes that "significant value would be realized if these specifications evolve with consideration to improved synergy between stateful processes and service-addressable stateful resources." Listing 7.2 lists the additional BPEL code required to manually invoke a WSRF service from BPEL (here: a simple service that only increments a number by the value passed in by the invoking client).

```
   <!-- Factory call -->
2  <!-- Initialize variable (creates corresponding message↵
     ) -->
   <assign>
4    <copy>
       <from>''</from>
6      <to variable="createCounterRequest" part="request" />
     </copy>
8  </assign>

10 <!-- create call information for createResource ↵
       operation -->
   <assign>
12   <copy>
       <from>
14       <literal>
           <wsa:EndpointReference
16         xmlns:s="http://counter.com/service">
             <wsa:Address>...</wsa:Address>
18           <wsa:ServiceName PortName="CounterPortTypePort">↵
                 s:CounterService</wsa:ServiceName>
             <wsa:ReferenceParameters>
20             <wsa:To>...</wsa:To>
               <wsa:Action>...</wsa:Action>
22           </wsa:ReferenceParameters>
           </wsa:EndpointReference>
24       </literal>
       </from>
26     <to variable="globusEPR"/>
     </copy>
28
     <copy>
30     <from variable="globusEPR" />
       <to partnerLink="globusPL" />
32   </copy>
   </assign>
34
   <!-- PERFORM createResource INVOKE -->
36
   <assign>
```

```
38  <!-- resource key extracted from reply and written ↵
       into EPR -->
    <copy>
40    <from variable="createCounterResponse" part="response↵
      ">
        <query>/globus:createCounterResponse/↵
          wsa:EndpointReference/wsa:ReferenceParameters/↵
          globus:CounterKey/text()</query>
42    </from>
      <to variable="globusEPR">
44      <query>/wsa:EndpointReference/↵
          wsa:ReferenceParameters/globus:CounterKey</query>
      </to>
46  </copy>
    <copy>
48    <from variable="globusEPR" />
      <to partnerLink="globusPL" />
50  </copy>
    </assign>
52  <invoke ... />
```
Listing 7.2: Invocation of WSRF service with plain BPEL

7.4.2 BPEL Extension: GridInvoke

Since it is unrealistic to assume that it is possible to change the WSDL interfaces of all WSRF services that one wishes to orchestrate with BPEL, the proposed solution does not require any changes to the orchestrated services. As a marginal note, one basic principle of service-oriented architectures would be violated by such an approach: Formal contracts (interface descriptions) should not be changed after publication. Therefore, in contrast to the solution presented above, no modifications to a service's WSDL document are required by the presented solution.

The proposed solution is based on introducing a new activity to the BPEL standard called `gridInvoke` (GI). It is derived from the `invoke` activity and transparently handles the invocation of state-aware WSRF services. This means that this new element of the language allows the invocation of state-aware services and the manipulation and querying of their resources.

As described above, the resources to be assigned to the state-aware service must be created prior to the invocation. Therefore, the activities `gridCreateResourceInvoke` (GCRI) and `gridDestroyResourceInvoke` (GDRI) which handle the creation and destruction of WS-resources are also introduced. The syntax of the constructs is described in Listing 7.3, lines 10–16.

```
    <partnerLinkSets>
2     <partnerLinkSet name="plsName">
        <resourceLink name="rlnName">
4         <factory name="factoryName" partnerLink="↵
            factoryPL"/>
          <resource name="resourceName" partnerLink="↵
            resourcePL"/>
6       </resourceLink>
      </partnerLinkSet>
8   </partnerLinkSets>
```

```
10   <gridCreateResourceInvoke resourceLink="rlnName"
                             partnerLinkSet="plsName" />
12   <gridInvoke resourceLink="rlnName" partnerLinkSet="↵
     plsName"
                operation="opName" inputVariable="inVar"
14              outputVariable="outVar"/>
     <gridDestroyResourceInvoke resourceLink="rlsName"
16                           partnerLinkSet="plsName"/>
```
Listing 7.3: Grid-specific extensions for the invocation of stateful WS

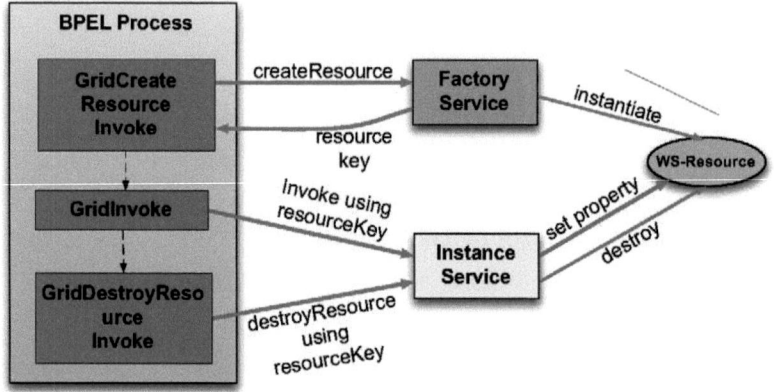

Figure 7.3: Execution chain of gridCreateResourceInvoke, gridInvoke and gridDestroyResourceInvoke

These activities (GCRI and GDRI) only need to be invoked once before and after using the service. The required information, such as the partnerLink of the factory service and the returned endpoint reference (EPR) pointing to the service to which the resource has been assigned, are stored in so-called partnerLinkSets. This is done automatically and transparently to the BPEL designer at runtime of the process by the BPEL engine. Lines 3–6 of Listing 7.3 define a resourceLink which consists of partnerLinks of the factory and instance service to be used. By using the resourceLink in the activities in lines 10–16, the BPEL engine automatically creates resources (GCRI) by invoking the createResource operation of the factory port type, uses the correct resources in gridInvoke, and destroys (GDRI) the resources upon request (line 15–16). As the listing shows, apart from once creating a partnerLinkSet, *only three lines*[1] (lines 12–14) of BPEL code are required to interact with stateful, WSRF compatible, Web services. Figure 7.3 illustrates the sequence of calls using the introduced additions to BPEL.

---
[1] One atomic activity without needing to copy data using assign.

7.5 Support for Grid Security Infrastructure

7.5.1 Status Quo and Requirements

The current approach of the BPEL standard does not encompass the more complex security requirements of the Grid environment which are supported by the Grid Security Infrastructure (see Section 7.2.1). To fully integrate with GSI, the workflow engine must be able to sign, verify, encrypt and decrypt outgoing and incoming messages (i.e. invocations of services and the corresponding replies) with all three of the aforementioned mechanisms. Furthermore, the workflow engine's security model needs to provide mechanisms to deal with proxy certificates which are required to authenticate the user on whose behalf the workflow is run. Furthermore, delegation must be supported since it is required by many standard Grid services, such as job submission, and is a basic usage paradigm of Grid computing. The workflow security approach must be extended to encompass temporal security issues since workflow execution times can far exceed Grid proxy certificate lifetimes. This entails lifetime monitoring and refreshing of proxy certificates. To fully benefit from BPEL's advantages (seamless integration with business applications), a solution must also support both web and Grid services within a single workflow instance. An example of a workflow incorporating Grid and Web services as well as all of the mentioned security mechanisms is illustrated in Figure 7.4.

7.5.2 Security Extensions to BPEL

The main design goal of the proposed security extensions is to equip the execution environment with the ability to create business processes which consist of both plain Web services and (secure) Grid services. It should be possible to use all three of the described security mechanisms simultaneously in a BPEL workflow. The idea is illustrated with a simplified workflow in Figure 7.4. The workflow simultaneously invokes two services (services A and B) at organizations A and B using GSISecureMessage and GSITransport. Afterwards, the services A and D are invoked at organizations A and B, this time using GSITransport and GSISecureConversation. Note that a different operation of Service A is invoked this time. Then, a plain Web service (E) is invoked at Organization C.

7.5.2.1 Syntactical Extensions

To allow the invocation of a service's different operations using distinct security methods, the security settings have to be modeled per-operation in BPEL and cannot be configured per partnerLink. Therefore, an addition to the previously described extensions (`gridCreateResourceInvoke`, `gridDestroyResourceInvoke` and `gridInvoke`) is introduced. The extension is modeled as the sub-element `<security>` in the activity's XML definition. The syntax is described in Listing 7.4.

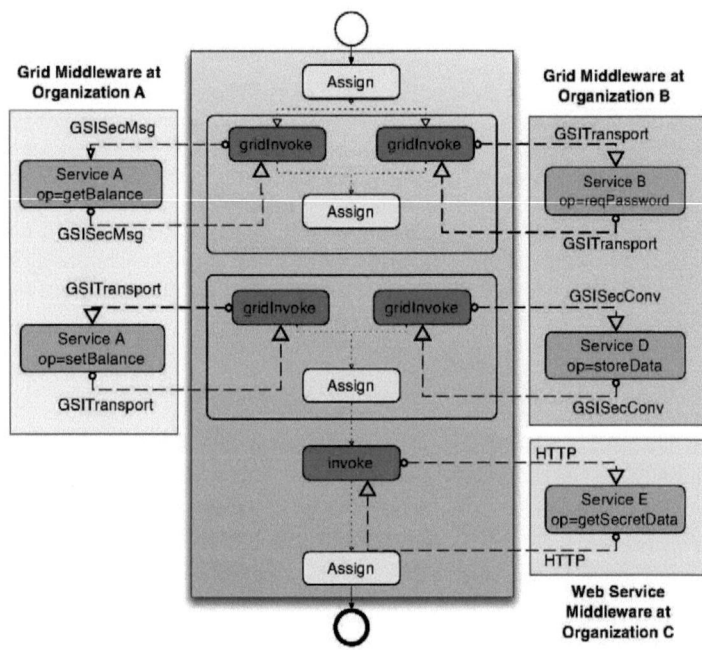

Figure 7.4: Schematic workflow incorporating Web and secure Grid services

```
  <gridInvoke ...>
2  <security
     method="GSITransport | GSISecureMessage | ↵
        GSISecureConversation"
4    level="privacy | integrity" ↵

     authz="none | self | host | anyString"?
6    peer-credentials="filename"? ↵

     anonymous="true | false"?
8    delegation="none | full | limited"? ↵

   />?
10 </gridInvoke>
```
Listing 7.4: Syntax of the security settings for invocation

In Line 3, the security method chosen by the workflow developer is stored; Line 4 represents the chosen security "level" (either signing/verifying messages (*integrity*) or (de/-)encryption (*privacy*)). The setting in Line 6 (peer-credentials) is only needed for GSISecureMessage and ignored for the other methods. Line 8 is only relevant for GSISecureConversation.

7.5.2.2 Certificate Management

Normally, the BPEL execution environment is not installed on the same machine from which a process is invoked. A common setup would be that the BPEL engine is installed on a cluster head node in a Grid. The client invoking a process could be a portal server (e.g., GridSphere) or a simple SOAP client installed on a user's laptop. Since the user's proxy certificate is needed in secure workflows (for encryption, signing and credential delegation), the user's proxy certificate must be made available at the engine's host. A very simple – and in terms of security poor – solution would be to store the user's credentials (including the private key) on the machine hosting the BPEL engine and create a proxy certificate when needed. This is not feasible, as the user's private key should not be spread and the user might not trust the provider of the hosting environment.

The solution to this problem consists of two mechanisms. Both add some information to the message header of the client's SOAP call. The advantage of modifying the header instead of the SOAP body is that the process' port type (i.e., the service's WSDL) does not need to be modified to accept any additional message parts than the process payload.

In the first case, an existing proxy certificate is read from the user's harddrive and transferred within the SOAP header to the engine. It is then retrieved from the header, stored to a file and used by the process.

The second solution does not require a pre-generated proxy certificate. It makes use of the MyProxy Credential Management Service [30]. MyProxy is a software for managing X.509 security credentials (private keys and certificates). It allows workflow users to generate proxy certificates from stored user credentials using a remote interface. The connection thereby is secured using Transport Layer Security (TLS/SSL)[2]. Within pre-configured intervals (since proxy certificates expire), the user has to log on to the machine where MyProxy is installed and create a proxy certificate. The generated proxy is then stored in a repository and is remotely accessible via (username, password) combination, where the password is chosen by the user when he/she generates the proxy and has the same lifetime as the proxy certificate. APIs in both C and Java exist to retrieve proxy certificates derived from the stored proxy certificate with a user-defined lifetime which cannot be longer than the original proxy's lifetime. The BPEL engine makes use of the Java API to retrieve a proxy certificate from the MyProxy server when needed. To do so, the required (username, password) combination has to be passed to the workflow engine using the SOAP header, like in the first solution.

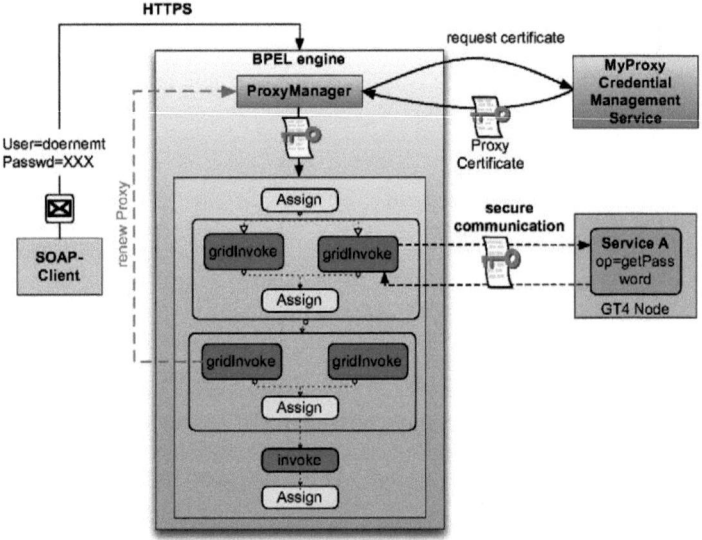

Figure 7.5: Schematic sequence of a workflow execution with automatic proxy management

Since the runtime of a process might be unknown and therefore longer than the proxy's lifetime, the solution consists of an additional feature: automatic renewal of proxy certificates (see dashed red line in Figure 7.5). The workflow engine monitors both the runtime of the process and the proxy's lifetime. If the proxy's lifetime is about to expire, the engine will renew the certificate if desired by the process' user. The (username, password) combination, the hostname of the MyProxy server, the desired proxy lifetime, and

---

[2]Secure Sockets Layer (SSL) is the more common term for the used cryptographic protocol. However, the latest release of the specification redefined the protocol's name to TLS.

a boolean `autoRenewal` are passed to the BPEL engine with the initial SOAP call that starts the workflow. If `autoRenewal` is set to `true`, the above-mentioned renewal of proxy certificates will be activated. The BPEL engine contacts the given MyProxy server and retrieves a proxy certificate with the given lifetime from the server. Figure 7.5 schematically illustrates this sequence. Since the whole conversation is secured using HTTPS (from client to BPEL engine) and pure TLS (from BPEL engine to MyProxy), it can be considered as secure. However, this solution assumes that the user trusts the carrier of the MyProxy server. This should be true in most cases, since MyProxy is typically installed along with the Globus Toolkit on the Grid head node of the user's home organization. Otherwise, the user could set up his/her own MyProxy server.

7.5.3 Automatic Security Configuration

The described security extensions allow workflow developers to make use of the security capabilities introduced by GT 4 within BPEL. However, the solution has a drawback that results from missing functionality in GT4. The workflow developer has to manually choose the security method to be used when the workflow is modeled. It would be more convenient and – for the long term – would require fewer changes in workflows if the user could simply choose the required security level (*integrity* or *privacy*) and decide whether *delegation* is required or not and leave the security configuration to the BPEL engine.

However, for some unknown reason[3], GT4 does not publish the security configuration of services. Hence, automatic security configuration is not possible without further preliminaries. This shortcoming may be bypassed using at least three different approaches: (1) one could simply try out all security mechanisms and use the one that does not result in an error, or (2) deploy a Grid service to the GT4 head node that reads all security descriptors and publishes the result so that one can access the security settings via SOAP call, or (3) use GT4's Monitoring and Discovery System (MDS) to publish the security settings.

While the first approach does not require any changes on the GT4 head node, it is still not feasible since it is inefficient (think of a large amount of services) and resembles a brute-force-approach. The second and third approach require administrative access to the GT4 head node to deploy either the developed service or a program that publishes the security information in MDS. Therefore, the third approach has been chosen because it relies on components already offered by GT4.

MDS is a collection of Grid services to monitor and discover Grid resources. It collects information about resources available in the Grid and their state. Information is stored in an XML structure; a WSRF-based query interface allows users to search for specific resources (using *XPath* queries). The resources are grouped according to the affiliation to so-called *Virtual Organizations* (VOs). Due to the hierarchical structure of MDS, it is therefore

---

[3]Globus Security Mailing List, post dating back to October 2007. https://lists.globus.org/mailman/private/security/2007-October/thread.html

sufficient to query the MDS service of *one* of a VO's sites to retrieve information concerning all resources (i.e. services). The second approach would require a query of *all* Grid sites.

The MDS-based approach collects information on the security settings when the GT4 software is started and publishes the settings (the information is automatically replicated to other MDS services, as configured during MDS setup). BPEL engines (and other clients) can then query MDS for these settings before invoking secured services. The syntax of the *security* tag was therefore extended by the method *automatic* (see Line 3 in Listing 7.4). Whenever a workflow uses the security method *automatic*, the BPEL engine checks whether or not is has already collected security information for the given service. If not, the MDS service (on the host where the target service is installed) is queried for the information. The retrieved information is then cached internally. The *Security Configurator* (see Figure 7.6) decides which method should be used; since the different security methods come with different overheads (refer to Section 7.7), the message size is taken as basis of for making this decision.

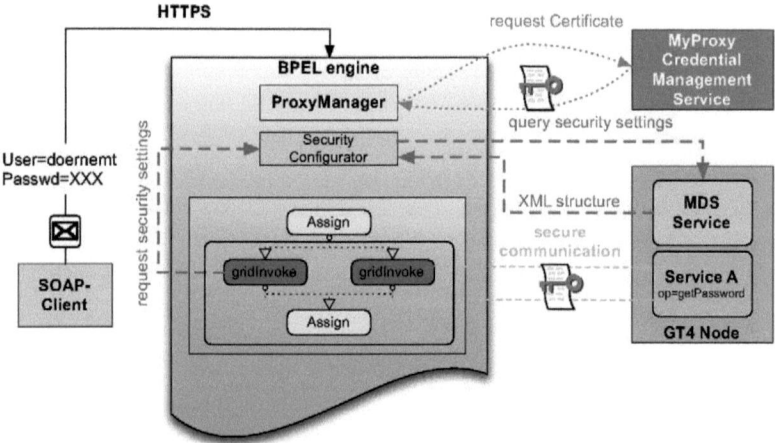

Figure 7.6: Automatic Security Configuration using Globus Monitoring and Discovery System

7.6 Implementation

7.6.1 WSRF Extensions

The implementation of the extensions to the BPEL standard is, as evidenced above, based on the BPEL engine developed by Active Endpoints [1] because the engine is very robust and the source code is available (GPL). Figure 7.7 gives an overview of the logical components of the ActiveBPEL engine. Of special interest for the WSRF extensions are the *Process Management* and the *Process* component itself (highlighted in the figure). The most important extension is the construct of PartnerLinkSets, which encapsulates the handling of WSRF resources. A SOAP handler component has been developed which automatically inserts the Resource Key and other information needed to identify the resources into the SOAP header of service calls. It is plugged into Apache Axis using the standard mechanism (client configuration file). Besides implementing classes for handling and storing properties of GridInvoke, GridCreateResourceInvoke and GridDestroyResourceInvoke, the ActiveBPEL management GUI (web-based) has been extended to reflect the additions to BPEL.

For each of the added activities, several classes had to be implemented to integrate them into the engine's architecture. In Figure 7.8, the different lifecycle states of a process in the BPEL engine along with the implementing classes are shown. `AeReaderVisitor` is responsible for parsing the process' XML description. Thereby, it passes every element defined in the process description. For every found element, a predefined handler is invoked (according to the *Visitor Pattern*). For instance, when a `<gridInvoke>` element is found, the method `public void visit(AeActivityGridInvokeDef aDef)` is invoked. It parses the XML and stores the retrieved parameters in an instance of `AeActivityGridInvokeDef`. The implementation of the validation step is quite similar. However, `AeDefValidationVisitor` does not operate on the process' XML, but on the `*Def` objects (i.e., the in-memory representation). After that step, the process is successfully deployed to the engine. When a process is invoked, each in-memory representation (`*Def`) is eventually instantiated; therefore, the corresponding (`*Impl`) classes are used (for instance, `AeActivityGridInvokeImpl`).

7.6.1.1 PartnerLinkSets

PartnerLinkSets may contain multiple resourceLinks, each corresponding to a WSRF resource. ResourceLinks consist of a factory service and a resource itself. Both, factory and resource, handle the concrete partnerLink which points to the services to be invoked. The information where the resource is located is retrieved from the factory service and automatically copied to the resourceLink by the implementation. The resource key, which is important for Grid middleware correlation, is delivered by the factory service and – together with the endpoint information of the instantiated WSRF resource – stored in the resource element of the resourceLink.

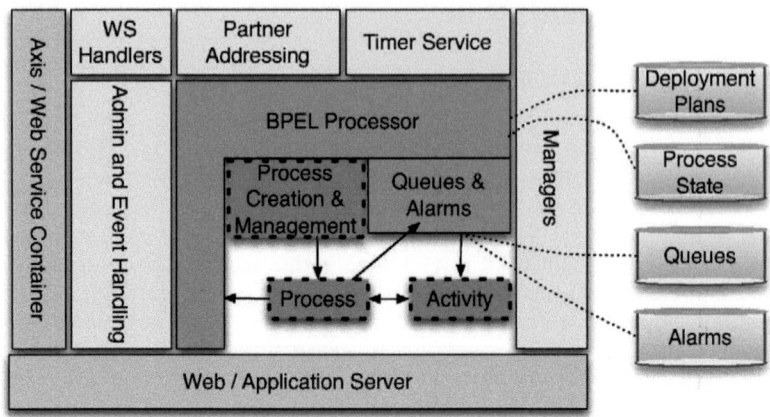

Figure 7.7: Logical components of the ActiveBPEL engine

7.6.1.2 Invoking a WSRF Resource

The gridCreateResourceInvoke activity identifies the corresponding partnerLinkSet before determining the resourceLink from it and constructing an invoke object. The created invoke object is added to the *execution queue* of the engine. As soon as the invoke is dequeued, any resourceLink information contained in that invoke is identified and the concrete endpoint is set in the Axis call. As soon as the response arrives, it is parsed and the resource key as well as the endpoint address are stored as a resource in the resourceLink. This information is handled by the partnerLinkSet data structure.

When gridInvoke is called, it searches for the partnerLinkSet and identifies the resourceLink that corresponds to it. The engine's natural strategy to resolve a partnerLink is to search for them by name. In order to use this mechanism, unique identifiers were introduced for resources which are stored in the invoke object. Hence, the engine can resolve the resourceLink during the creation of an Axis call object. Subsequently, the correct endpoint information is saved within the call and the information about the resource key is put into the *MessageContext* (see SOAP Handler below).

GridDestroyResourceInvoke is used when a WSRF resource is not required anymore and therefore its lifetime should end. It constructs an invoke object in the same way gridInvoke does (but with the intention of destroying the resource). After a response arrives, the resource is removed from the partnerLinkSet.

7.6.1.3 SOAP Handler

The SOAPHandler is integrated into the handler chain of Apache Axis. It inspects the MessageContext for given resourceKey information. If some information is found, the resource key is added to the SOAP header of the message, so that the Grid middleware can correlate the call with the correct

WSRF resource. If no information is found, the call remains unchanged. In any case, the handler chain continues processing it.

7.6.2 Support for Grid Security Infrastructure

The implementation of Grid-related security extensions is built on the extensions described in the previous section. In order to integrate the BPEL engine with the Grid Security Infrastructure implemented by the Globus Toolkit 4 (GT4), several changes and additions to the engine (see Figure 7.7) had to be made.

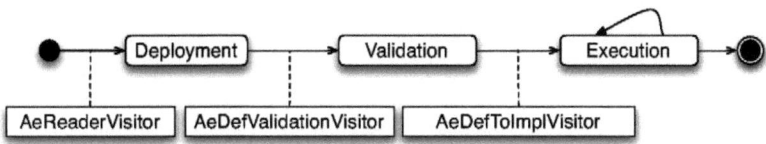

Figure 7.8: Process lifecycle and its implementing classes

First of all, there were compatibility issues to be solved. GT4 uses a different version of the SOAP engine Axis (Version 1.2.1RC2), which is incompatible with ActiveBPEL, as it uses Axis 1.2.1 (final version). Therefore, a variety of minor changes to the BPEL engine had to be made so that it runs with Axis 1.2.1RC2.

As described above, AeReaderVisitor (see Figure 7.8) is responsible for parsing the process' XML description. To do so, it passes every element defined in the process description. For every element found, a predefined handler is invoked. In particular, whenever a security descriptor is found, the method public void visit(AeSecurityDescriptorDef aDef) is invoked. It parses the XML and stores the retrieved parameters in an instance of AeSecurityDescriptorDef, which is then attached to the object representing the corresponding activity (GridCreateResourceInvoke, GridInvoke oder GridDestroyResourceInvoke). The implementation of the validation step is quite similar. However, AeDefValidationVisitor does not operate on the process' XML, but on the ADef objects (i.e., the in-memory representation).

When a process is invoked, the SOAP message is passed to a new SOAP handler that has been developed. The SOAP handler examines the SOAP header for the element soapproxycert. If the element is present in the SOAP header, the method handleProxyHeader is invoked.

The method handleProxyHeader examines the soapproxycert header element (see Listing 7.5). If myproxyuser, myproxypasswd and myproxyhost are set (Line 45), it uses the class MyProxyConnector to connect to MyProxy using the given credentials and retrieves a proxy from it. If autoRenewal is enabled, the proxy's lifetime is determined and a thread to monitor the lifetime of the certificate is started. In the event that the workflow runs longer than the proxy's lifetime, it is automatically renewed (implemented in `ProxyCertMap`, not listed here). Otherwise, the proxy must have been passed as a binary in the SOAP element and is extracted. Then, it is temporarily saved to disk. In both cases (Line 60 and following), the credential is initialized as a `GlobusGSSCredentialImpl` object and then stored in a HashMap.

```
   private void handleProxyHeader(SOAPHeaderElement he,
2    MessageContext ctx) throws SOAPException {

4    String user = he.getAttribute("myproxyuser");
     String password = he.getAttribute("myproxypassword");
6    String host = he.getAttribute("myproxyhost");
     String _lifetime = he.getAttribute("lifetime");
8    String _autoRenew = he.getAttribute("autoRenewal");
     int lifetime = 3600;
10   boolean autoRenew = false;

12   // Valididy checks on parameters.
     // ...
14
     String tmpDir = System.getProperty("java.io.tmpdir")+
16           File.separator+"proxy";
     new File(tmpDir).mkdirs();
18
     // Error handling
20   // ...

22   String fName = tmpDir+File.separator+"x509up_u_" +
                                    he.hashCode();
24   // =======================================
     // No user name, password or host given... assume
26   // that proxy is sent binary
     // =======================================
28   if ( (user == null || user.isEmpty()) ||
          (password == null || password.isEmpty()) ||
30        (host == null || host.isEmpty()) ) {

32     Object o = he.getObjectValue();
       if (o instanceof byte[]) {
34       byte[] outputBytes = (byte[]) o;
         writeProxyToFile(fName, outputBytes);
36     } else
         // No credentials and no proxy in message
38       throw new SOAPException("Structure of "+
         "soapproxycred element wrong!");
40   }
     // =======================================
42   // MyProxy User, password and host given =>
     // connect to MyProxy
44   // =======================================
     else {
46     MyProxyConnector conn = new MyProxyConnector(host, ↩
                 user, password, lifetime);
       try {
48       conn.saveProxyCertificateToFile(filename);
```

```
         } catch (Exception e) {
50           throw new SOAPException("MyProxyConnector error: ↵
             ", e);
         }
52
         // Store MyProxy settings (needed for renewal)
54       ProxyCertMap map = ProxyCertMap.getInstance();
         MyProxyPropertiesHolder propH = new ↵
             MyProxyPropertiesHolder(
56           user, password, host, filename, lifetime, ↵
                 autoRenew);
         map.addMyProxyPropertiesHolder(filename, propH);
58       }

60       // No error so far -> create GSSCredential object
         ProxyCertMap map = ProxyCertMap.getInstance();
62       // Store the proxy in our internal data structure
         map.addProxyCertificate(filename);
64       // Save the key in the context to retrieve it
         // in AeBpelHandler
66       ctx.setProperty("proxyCertKey", filename);
         }
```

Listing 7.5: Excerpt of class de.fb12.soap.proxyCert.SOAPHandler: handling of proxy information

When the SOAP handler has finished, corresponding implementation objects, like AeActivityGridInvokeImpl, are created for all *Def objects. They contain concrete runtime information like endpoint addresses of services. The execute method had to be extended to pass the security descriptor to AeBusinessProcess via the queueInvoke method. AeBusinessProcess creates an instance of AeInvoke, sets all runtime data and retrieves the corresponding proxy certificate from the ProxyManager's credential HashMap if the current operation has a security descriptor. The proxy is then attached to the AeInvoke object which is executed as soon as it is dequeued. The execution is done by AeInvokeHandler which required the most extensive extensions (an excerpt is given in Listing 7.6). The method handleInvoke(IAeInvoke obj, String query) receives the above mentioned AeInvoke object and creates the SOAP call. Thereby, the security descriptor is used to determine the security settings (Line 4). All settings are passed to the call via call.setProperty-(key, value), for instance call.setProperty(Constants.GSI_-SEC_MSG, Constants.SIGNATURE) for GSISecureMessage with message integrity (see Line 37).

```
1 // ...
  public IAeWebServiceResponse handleInvoke(IAeInvoke ↵
      aInvokeQueueObject, String aQueryData) {
3 // ..
     IAeSecurityDescriptorDef secDesc = ↵
         aInvokeQueueObject.getSecurityDescriptor();
5
     if(secDesc != null) {
7      String method = secDesc.getMethod();
       String protection = secDesc.getLevel();
```

```
 9    String authz = secDesc.getAuthz();

11    Integer level = new Integer(-1);

13    if("privacy".equals(protection))
        level = Constants.ENCRYPTION;
15    else if("integrity".equals(protection))
        level = Constants.SIGNATURE;

      Authorization authzImpl = null;
19    if(authz != null) {
       if(authz.equalsIgnoreCase("self"))
21        authzImpl = SelfAuthorization.getInstance();
       else if // ... ( other cases omitted)
23     else
          authzImpl = NoAuthorization.getInstance();
25    }
      else
27     authzImpl = NoAuthorization.getInstance();

29    call.setProperty("org.globus.security.authorization"↵
         , authzImpl);

31    // TRANSPORT
      if("GSITransport".equals(method)) {
33     call.setProperty(Constants.GSI_TRANSPORT, level);
      }
35    // GSISecureMessage
      else if("GSISecureMessage".equals(method)) {
37     call.setProperty(Constants.GSI_SEC_MSG, level);

      /* Generate credentials */
39    String peerCredentials = secDesc.↵
         getPeerCredentials();
41    Subject subject = new Subject();
      X509Certificate serverCert =
43       CertUtil.loadCertificate(peerCredentials);
      EncryptionCredentials encryptionCreds =
45       new EncryptionCredentials(new X509Certificate[]{↵
           serverCert});
      subject.getPublicCredentials().add(encryptionCreds)↵
          ;
47
      call.setProperty(Constants.PEER_SUBJECT, subject);
49    }
      // GSISecureConversation
51    else if("GSISecureConversation".equals(method)) {
      call.setProperty(Constants.GSI_SEC_CONV, level);
53
      String delegation = secDesc.getDelegation();
55    if("full".equals(delegation)){
       call.setProperty(GSIConstants.GSI_MODE,
57              GSIConstants.GSI_MODE_FULL_DELEG);
      } else if // ... other cases omitted
59    }

61    GSSCredential proxyCert = secDesc.getProxyCertificate↵
```

```
                ();
        if(proxyCert != null)
63          call.setProperty(GSIConstants.GSI_CREDENTIALS, ↩
               proxyCert);
        }
65  //   ... perform the actual invoke operation
```
Listing 7.6: Except of class org.activebpel.rt.axis.bpel.AeInvokeHandler: addition of security settings to SOAP call

Then, the call is executed, which means that it passes the Axis handler chain defined in the Axis deployment descriptor `ae-client-config.wsdd`. By adding Globus' message and security handlers to the chain, they automatically encrypt and sign messages if the mentioned properties are set in the call. The response is also handled by the Axis handler chain so that no custom implementation to take care of decryption and verification was required.

To simplify development of appropriate clients to invoke GSI-enabled BPEL workflows, a library which offers methods for adding the required SOAP header elements (see Listing 7.7) has been developed and published on the research group's website along with the implementation of the engine itself, including all extensions.

```
1 setProxyCertificate(Call call,
                      String pathToProxyCert)
3
   setCredentials(Call call, String myProxyHost,
5           String userName, String passwd,
           int lifetime, boolean autoRenewal)
```
Listing 7.7: Extract of the client API

7.6.3 Automatic Security Configuration

The implementation of automatic security configuration for Globus Toolkit 4 required additions and changes in two different places: (1) within GT4 and (2) within the BPEL engine.

As stated above, the Globus Toolkit 4 Monitoring and Discovery System (MDS) is used to register and query the services' security settings. The *Execution Aggregator Source* mechanism of MDS is used ro collect the services' security settings. It allows users to add custom programs to the Globus container's startup procedure that collect and register arbitrary data. To do so, two parameters had to be added to the configuration file `server-config.wsdd` of Globus (see Listing 7.8).

```
  <!-- ... -->
2 <parameter name="providers" value="org.globus.mds.↩
     usefulrp.rpprovider.↩
     ResourcePropertyProviderCollection" />
  <parameter name="rpProviderConfigFile" value="/etc/↩
     globus_wsrf_mds_index/csi-provider-config.xml"/>
4 <!-- ... -->
```
Listing 7.8: Additions to server-config.wsdd configuration file

In the file `csi-provider-config.xml`, the program to be executed to collect the security information is configured. The program, `collectSecurityInformation.sh` (located in directory `libexec`), is a bash-script that basically scans Globus' directory where the services are stored and parses each service's configuration file in which the security settings are located. The discovered security settings are encoded as XML entities and stored in MDS (as child elements of the element `SecurityInformationProvider`).

The BPEL engine had to be extended such that, whenever a `<security>` element with attribute `method` set to `automatic`, it queries the corresponding Globus MDS to retrieve the possible security settings and chooses the best fitting one. To do so, it marks all partnerLinks that point to security-enabled services during the deployment phase. During validation phase (see Listing 7.9), the class `FB12SecurityInformationCollector` then queries the MDS system(s) and stores the retrieved information in the corresponding activity's *security options* data structure (a `HashMap`).

```
   private void checkSecurityDescriptor(IFB12SecureInvoke ↩
       aDef){
 2   AeSecurityDescriptorDef secDef = aDef.↩
       getSecurityDescriptor();
     if(secDef == null)
 4     return;

 6   String method = secDef.getMethod();
     if("automatic".equals(method)) {
 8     FB12SecurityInformationCollector secCollector = new↩
         FB12SecurityInformationCollector();
       // ...
10
       boolean success = secCollector.↩
         collectSecurityInformation(address);
12     FB12ServiceSecurityOption secOpt = secCollector.↩
         getSecurityOptions(address);

14     // ... perform validation ...
     }
16 }
```

Listing 7.9: Verification of security configuration using automatic determination of settings

At execution time, the engine has to actually set up the SOAP call to the security-enabled service. This is, as seen above, done in class `AeInvokeHandler`, which had to further be extended. Listing 7.10 contains only the most important parts of the selection process. It is noteworthy that if the target service offers more than one security method, the class `FB12SecurityModeDecider` is used to determine the best-fitting one. The decision is based on two factors: (1) capabilities of the offered security methods[4] and (2) size of the message to be signed or encrypted. Details on this topic are given in Section 7.7.

---
[4] For instance, when delegation is required, only SecureConversation may be chosen since the other methods do not support delegation.

```
   if("automatic".equals(method)){
2    Map secOptions = aInvokeQueueObject.↵
        getSecurityOptions();
     // ... determine hostname, service name ...
4    Map secOptMap = (Map)secOptions.get(serviceHost);
     FB12ServiceSecurityOption secOpt = null;
6    if(secOptMap != null){
        secOpt = (FB12ServiceSecurityOption)secOptMap.get(↵
           serviceName);
8    }

10   if(secOpt != null){
        int msgSize = determineMessageSize(↵
           aInvokeQueueObject);
12      FB12SecurityModeDecider decider = new ↵
           FB12SecurityModeDecider();
        decider.decide(msgSize, secOpt, secDesc.↵
           getDelegation());
14      method = decider.getMethod();
        protection = decider.getProtection();
16   }
```

Listing 7.10: Actual automatic selection of security method during execution time

7.7 Evaluation

In this section, experimental results with respect to the performance of the different security methods are presented. The measurements compare the execution times of all three security methods using both a "hand written" Java Globus client and BPEL processes when performing exactly the same operations. A simple Globus service offering some basic operations has been written for the evaluation. The invoked service's operations do nothing but return the input value. Therefore, the runtime of the operations can be treated as zero. To obtain reliable results, every run was repeated fifty times and the arithmetic mean of the results was computed.

The machine hosting the Globus environment was a Pentium IV 3 GHz with Hyper-Threading and 1 GB of RAM running Linux (kernel 2.6). The workflow engine as well as the Globus clients were installed on a 1.7 GHz Pentium M machine (1 GB of RAM) running Windows XP SP 2. The hosts were connected using the 100 MBit switched Ethernet network of our department.

The execution times of workflows as well as Globus clients with 1, 10 and 50 (sequential) service invocations are shown in Tables 7.1, 7.2, and 7.3. The results represent two aspects: overhead of the (implementation of the) security protocols used, and client and workflow execution time, respectively. For comparison purposes, the execution times for workflows and Globus clients with security disabled (see Table 7.4) were also measured. The overhead of the BPEL implementation is approximately 45% compared to a hand-written Globus client when pure HTTP is used for transmission. This overhead reduces to about 13% to 19% when encryption is used, and 0% to 15% when integrity is of interest. Therefore, it is evident that the entire runtime is clearly dominated by security aspects rather than by the overhead introduced by the workflow engine.

Table 7.1: Experimental results in milliseconds for GSITransport using encryption and integrity.

Calls	GSITransport Integrity			GSITransport Encryption		
	Globus	BPEL	Overhead BPEL	Globus	BPEL	Overhead BPEL
1	350	624	78.29 %	375	622	65.87 %
10	1805	2488	37.84 %	1838	2167	17.90 %
50	7952	9164	15.24 %	8299	9861	18.82 %

Table 7.2: Experimental results in milliseconds for GSISecureMessage using encryption and integrity.

Calls	GSISecureMessage Integrity			GSISecureMessage Encryption		
	Globus	BPEL	Overhead BPEL	Globus	BPEL	Overhead BPEL
1	794	1586	99.75	1108	1861	67.96 %
10	4305	4755	10.45	5803	6483	11.72 %
50	19460	21060	8.22 %	26313	30040	14.16 %

Table 7.3: Experimental results in milliseconds for GSISecureConversation using encryption and integrity.

Calls	GSISecureConversation Integrity			GSISecureConversation Encryption		
	Globus	BPEL	Overhead BPEL	Globus	BPEL	Overhead BPEL
1	1615	747	-53.75 %	1583	808	-48.96 %
10	3633	2818	-22.43 %	3335	2693	-19.25 %
50	12507	12489	-0.14 %	11182	12602	12.70 %

Obviously, the BPEL processes have an initialization overhead which only carries weight when only a few services are invoked during the run. Since typical workflows consist of several invocations, the initialization overhead does not play an important role. The results for 50 invocations show that the overhead when using BPEL is between 0% and 19%, depending on the security method used. This overhead is definitely acceptable when taking into account that the normal runtime of a service is between hours and days (compared to milliseconds in the conducted tests). Then, a few milliseconds more or less required for the invocation of the service do not matter at all. Interestingly, when GSISecureConversation is used, the BPEL implementation performs better than a Globus client when a few services are invoked (overhead -0.14%). This implies that Globus has a high initialization overhead for this particular security method. When many services are invoked, the Globus implementation performs better (about 12% faster).

Table 7.4: Experimental results in milliseconds using pure HTTP.

Calls	HTTP		
	Globus	BPEL	Overhead BPEL
1	90	129	43 %
10	293	416	42 %
50	1076	1559	45 %

Obtaining a proxy certificate from MyProxy took between 900 to 1000 milliseconds. This is independent of the security method used as well as whether BPEL or Globus clients were used. Thus, when MyProxy is used instead of locally stored certificates, this time has to be added to every value in the tables above.

Automatic security configuration has also been analyzed in terms of produced overhead. Thereby, the same machine and network setup as above was used. It turned out that the overhead induced by collecting security information from Globus head node can be neglected, as it takes about 250 ms to collect this data. Moreover, the BPEL engine caches those values, meaning that the operation only has to be carried out very rarely. To measure the performance of the different security methods, a sample workflow was developed that basically consists of one *gridInvoke* operation (along with *gridCreateResourceInvoke* and *gridDestroyResourceInvoke*). The invoked service "echoes" the input (given as datatype string). Tests were performed using messages ranging from 1 Byte to 1000 Kbytes; the *gridInvoke* operation was carried out using all possible security mechanisms and levels (six in total: GSITransport with encryption and signature, GSISecureMessage with encryption and signature, GSISecureConversation with encryption and signature). The results are shown in Figure 7.9. Obviously, the duration of workflow execution grows linearly with the message size. GSITransport is clearly the best performing method, followed by GSISecureConversation and GSISecureMessage. However, it does not support delegation. Therefore, when offered by the service and delegation is not required, it should be given preference. Otherwise, GSISecureConversation should be selected.

To summarize, BPEL is suitable for Grid workflow modeling since it pro-

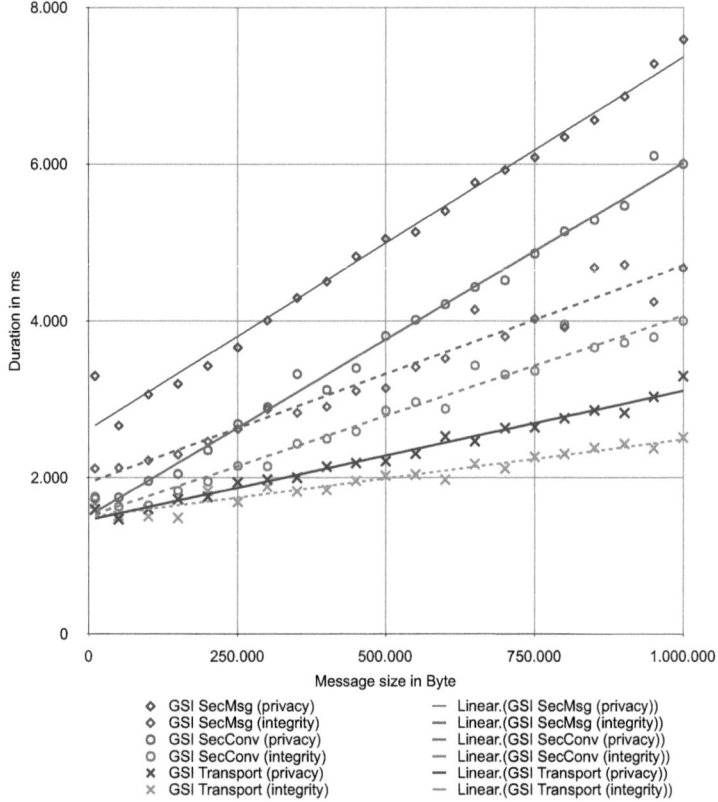

Figure 7.9: Duration of service invocation using different security mechanism and message sizes

vides a powerful way to build Grid applications while introducing a moderate overhead. When security is involved, the overhead even decreases. Using the graphical modeling tools developed during the course of this thesis, the error-prone task of hand-writing security enabled Grid clients is replaced by an intuitive, graphical way of composing services in a secure manner.

7.8 Summary

This chapter has presented Grid-related extensions to the BPEL standard. First, language extensions that allow workflow developers to integrate WSRF-based services into BPEL workflows were introduced. *gridInvoke*, *gridCreateResourceInvoke* and *gridDestroyResourceInvoke*) map the *factory pattern* of WSRF to BPEL. This dramatically eases workflow modeling and is a good extension point for security-related extensions. Second, it has been described how Grid Security Infrastructure (GSI) can be used within BPEL. Therefore, the language standard was further extended. The presented solution allows users to use all security mechanisms offered by Globus Toolkit 4 and also features certificate lifetime management. Moreover, an approach to automatic security configuration of workflows has been presented. Implementation details were discussed in Section 7.6, whereas an evaluation was presented in Section 7.7.

Chapter 8
Development Tools

Contents

8.1	Introduction	153
8.2	Related Work	155
8.3	Design of the Development Suite	157
	8.3.1 Domain-adaptable Visual Orchestrator	157
	8.3.2 SimpleBPEL	162
8.4	Implementation of the Development Suite	167
	8.4.1 Domain-adaptable Visual Orchestrator	167
	8.4.2 SimpleBPEL	172
8.5	Use Cases	179
	8.5.1 Service-oriented Grid Computing	179
	8.5.2 Time-constrained Web Services for Industrial Automation	180
	8.5.3 SimpleBPEL	187
8.6	Summary	189

8.1 Introduction

Due to the complex nature of Web service standards, the definition of a workflow is quite error-prone and time-consuming without tool support. As a result, several research and commercial activities concentrate on the design and development of graphical BPEL workflow editors focusing on a clear visualization and a syntactically correct mapping of the graphical representation to BPEL code. Thus, existing BPEL workflow editors are only suitable for Web service experts who are familiar with the details of Web services and BPEL. Non-Web service experts are normally overburdened by these editors.

This motivated the development of an BPEL modeling tool that offers greater flexibility and adaptability to certain application domains. The tool, *Domain-adaptable Visual BPEL Orchestrator (DAVO)*, provides abstractions for process modeling and is designed for non-Web service experts. DAVO is a domain-adaptable, graphical BPEL workflow editor. The key benefits that distinguish DAVO from other graphical BPEL workflow editors are the *adaptable data model* and *user interface* which permit customization to specific domain needs. This increases usability for non-Web service experts.

To meet the specific requirements of Grid environments, the adaptability of DAVO is used to create a tool specifically for Grid-based workflows. The tool, *Visual Grid Orchestrator (ViGO)*, offers – as its name suggests – extensions for service-oriented Grid computing based on WSRF to simplify the integration of stateful Web services into BPEL workflows. Moreover, it features graphical dialogs to configure the security settings (for usage of Grid Security Infrastructure) and presents a visual feedback whether workflow operations use security or not.

The cooperation with scientists from other disciplines has shown that further simplifications in workflow modeling are desirable. Especially when used by scientists from non-computer science domains, the generic nature of BPEL has some drawbacks, as BPEL modeling is quite complex and requires knowledge in some of the standards of the Web service "universe," such as WSDL, SOAP, XML Schema and XPath. Furthermore, scientific workflows for experimental data analysis and computer simulations often consist of recurring fragments. Hence, it would be highly beneficial to have a BPEL modeling tool that simplifies workflow composition without introducing another modeling language. As a consequence, the idea of separating workflow development into two distinct roles with clear areas of responsibility has emerged. Experienced users (BPEL experts) carry out the development of BPEL fragments for the needs of the given application domain. This task requires a standard BPEL modeling tool with the capability of storing these fragments. The second role is carried out by a domain expert who simply has to combine the fragments, as required for his/her application. Here, a tool is required that enables the domain expert to intuitively model his/her experiments, or his/her application in general. To achieve this goal, DAVO is extended to enable users to save BPEL fragments (called *SimpleBPEL fragments* or SBFs for short in the following) to a library. A end user may use another tool, *SimpleBPEL Composer*, to model a workflow from existing SBFs. Thereby, no knowledge about BPEL or Web services is required.

The rest of this chapter is organized as follows: In Section 8.2, related work is discussed. The first part of Section 8.3 outlines the architectural blueprint of DAVO and describes its main features including the domain-adaptable data model and user interface. In the second part, the design of SimpleBPEL is explained in detail. Implementation details are discussed in Section 8.4. In Section 8.5, use cases from the Grid computing and industrial automation domain show how DAVO can be adapted to different fields of application. Furthermore, using the medical use case, the simplified modeling approach of SimpleBPEL is demonstrated. Finally, Section 8.6 summarizes the chapter.

Parts of this chapter have been published [51, 52, 55, 56, 85, 104].

8.2 Related Work

Since BPEL is an industry-backed standard, a variety of commercial modeling tools exist. What is more, several scientific approaches to ease BPEL modeling have been introduced. They range from highly abstracted modeling approaches like describing Web service interactions by message sequence charts to pragmatic solutions that more or less emulate the functionality of commercial tools and add some abstractions to ease modeling for scientists. Due to this high number of related tools, only representatives for each category are discussed here.

Martinez et al. [100] present a visual Web service composition tool based on BPEL called *ZenFlow*. ZenFlow focuses on the visualization of a workflow by five different views: *flow chart view* (a graphical representation of the control flow of a business process), *form view* (a textual representation of the properties of a BPEL activity), *text tree view* (an tree-like excerpt of the most-relevant BPEL activities), *error view* (a list of warnings and syntactic errors), *free text view* (a plain text editor that permits the manual modification of the BPEL code), and *execution view* (a graphical representation of the workflow execution). The design and implementation of ZenFlow and DAVO differ significantly: whereas ZenFlow focuses on the visualization of a workflow by different views, DAVO offers an extensible data model supporting adaptability to different domains. Consequently, ZenFlow and DAVO may complement each other.

Foster et al. [64] present a model-based approach for the formal description of Web service interactions. The Labelled Transition System Analyser (LTSA) permits the specification of Web service interactions using message sequence charts, verification of these specifications using labeled transition systems, and generation of orchestration and choreography descriptions using BPEL and WS-CDL. Consequently, a workflow designer never composes a workflow directly using BPEL, but starts with definition and verification of the interaction. An abstraction of the Web service composition process permits the formal verification of the Web service interaction which is undoubtedly useful in some cases. However, another level of abstraction additionally exacerbates the composition process for non-Web service domain experts.

McGough et al. [106] present the GRIDCC project, whose main objective is the integration of instruments, e.g. telescopes, particle accelerators or power stations into a Grid computing environment respecting Quality of Service (QoS) parameters. The *GRIDCC Workflow Management Service (WfMS)* contains several functional components: the workflow editor allows users to compose new workflows using BPEL, the workflow planner is used to select an appropriate resource for the defined QoS parameters, and the workflow observer monitors whether a running workflow holds its QoS parameters. The main focus of GRIDCC is a QoS-aware scheduling and runtime monitoring of BPEL workflows within the service-oriented Grid computing domain. Consequently, an adoption of GRIDCC technologies within other domains is difficult in comparison with DAVO.

Held et al. [81] present a collaborative BPEL environment based on Web 2.0 technologies. It offers browser-based collaborative workflow modeling using *Hobbes*, a BPEL design tool running on a central server. The modeling tool features graphical editing of standard BPEL processes with sophisticated locking mechanisms. Therefore, it holds a process' object model (*BPEL object model (BOM)*) in an object tree on the server. Unfortunately, the authors do not provide any information whether the model is extensible or not. The implementation is based on the proprietary Adobe Flex framework which requires the Adobe Flash plug-in to be installed on client machines.

Within the OMII-BPEL project, the graphical BPEL modeler Sedna [137] has been developed. In addition to the modeling with plain BPEL activities, it introduces two levels of abstraction to ease the composition of workflows. The first level of abstraction is called Scientific PEL and offers pre-defined function blocks that are often utilized in scientific workflows, like parallel loops. The second level of abstraction is Domain PEL which allows developers to define domain-specific BPEL function blocks. These functions blocks are coined macros and, like in SimpleBPEL, can contain several BPEL activities. Major design goals where reusability, an increase of clearness and an ease of development. However, Sedna provides no means for a separation of roles between BPEL experts and domain experts, meaning that one can use macros to model workflows, but one also has to deal with BPEL constructs. The authors of Sedna state that "Computational scientists can [...] be regarded as highly computer literate [...]. We can expect to find some programming skills." While this statement might be true for scientists from natural sciences, it does not hold for other domains like medicine, systems biology and media research, as my experience shows. The authors state that Sedna is extensible as it is an Eclipse plug-in. However, they do not provide any further interfaces to extend the data model for adaptation to specific application domains.

Eclipse BPEL Designer [57] is a classic BPEL modeler that uses the aforementioned one-to-one mapping. It does not provide any means for abstracting from the complexity of BPEL modeling. In his master's thesis, Streule [125] developed a plug-in for Eclipse BPEL Designer, that allows users to create different views on BPEL processes. This feature may be used, for instance, to hide confidential data when a processes is handed over to business partners or to ease readability of large, complex processes. As described, the plug-in only provides simplified *views* of processes, but does not allow users to modify processes. In conclusion, one can say that the tool is very useful for *understanding* existing BPEL processes, but it does not help a non-BPEL expert to develop processes.

ActiveVOS [20] is a commercial BPM suite (Business Process Management) developed by Active Endpoints. It features the creation of so-called BPELets, reusable BPEL components, that are added to the editor's palette after creation and can be utilized to model processes. Like Sedna, ActiveVOS does not provide a separation between the development of BPELets and the composition of workflows from BPELets. Instead, it allows users to mix BPELets with plain BPEL activities and is mainly focussed on BPEL

experts who wish to reuse commonly required BPEL fragments.
Representative for a variety of BPMN-based (Business Process Modeling Notation) modeling tools, Intalio|Designer is discussed. BPMN is a graphical notation for specifying business processes. It is quite similar to activity diagrams in UML and was designed to support business process management for both technical and business users. BPMN processes are abstract and cannot directly be executed by a workflow engine. However, it is possible to enrich (annotate) the process with technical information like WSDL message definitions, service endpoints and so forth and perform a mapping to BPEL. The mapping from BPMN is not straightforward and not even always possible, as discussed for instance by Ouyang et al. [116]. Among others, one of the main reasons is that BPMN and BPEL are fundamentally different languages: BPMN is graph-oriented while BPEL is mainly block-structured. The vendors of BPMN-to-BPEL translation tools circumvent this problem by limiting the BPMN vocabulary to constructs that can be unambiguously mapped to BPEL. The BPMN-based modeling approach is not able to completely hide technical details from the workflow developer, since one has to deal with WSDL messages, service port types, operations and so forth.

8.3 Design of the Development Suite

8.3.1 Domain-adaptable Visual Orchestrator

The main goal developing DAVO is to build an easy-to-use BPEL editor that supports the entire BPEL standard and offers great flexibility for adaptions to specific application areas. Therefore, the key requirement of DAVO's architecture is *extensibility*, especially with respect to the data model.

As the basis for DAVO, the Eclipse Rich Client Platform (RCP) [6] has been chosen because it offers a very powerful and easy-to-use extension mechanism that in turn is based on a Java component model defined by the OSGi Alliance[1]. The Eclipse platform implements the OSGi specification (their implementation is called Equinox[2]) and allows developers to define so-called *extension points* for applications. The mechanism provides a very convenient way to develop extensible software. For example, this mechanism allows the developer to integrate features like version control by simply adding a third-party Eclipse plug-in like Subversive [13] to an existing application.

Eclipse RCP applications are designed as plug-ins that extend the basic functionality of the Eclipse runtime environment. A plug-in itself may offer extension points to facilitate that other plug-ins may contribute functionality to the plug-in offering the extension point. An extension point contains a definition that describes how other plug-ins can contribute its functionality, e.g., which interfaces have to be implemented by the contributing plug-in. It is up to the plug-in offering the extension point to integrate the functionality

---
[1] http://http://www.osgi.org/Specifications/HomePage
[2] http://www.eclipse.org/equinox/

of plug-ins that provide the extension[3].

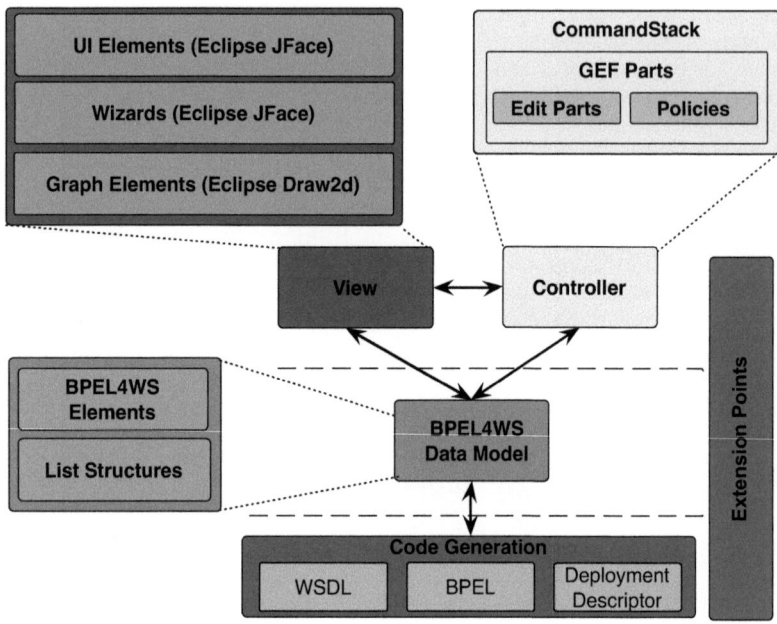

Figure 8.1: Conceptual overview of the core components of DAVO

Figure 8.1 shows a conceptual overview of the core components of DAVO. The architecture is based on a model-driven approach and follows the model-view-controller (MVC) design pattern [76]. Every element of a workflow is presented to the user through a view component with a corresponding controller, allowing editing operations. By visually adding elements to a workflow, changing properties and so on, the controller object corresponding to the action performed makes changes to the internal data model. Vice versa, changes to the internal data model trigger controller objects to update the visualization. The mapping from the internal data model to executable BPEL code is performed by a code generation component. It generates at least three files from the internal model: a ".bpel" file that contains the logic of the workflow, a ".wsdl" file with the workflows interface description and a (non-standardized) deployment descriptor, which contains runtime information like service endpoints.

The design of the mentioned functional components will be described in the following subsections.

---

[3]Technically speaking, the plug-in has to query the *Eclipse Extension Registry* for its extension point's name and integrate the plug-ins (by loading or calling them) that connect to the extension point.

8.3.1.1 Data Model

BPEL workflows may be composed of basic and structured activities which may be nested. This leads to the obvious decision to represent the internal data model in a tree-like manner. The process itself forms the root of the tree with structured child elements, which may also contain subtrees. According to the BPEL standard, each activity used within a workflow is defined by its *type*, a specific set of *attributes* (e.g., name), and specific *nested elements* (e.g., for exception handling purposes). In the case of structured activities, the nested elements can be other activities as well. In DAVO, the activities are represented using objects of the class hierarchy shown in Figure 8.2. *Element* is the parent class of all activities, whereas *ContainerElement* is the parent class for all structured activities. The actual class hierarchy is more sophisticated than the one outlined in the figure. *ConnectedElement* contains several attributes referring to other Web services (e.g., port types and operation names) and is the parent class of the *invoke*, *receive*, and *reply* activities. A *SequentialContainer* is a container whose nested activities are executed in the given order. SequentialContainer is the parent class of *sequence* and *while* for example.

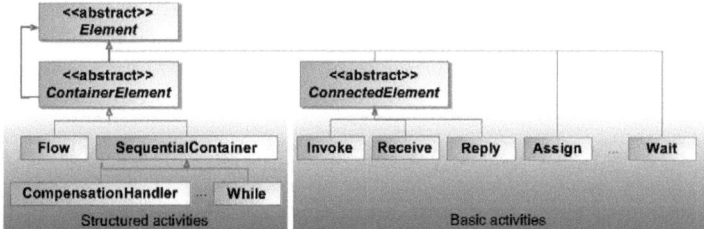

Figure 8.2: A simplified `Element` class hierarchy.

To fulfill the major design goal of (domain) extensibility, the data model must be extensible in two ways: (1) the model must allow developers to add new activities and (2) existing elements must be extensible. The first type of extensibility is required to support the addition of constructs like *gridInvoke*. It might be realized using the standard Eclipse mechanism of extension points. The extension points defined by DAVO are explained in Section 8.3.1.3. The second type of extensibility is required to allow developers to define certain properties that might be required for special application domains, like the real-time service environment presented in Section 8.5. To support this type of extensibility, the data model must innately support the modification of existing elements by contributing plug-ins. In this case, extensibility may mean adding, modifying or removing attributes. To ensure the validity of the model, an extensible validation mechanism is needed. The presented solution provides a factory component to instantiate activities. These activities may be extended or changed by implementations using

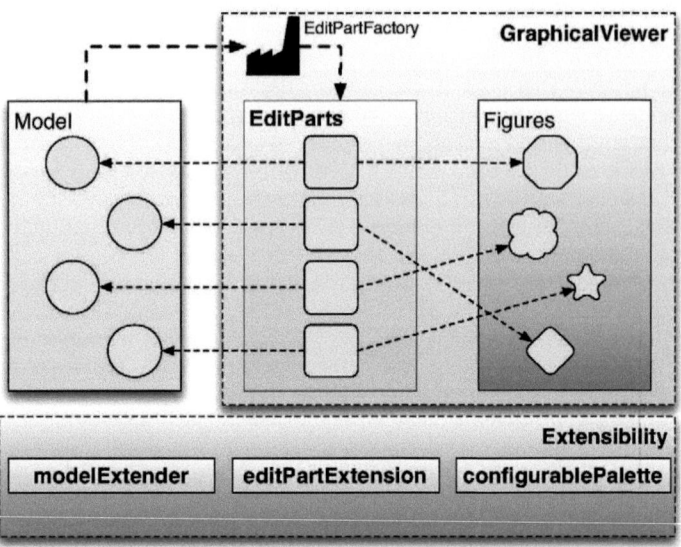

Figure 8.3: Relationship between EditParts, Figures and the data model in GEF

an element extender that registers extensions and is able to remove existing ones.

Furthermore, an event mechanism is needed that automatically performs updates – for instance, on an element's visual representation – whenever an external event occurs. The solution described in Section 8.4.1.1 solves these issues without the need for registering listeners for every event.

8.3.1.2 Views and Controllers

DAVO's graphical user interface is composed of several views that present a variety of information and allow users to perform different actions. Figure 8.4 shows a screenshot in which the views' names have been annotated. Within the editor view, graphical objects are represented by Eclipse Draw2D [4] objects. The view allows the workflow developer to graphically compose a BPEL workflow from BPEL activities that may be chosen from the palette to the right.

Typically, Eclipse displays the properties of an object (here: the BPEL activity currently selected in the editor view) in a property view, which tabularly shows properties in key/value manner. It also allows the programmer to group elements and add more sophisticated user interface elements to ease editing. Since this is quite complicated to implement and would have to be done for every extension, the described solution provides a much simpler, but powerful mechanism. It automatically creates visual representations of the properties of an activity using the adapter pattern [76].

In the MVC design, controllers manage the presentation layer by reacting on user actions. It is responsible for determining which data in the underlying model has to be changed in reaction to a user action. The model change itself is not carried out by the controller object, but delegated to the model. In DAVO, controllers are represented by corresponding Eclipse GEF `Edit-Parts` [5]. EditParts in turn are equipped with so-called *Policies* that are registered to handle certain user actions. In GEF, any modifications to the underlying data model must be carried out by *commands* that are executed by the aforementioned policies.

A factory component allows developers to register visual representations and controllers for standard and new activities. For every element of the data model, it stores the class name and the corresponding `EditPart` which refers to its corresponding `Figure`. The principle is sketched in Figure 8.3.

8.3.1.3 Extension Points

DAVO is designed to be a general-purpose BPEL editor with a special focus on extensibility and adaptability to certain application domains. Therefore, as sketched above, the data model has to innately support extensibility. Moreover, the user interface should be as extensible as possible.

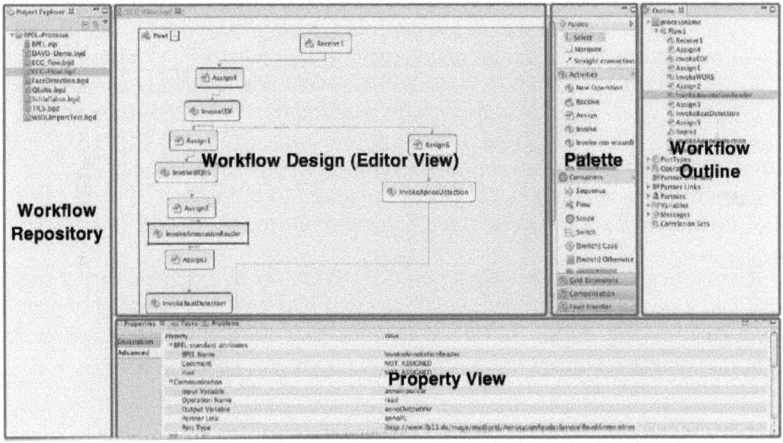

Figure 8.4: Main functional areas of DAVO's user interface.

DAVO relies heavily on the concept of extension points in Eclipse to offer extensibility on all layers (user interface, data, model transformation). The main functional areas of the user interface are depicted in Figure 8.4, as the general outline of the user interface (UI) is required to understand the location and purpose of the different extension points that enable the extensible of the UI. The extension points are:

configurablePalette Allows developers to contribute new items to the editor's palette. The contributor may thereby influence the placement of the item within the palette and even define a new group within the palette. The developer must also implement the *editPartExtension* extension point to provide the corresponding edit part.

multiPageEditorExtension By implementing this extension point, a contributor may provide an editor view. If more than one editor is available, they are displayed as "tabs" below the editing view. By clicking on the different tabs, the user may switch between available editors. Thereby, all editors operate on the same data model, meaning that changes in one editor are reflected in the other editor views as well.

modelExtension The extension point allows extension developers to add, modify or remove properties from existing elements in DAVO's internal data model (referred to as Type 2 extensibility in Section 8.3.1.1).

editPartExtension The extension point allows extension developers to contribute new elements (BPEL activities) to DAVO. Thereby, the developer has to provide model classes and edit parts. Where appropriate, corresponding commands and figures also have to be provided.

shadowFactoryExtension By implementing the extension point, one may add logic to DAVO that is responsible for the mapping between the editor's internal data model and actual BPEL code. It is required during the "export" of a workflow (to BPEL) when new elements are added to DAVO, as it does not know how to map them to the BPEL standard.

invokeHandlerExtension Allows developers to provide additional logic and user interface components that are required to place custom invoke handlers in a process' deployment descriptor during the export process.

Using the described extension points, DAVO may be extended in any way; one can contribute additional activities (that may even be mapped on standard BPEL using the shadow(Factory) mechanism), add simplified or more powerful editors, change or enrich existing activities, and so forth.

8.3.2 SimpleBPEL

This section presents the design of SimpleBPEL, an approach that simplifies modeling of BPEL workflows. The basic idea is to design a graphical modeling tool that enables a domain expert to model his/her application without being distracted by any technical details. To simplify workflow composition, the domain expert creates workflows based on so-called SimpleBPEL fragments (SBFs), an arbitrary but valid combination of BPEL activities. A SimpleBPEL fragment is basically a valid BPEL process without receive and reply activities, in combination with a description of input and output connectors to interface with other SBFs. Those fragments are modeled by BPEL

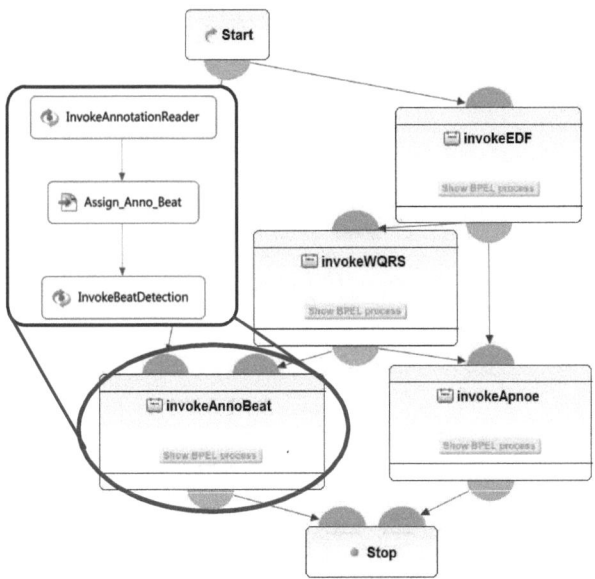

Figure 8.5: Modeling of the medical use case in SimpleBPEL Composer using SBFs defined in DAVO

experts using an extended version of DAVO and are stored in libraries (Domain Profiles) that can be shared between scientists. A newly developed tool, the SimpleBPEL Composer, allows the domain expert to build workflows by simply connecting the input connectors of SBFs with the output connectors of other SBFs. The system automatically verifies whether the blocks are compatible and can be connected or not. In the first case, the required glue code is automatically generated, such that the created SimpleBPEL workflow is exported to a standard-conform BPEL workflow.

An example, in which the medical workflow is modeled in SimpleBPEL Composer, is given in Figure 8.5. Within the SBF "invokeAnnoBeat", the annotation reader and beat detection services have been combined to one fragment.

After a discussion of the modeling of function blocks (process fragments) within DAVO, the design of the SimpleBPEL Composer itself is described.

8.3.2.1 Extensions to DAVO

Since SimpleBPEL fragments are BPEL processes with some restrictions (see below) and can utilize the full expressiveness of BPEL, a suitable modeling tool is inevitable. Ideally, it should be integrated into an existing BPEL editor such that a BPEL expert does not need to learn how to use a new tool for modeling the SBFs. Despite the advantage for BPEL developers, integrating the required functionality into an existing BPEL modeling tool has the advantage that less code has to be developed to create the tool itself. As presented, DAVO supports the complete BPEL standard and is therefore suitable as a basis for the SimpleBPEL Composer. Its extensibility mechanisms allowed to integrate the required functionality for modeling SBFs.

Restrictions on SBFs. To assemble SimpleBPEL fragments to a BPEL workflow, the fragments have to fulfill some constraints that have to be enforced by the modeling tool: (1) the SBF may not have a *receive* or *reply* activity and (2) SBFs must have (one or more) distinguished input and output variables. Without restriction (1), a SBF would already be a complete BPEL workflow and could not be added as part of another workflow. The variables represent the input and output for an entire SBF and define its data exchange capabilities with other SBFs. Moreover, SimpleBPEL fragments are automatically wrapped by a BPEL *flow* activity. This is required when the BPEL developer ordered the workflow steps using connections (BPEL links) without an enclosing flow element. Another solution would be to check whether the fragment's root element is either a flow or a sequence and print an error message in case the developer did not follow the rule. However, putting another flow around a flow (or a sequence) does not change the semantics at all; therefore, the mechanism does not cause any harm, but eases development.

Domain Profiles. A SBF represents exactly one (part of a) BPEL workflow. If, for example, a media researcher models a video analysis, he/she wants to compose several fragments that belong to the same domain (such as face recognition, cut detection etc.) into a workflow. To aggregate multiple SBFs of one domain into a library, so-called *Domain Profiles* are used that basically represent a binding of SBFs into a single XML file. Thereby, profiles can easily be shared among different developers/researchers. The relation between fragments and profiles is depicted in Figure 8.6. Furthermore, the figure also implies that a fragment-level validation mechanism (*ReceiveReplyModelValidator*) exists, which ensures that the restrictions mentioned above are met.

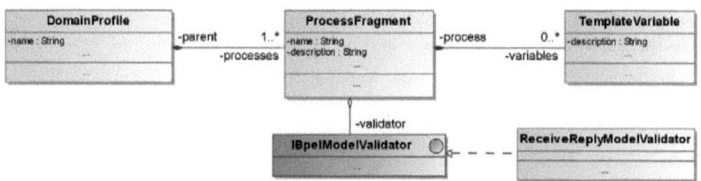

Figure 8.6: Data model of the Domain Profile

8.3.2.2 SimpleBPEL Composer

Architecture. The SimpleBPEL Composer must be able to import Domain Profiles and to offer the contained SBF to the domain expert, who in turn can compose a SimpleBPEL workflow based on them. The graphical representation of a SBF has to reflect its input and output variables so that the domain expert can gain an intuitive overview of all possible connections between SimpleBPEL fragments.

The model of the SimpleBPEL Composer basically consists of two types of elements. On one hand, there are `ProcessModules` that are represented by start, end, and function modules. On the other hand, function modules are interconnected via `VariableConnections`. Each end of such a connection is represented by an input or an output variable of a fragment. The UML diagram of the data model of the SimpleBPEL Composer is illustrated in Figure 8.7.

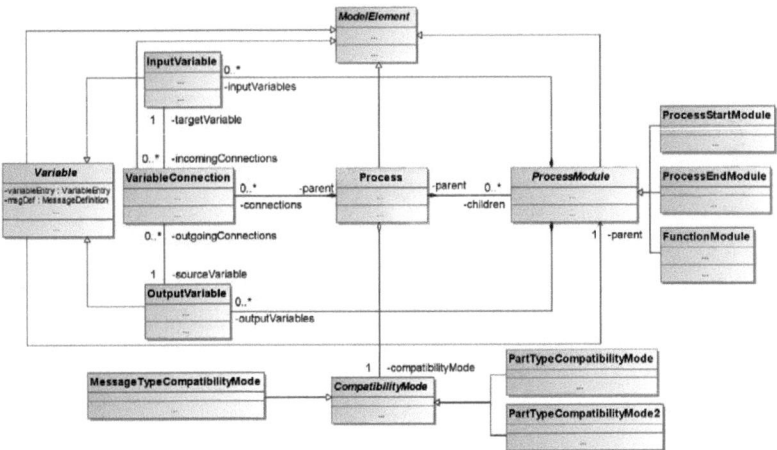

Figure 8.7: Data model of the SimpleBPEL Composer

Since not all connections between SBFs are reasonable, a validation has to be performed whenever the user attempts to connect SBFs. It has to check whether an assignment between two selected variables is reasonable and present the result in an adequate way. Since variables are based on WSDL messages that in turn are sets of parts, different validation strategies are possible. A part can either be a simple type (like an integer or a string) or a complex type that is comparable to a data structure in traditional programming languages. Thus, the validation can be performed on two different levels. The first one is to compare the qualified name (*QName*) of the messages themselves (*MessageTypeCompatibilityMode* in Figure 8.7). A connection is valid if the *QNames* coincide. The second validation is to check whether all data types used within the messages conform to each other (*PartTypeCompatibilityMode*). In some special cases, where an in-order mapping is too strict, a bijective mapping between the fields of the message is more appropriate (*PartTypeCompatibilityMode2*), see also Figure 8.8). Since this mapping can be ambiguous, it is only useful under special circumstances. In-order mapping is set as a default, but the SimpleBPEL user may choose which type of compatibility checking should be used within the SimpleBPEL Composer UI.

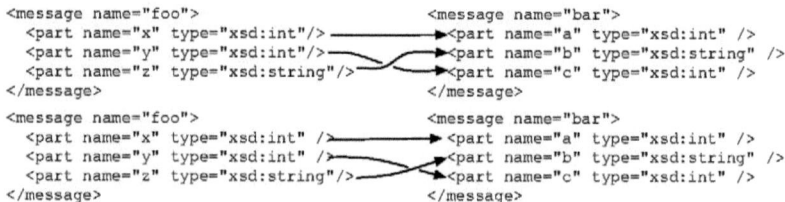

Figure 8.8: Bijective mapping between two messages

Export. To be executable by a BPEL engine, a SimpleBPEL workflow has to be transformed into a BPEL workflow following the language standard. The occurrence of variables with the same name within different fragments may cause conflicts since the variables might overwrite each other. To guarantee the correctness of an exported workflow, it is necessary to encapsulate the SBFs. Thus, the BPEL code represented by a fragment has to be embedded into a `scope` activity. Therefore, two `assign` elements are necessary, one to initialize the input variable(s) and one to copy the output into the succeeding SBF(s), as illustrated in Figure 8.9.

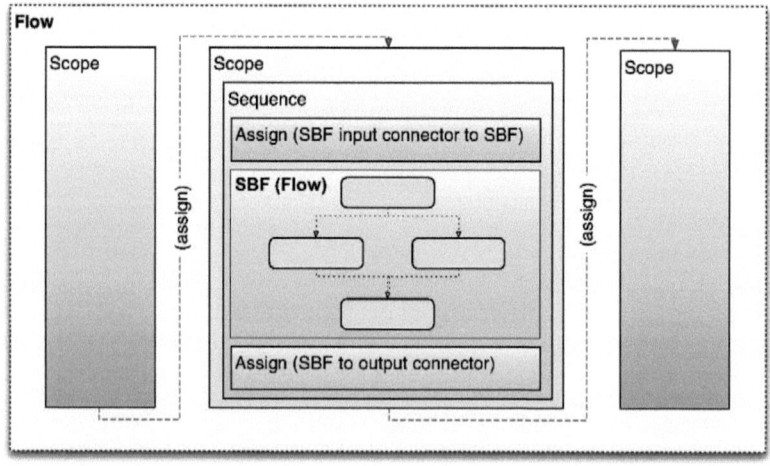

Figure 8.9: Integration of process fragments into a BPEL workflow

Once all the fragments have been wrapped by their corresponding *scope* activities, the start and stop elements of the SimpleBPEL workflow have to be transformed, too. They are represented by a *receive* and a *reply* activity, respectively. Both receive and reply use variables to transfer input data (and output data, respectively). The exact definition of the activities's variables depends on the SBFs that are connected to them. In the case of the start element, the input variables of the fragments that are connected to it are introspected. Each part of their messages is aggregated into a new message that in turn serves as the message type for the variable used by the receive activity.

As a last step, the assign operations that copy variable contents between the different scope containers have to be generated. Which part of the underlying source message is copied to which part of the destination message depends on the chosen compatibility mode (see above).

The fragments use DAVO's internal model representation instead their own data model. This provides the possibility of reusing all the functionality available in DAVO, such as the export of the BPEL workflow into a deployable archive, which includes functionalities like generating the WSDL of the workflow and the deployment descriptor.

8.4 Implementation of the Development Suite

In this section, some aspects of the implementation of DAVO and SimpleBPEL Composer are briefly discussed. Both DAVO and the SimpleBPEL Composer have been implemented as plug-ins for the Eclipse RCP Platform. Using Eclipse has various advantages compared to implementing applications without using a framework. For instance, Eclipse features a powerful framework for drawing graphs and figures, the Graphical Editing Framework (GEF), that has extensively been used in this work. The implementation makes use of Eclipse's extensibility mechanisms (extension points, OSGi bundles). For example, DAVO's user interface has been extended by a view that allows the user to store function blocks as a SimpleBPEL profile.

8.4.1 Domain-adaptable Visual Orchestrator

In this section, some details regarding the implementation of DAVO are presented. Since the implementation is quite complex in its entirety (about 43,000 lines of code), only the parts of the implementation that are relevant to extensibility are discussed.

8.4.1.1 Data Model

While it is sufficient for a standard BPEL workflow editor to use a simple data model to store the process' information, i.e. information about elements and attributes, this approach is not feasible with regard to extensibility. For the use of BPEL within and the adaptation of DAVO to specific domains (e.g., industrial automation), it is necessary to associate additional information with an activity (e.g. the average and worst-case execution time). DAVO uses named properties to associate arbitrary information with activities.

Besides name and value, these properties also contain an `IValidator` which can be used to check validity when `setValue()` is called. Additionally, the properties themselves have various meta-properties (see Figure 8.10), such as:

- `persistent` determines if the property value is stored together with the DAVO data model.

- `readOnly` and `visible`, which are used (together with various other meta-properties) to control the automatic creation of property views, as described in Section 8.4.1.2.

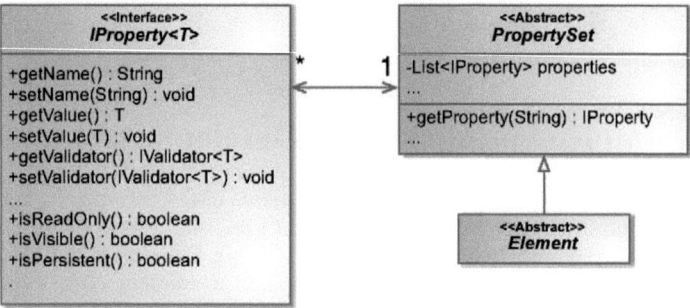

Figure 8.10: The property model of DAVO

There may be various dependencies between the properties of an `Element`. For instance, an *operation name* depends on the *port type*, which in turn depends on the *partner link*. Additionally, dependencies to external events may be presented. For instance, a list of variables, shown in the property view, needs to be updated whenever the variable set of the process or scope changes. All of these dependencies are automatically managed by the `Element`. For internal dependencies, a property simply needs to implement an interface giving `Element` access to the names of the properties on which it depends; it must also provide a callback method that will be invoked automatically. For external dependencies, a similar interface exists that gives access to a list of events of which the property needs to be notified. External events are automatically propagated through the workflow by the `ContainerElements`. Due to this design, it is not necessary for properties to be registered as listeners. Since an `Element` is a set of properties plus additional information, an `Element` inherits from `PropertySet` (see Figure 8.10).

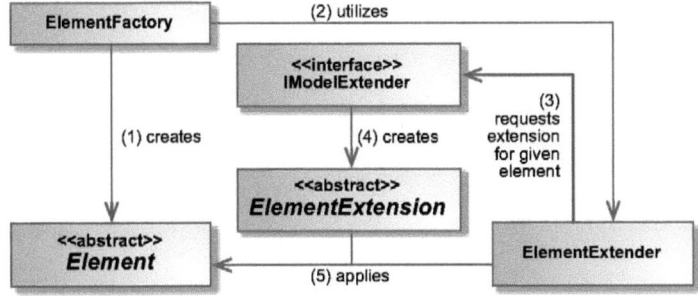

Figure 8.11: The Element extension mechanism is used when extension point *modelExtension* is implemented

The extension mechanism is illustrated in Figure 8.11. The core of each DAVO extension is an implementation of the IModelExtender (the interface required to implement to connect to the extension point *modelExtension*). A specific IModelExtender implementation knows the ElementExtension for each Element. After the ElementFactory has created the Element (1), it passes it to the ElementExtender (2), which then asks the IModelExtender for extensions for the given Element (3). After the IModelExtender has created the extension for the given Element (4), it is added to the Element (5). The ElementExtension can modify the Element in many ways. For example, it can add new properties or hide existing ones.

Using DAVO's extensions points (*configurablePalette* and *editPartExtension*), new activities can be added by simply inheriting an arbitrary class from the hierarchy and registering the new activity. As a consequence, the new activity is added to DAVO's graphical user interface, as described below.

8.4.1.2 Views and Controllers

Eclipse and GEF make heavy use of the MVC design pattern. For example, an IFigure is used as view and an EditPart is used as controller of an activity. An IFigure is the graphical representation of an activity, the EditPart permits the interaction (e.g., moving, resizing) with its graphical representation.

The abstractions realized by the data model are reused here to create a minimal hierarchy of view and controller implementations. The controller hierarchy shown in Figure 8.12 is very similar to the data model. Analogously, it contains the same main abstractions ElementEditPart and ContainerElementEditPart, a concrete controller for basic activities (BasicElementEditPart), and two controllers for structured activities (SequentialElementEditPart and NonSequentialElementEditPart). The hierarchy of view classes is organized in a similar fashion. In both cases, a factory is used to create instances of views and controllers (see Figure 8.3). It automatically chooses the concrete type accord-

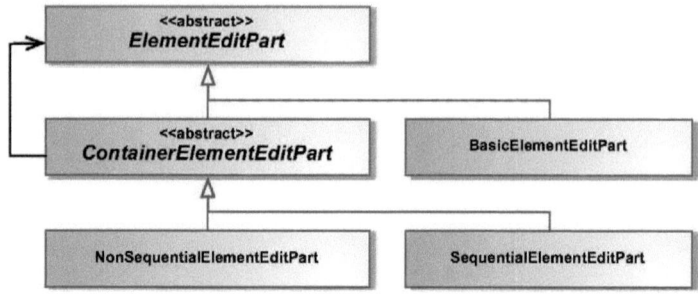

Figure 8.12: The EditPart type hierarchy

ing to the activity's type. An extension may register new views or controllers with the factories and associate them with the Elements.

In DAVO, activities are represented by graphical widgets containing the *name* of the activity and an *icon* to easily distinguish the different activities. Additionally, one or more *status icons* can be added to the activities. Together with new properties, DAVO extensions may also add corresponding status icons to the activities. For example, for the development of security-enabled Grid workflows, a status icon could reflect whether or not security is enabled. Figure 8.13 shows a screenshot of the actual implementation of the security settings (property) view and the corresponding status icon change.

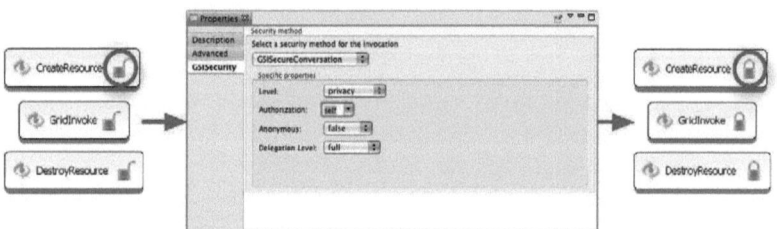

Figure 8.13: State change of a property (gridInvoke security setting) reflected by a change of the corresponding status icon

Apart from the graphical workflow view, the most important part of DAVO is the property view that allows the user to assign values to the properties of an activity. The property view is one of Eclipse's core views. It contains a table of property names and values, which can either be directly entered or selected from a list of possible values. In addition, groups of user interface controls, so-called sections, can be added to the property view to edit a group of properties in a more sophisticated way. In that case, the property view uses tabs to switch between the basic property view and the other sections. Because detailed knowledge of the Eclipse Standard Widget Toolkit (SWT) is required to create such sections, an easy way to use the standard property view is desirable.

Eclipse defines two interfaces which have to be implemented to edit properties of any object: IPropertySource and IPropertyDescriptor. IPropertySource contains methods to read and change the values of properties and to return a list of IPropertyDescriptor objects. An IPropertyDescriptor object describes one of the available properties. The adapter design pattern is used to dynamically create wrapper objects for Elements of the data model, if they are selected. This procedure is shown in Figure 8.14. When an activity, or more precisely, the EditPart belonging to its graphical representation, is selected, Eclipse tries to update the properties view. It discovers that the EditPart does not implement IPropertySource and uses an adapter factory to create a valid adapter, which is an instance of PropertySetAdapter in this case (Element inherits from PropertySet since it is a set of properties plus additional information. For simplicity reasons, this is not shown in Figure 8.2). This instance will create the list of IPropertyDescriptors using the meta-properties mentioned earlier. For instance, properties whose visible meta-property is set to false will not be shown, whereas properties whose readOnly meta-property is set to false will be shown, but will not be editable. Calls to read or change the value of a property are delegated to a PropertyAdapter that wraps the property (a subclass of IProperty) and is responsible for value conversion, as the property view only accepts strings.

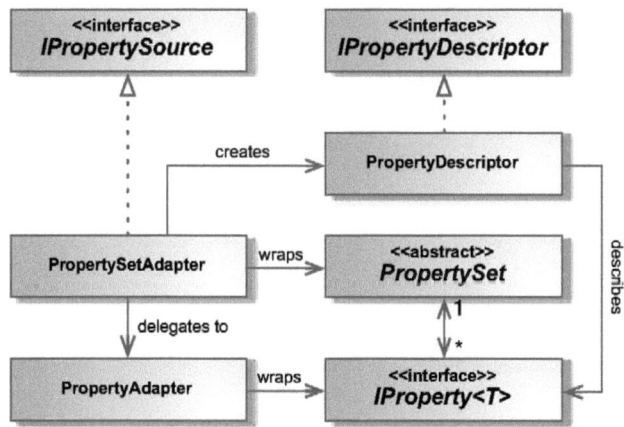

Figure 8.14: The Property adapter model

8.4.1.3 Shadow Model

Translating the workflow from the data model to actual BPEL code is done using the so-called *shadow model*, a second class hierarchy equivalent to the data model. The use of a separate model for translation purposes prevents that changes to the translation process may influence the data model. The model contains an ElementShadow class for every Element, whose sole purpose is the conversion of the values stored in the properties of its associated Element to an XML element representing the corresponding BPEL activity. The translation process is coordinated by the Exporter, which generates the BPEL document. The document contains the activities and other meta-information as well as auxiliary files needed to deploy the workflow. All classes involved in the conversion process are shown in Figure 8.15.

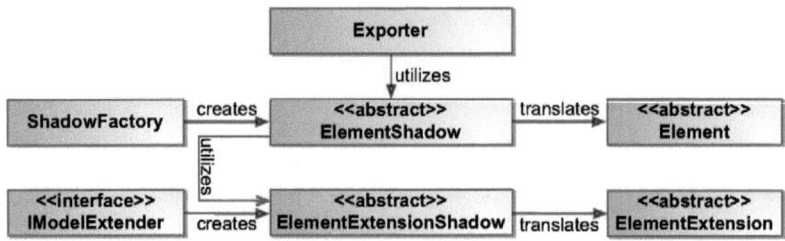

Figure 8.15: A BPEL translation process using the shadow model

A DAVO extension that adds new Elements to the data model must register the corresponding ElementShadows with the ShadowFactory. If the extension does not add new Elements, but instead modifies existing ones by means of an ElementExtension, it is required to provide an appropriate ElementExtensionShadow that is capable of translating the auxiliary information.

8.4.2 SimpleBPEL

This section sketches some implementation details of SimpleBPEL. The entire implementation of the plug-in consists of about 16,000 lines of code and is thus too extensive to be discussed in details. On that score, only the most important aspects are sketched in the following.

8.4.2.1 Extensions to DAVO

The Profile Editor has been implemented as an extension to DAVO and consists of additions to the user interface. The graph-based workflow editor and data model of DAVO could be used because SBFs are (incomplete) BPEL processes. In Figure 8.16, the user interface of the Profile

Editor is shown. It is implemented as a view (extending the base class
org.eclipse.ui.part.ViewPart) and registered at the extension point
org.eclipse.ui.views that is offered by the Eclipse platform.

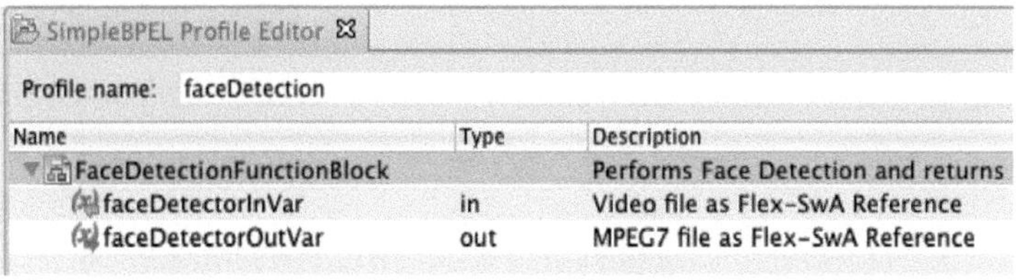

SimpleBPEL Profile Editor ⊠		
Profile name: faceDetection		
Name	Type	Description
▼ FaceDetectionFunctionBlock		Performs Face Detection and returns
faceDetectorInVar	in	Video file as Flex-SwA Reference
faceDetectorOutVar	out	MPEG7 file as Flex-SwA Reference

Figure 8.16: Profile Editor

The user interface can be used to model SBFs, add descriptions and define whether a variable is input or output of the SBF. When a SBF is added to a profile, the editor performs a validation according to the rules defined in Section 8.3.2.1. The validation process may be further extended and is based on the interface IBpelModeValidator. It declares the methods boolean validate(Process process) and String get-InvalidMessage(). The latter represents the error message to be displayed when the validation fails. The "receive-reply" validator assures that a fragment does not contain receive and reply activities. Its source code is listed in Listing 8.1. As the import statements illustrate, DAVO's data model is used to model the internals of fragments.

```
2 package de.fb12.gdt.bpel.simplebpel.model.xmlprofile.↵
    validators;

4 import de.fb12.gdt.bpel.model.ContainerElement;
  import de.fb12.gdt.bpel.model.Element;
6 import de.fb12.gdt.bpel.model.Process;
  import de.fb12.gdt.bpel.model.Receive;
8 import de.fb12.gdt.bpel.model.Reply;

10 public class ReceiveReplyModelValidator implements ↵
    IBpelModelValidator {
    @Override
12  public boolean validate(Process process) {
      return containsReceiveOrReply(process);
14  }

16  private boolean containsReceiveOrReply(↵
      ContainerElement container){
      boolean flag = true;
18    for(Element element:container.getChildren()){
        if(element instanceof ContainerElement){
20        flag = flag && containsReceiveOrReply(((↵
            ContainerElement)element));
        } else if(element instanceof Receive){
```

```
22        flag = false;
      } else if(element instanceof Reply){
24        flag = false;
      }
26    }
      return flag;
28  }

30  @Override
    public String getInvalidMessage() {
32      return "Contains Receive or Reply";
    }
34 }
```
Listing 8.1: Validation of SimpleBPEL fragments

Once a profile is completed, the developer may export it to share it with other SimpleBPEL users. The profile is stored in a ZIP file that contains the profile's XML-based description (particularly the discussed input and output variable definitions) as well as the functions blocks as well as screenshots of the function blocks to allow a quick look into a function block's intrinsics in the SimpleBPEL Composer. The XML format is shown in Listing 8.2.

```
2 <domainProfile name="NAME">
  <process name="NAME">+
4   <description>DESCRIPTION</description>
    <processFilename>FUNC_BLOCK_FILE</processFilename>
6   <variable name="NAME">+
    <description>DESCRIPTION</description>
8   <type>in | out</type>
    </variable>
10 </process>
   </domainProfile>
```
Listing 8.2: Schema definition of domain profiles

8.4.2.2 SimpleBPEL Composer

The SimpleBPEL perspective consists of a navigation view on the left where existing SimpleBPEL workflows are listed as well as a graph-based editor where the modeling takes place. The editor has a palette where active profiles and their SBFs are displayed. Users can add SBFs to a SimpleBPEL process by dragging them from the palette to the editing area. Thereby, `SimpleBpelPaletteFactory` invokes `createModule` on the model element (class `ProcessFragment`) that represents the selected fragment. In Listing 8.3, both the addition of a domain profile's fragments to the palette and the code that instantiates the function modules is shown. The code is executed when the user opens a SimpleBPEL process by clicking on it. Then, `de.fb12.gdt.bpel.simplebpel.SimpleBPELEditor` is instantiated and populated with the XML description of the process (using the method `setInput(IEditorInput input)`). Within the method, all attached domain profiles are decompressed and `createModulesDrawer` is executed for each domain profile.

```
1  public static PaletteEntry createModulesDrawer(↵
       DomainProfile profile, final SBProcess diagram) {
       // Name the drawer after the profile's name
3      PaletteDrawer componentsDrawer = new PaletteDrawer(↵
           profile.getName());
       List<ProcessFragment> pfs = Arrays.asList(profile.↵
           getProcesses());
5      // Sort fragments by name before adding them to the ↵
           palette
       Collections.sort(pfs, new Comparator<ProcessFragment↵
           >() {
7          @Override
           public int compare(ProcessFragment o1, ↵
               ProcessFragment o2) {
9              return o1.getName().compareTo(o2.getName());
           }
11     });
       // Add all fragments to the drawer
13     for(final ProcessFragment bp:pfs){
           PaletteEntry component = new CreationToolEntry(
15             bp.getName(),
               bp.getDescription(),
17             new CreationFactory() {
                   public Object getNewObject() {
19                     return bp.createModule(diagram);
                   }
21                 public Object getObjectType() {
                       return FunctionModule.class;
23                 }
               },
25             SBEditorPlugin.getImageDescriptor("module.png")↵
               ,
               SBEditorPlugin.getImageDescriptor("module.png")↵
               );
27         componentsDrawer.add(component);
       }
29     return componentsDrawer;
   }
```

Listing 8.3: Addition of SimpleBPEL fragments to the editor palette

`createModule` deserializes the XML description, loads the underlying BPEL code (using `ProcessUtils` utility class) into the data model, instantiates both the corresponding GEF *edit part* and the corresponding figure class that draws the graphical representation. An excerpt of the corresponding source code is presented in Listing 8.4.

```
   public FunctionModule createModule(SBProcess sbProcess)↵
       {
2  if (profileFilename == null || profileFilename.length↵
       () == 0)
       return null;
4  Process process = ProcessUtils.getProcess(↵
       processFilename, profileFilename, null);
   if (process != null) {
6      FunctionModule fmi = null;
       // only one Invoke element => construct a ↵
           SimpleFunctionModule
```

```
8    if( process.getChildren().size() == 1 &&
          process.getChildren().iterator().next() ↵
          instanceof Invoke) {
10       fmi = new SimpleFunctionModule(process, name, ↵
             description, sbProcess);
         Invoke iv = (Invoke) process.getChildren().↵
             iterator().next();
12    } else {
         fmi = new FunctionModule(process, name, ↵
             description, sbProcess);
14    }
      // Add variables depending on their type (in- or ↵
          output)
16    InputVariable inVar;
      OutputVariable outVar;
18    for (TemplateVariable var : variables) {
         if (var.getType().equals("in")) {
20          inVar = new InputVariable(var, fmi);
            inVar.setVariableEntry(process.getVariable(var.↵
                getName()));
22          inVar.setMessageDefinition(process.↵
                getMessageDefinitions().get(inVar.↵
                getVariableEntry().getType()));
            fmi.addInputVariable(inVar);
24       } else if (var.getType().equals("out")) {
            outVar = new OutputVariable(var, fmi);
26          outVar.setVariableEntry(process.getVariable(var.↵
                getName()));
            outVar.setMessageDefinition(process.↵
                getMessageDefinitions().get(outVar.↵
                getVariableEntry().getType()));
28          fmi.addOutputVariable(outVar);
         }
30    } ↵
```

Listing 8.4: Instantiation of SimpleBPEL fragments (represented by class `FunctionModule`)

In Lines 15–30 of Listing 8.4, variable definitions are added to the mode representation of each SimpleBPEL fragment. Each variable definition has a visual representation in the fragment's figure, as shown in Figure 8.17.

One of the most important implemented commands is `Connection-CreateCommand`. It is executed whenever the user wishes to connect a SBF's output with another SBF's input. The source code is printed in Listing 8.5. It must ensure that only SBFs that "fit" together can be connected. Therefore, it uses the configured `CompatibilityMode` (confirm Line 4) to check whether or not the selected function blocks can be tied (confirm Line 27). In the latter case, `canExecute()` would return `false`. The visual representation of the command's results is shown in Figure 8.18. It provides realtime feedback to the user; grayed out input connectors may not be used to connect with the selected (output) fragment.

```
   public boolean canExecute() {
2     CompatibilityMode cm = null;
      try{
```

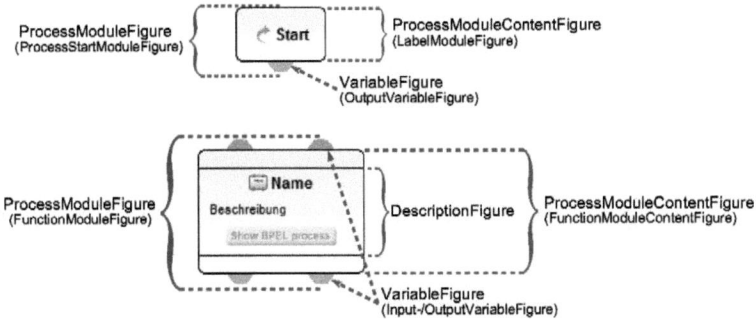

Figure 8.17: Visual representation of SimpleBPEL fragments. Next to each figure, the super class name is given. Below (in brackets), the name of the actual implementation class is shown

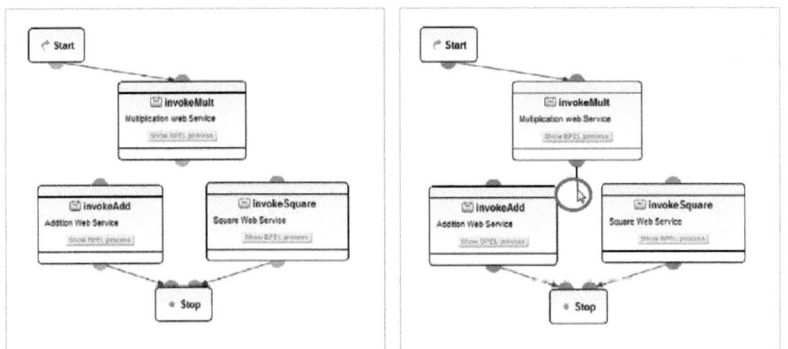

Figure 8.18: Graphical representation of the message compatibility check. On the left side, the SimpleBPEL process before the connection attempt is shown. Note that non-fitting input connectors are grayed out (right side)

```
 4      cm = ((VariableConnection)request.getNewObject())↵
            .getCompatibilityMode();
        } catch(Exception iae){
 6         cm = parent.getCompatibilityMode();
        }
 8      if (endModule == null) {
          if (source == null || target == null) {
10          return false;
          }
12        // Parent module mustn't be the same
          if (source.getParent().equals(target.getParent())↵
            ) {
14          return false;
          }
16        // Check for circular connections
          for(VariableConnection vc:source.↵
            getOutgoingConnections()){
18          if(vc.getTargetVariable() == target){
              return false;
20          }
          }
22        // All message parts have already been mapped
          if(target.isComplete())
24          return false;

26        // Only connect when the VariableTypes are ↵
            compatible
          if (source != null && target != null){
28          if (!cm.check(source, target)) {
              return false;
30          }
          }
32      } // endModule == null
        else {
34        if (source == null) {
            return false;
36        }
        }
38          // All (negative) checks passed => connection ↵
              allowed
        return true;
40    }
```

Listing 8.5: Validation of connection requests in `ConnectionCreateCommand`. Source and target are intrinsic variables of connection command and refer to the connection's source and target object, respectively

The *Process Exporter* sub-component is clearly the most important and complicated part of the SimpleBPEL Composer. It is responsible for creating a standard-compliant, executable BPEL process from the composed SimpleBPEL fragments. The export procedure consists of approximately 800 lines of code that are split over five steps:

1. *initializeProcess* sets parameters, such as process name and namespace.

2. *addSBF* adds all SimpleBPEL fragments using the container structure

(*scope*); further information from each SBF, like variables, messages, portTypes, and partnerLinkType definitions are extracted and attached to the process model.

3. *initReceiveReply* creates the start and end point of the process by creating input and output variables, messages and a *portType*.

4. *addAssignActivities* generates *assign* activities that convert output data of SBFs to the required input data format of dependent SBFs. Behind the scenes, XPath expressions that copy data from the output message parts of one function block to the input message part of succeeding function blocks are generated.

5. *finalize* wraps the created process elements in a *flow* element and writes the created process to disk using DAVO's export mechanism, since at this point a complete BPEL process has been created in DAVO's internal data model.

8.5 Use Cases

This section presents two use cases to exemplify the adaptability of DAVO to specific domain needs. More precisely, an extension for service-oriented Grid computing called Visual Grid Orchestrator (ViGO) and an extension for industrial automation called Time-Constrained Services (TiCS) Modeler [102] are presented. The latter use case stems from a joint work with Markus Mathes who defined and implemented a Web service-based realtime framework for industrial automation in the context of his dissertation [101]. The third part of this section exemplifies how the modeling abstractions introduced with SimpleBPEL can be applied practically. To ease understanding of the use case (particularly the function of the services wrapped into SimpleBPEL fragments), the medical use case is used for demonstration purposes.

8.5.1 Service-oriented Grid Computing

Modern Grid middleware environments like Globus Toolkit 4 [8] are built on the Web Services Resource Framework (WSRF) [11], as detailed in Chapter 7. WSRF enables developers to create *stateful Web services*, which can store the state of operations and other properties without breaking the compatibility to standard Web services. Since BPEL innately does not explicitly support the underlying *factory pattern*, BPEL extensions (*gridCreateResourceInvoke*, *gridInvoke*, and *gridDestroyResourceInvoke*) have been proposed and integrated into the ActiveBPEL engine.

To ease the work of workflow designers, a Grid-specific version of DAVO, named ViGO (Visual Grid Orchestrator), has been created. It makes use of DAVO's extensible data model to introduce new model elements for the aforementioned new BPEL activities. Moreover, it uses the offered extension points to register the new elements in the palette, provide serialization classes (shadow model) and offer wizard dialogs to ease the modeling of the invocation of stateful services. Figure 8.19 shows two steps of the "GridInvoke wizards" and the resulting BPEL activities that are added to the workflow. Note that some intermediate wizard steps have been omitted in the figure. The output of the wizard operation consists of three BPEL elements: *gridCreateResourceInvoke*, *gridInvoke*, and *gridDestroyResourceInvoke*

The Grid-related activities make use of the status icon feature that allows figures to provide an icon next to the textual description. The status icon displays whether the operation uses the Grid security features (as discussed in Section 7.5). Figure 8.20 shows the modeling of a security-enabled workflow. The property view automatically displays a tab "GSISecurity" when Grid-related activities are selected in the editor view. The GSISecurity tab allows the developer to configure all GSI-related settings for WSRF service invocations. As soon as the configuration is complete, the status icon of the corresponding activity changes (from opened lock to a closed one).

The extensions for service-oriented Grid computing and ViGO have been successfully used as the main workflow execution and modeling tools in several projects of the German Grid Initiative (D-Grid) [42]: In-Grid and GDI-Grid (Geodateninfrastruktur-Grid) [107]. Currently, they are used extensively in the MediaGrid [108] project, also part of the German Grid Initiative.

8.5.2 Time-constrained Web Services for Industrial Automation

Industrial automation is aimed at monitoring and controlling an industrial plant via hard- and software with minimized human intervention during operation. A main characteristic of industrial automation is that real-time processing is required [124], i.e., a task is completed correctly within a given time constraint. Industrial automation processes generally consist of several consecutive production steps. Consequently, a single Web service is not suitable to model the entire manufacturing process, but a workflow is required.

In order to be used in the industrial automation domain, DAVO was extended by time-related functionalities. In the context of industrial automation, the *average* and the *worst-case execution time* of a single Web service and of an entire workflow are of particular interest. This permits the assisted composition of manufacturing processes and eases the work of automation engineers. An automation engineer defines the desired average and worst-case execution time for a new workflow, and the current average and worst-case execution time are calculated automatically during the composition process.

The DAVO plug-in for industrial automation is part of the Time-Constrained Services (TiCS) framework [101, 102, 105] and is called *TiCS Modeler*. Figure 8.21(a) shows an input mask to enter the aforementioned time-related values, whereas Figure 8.21(b) displays the result of the automated execution time calculation.

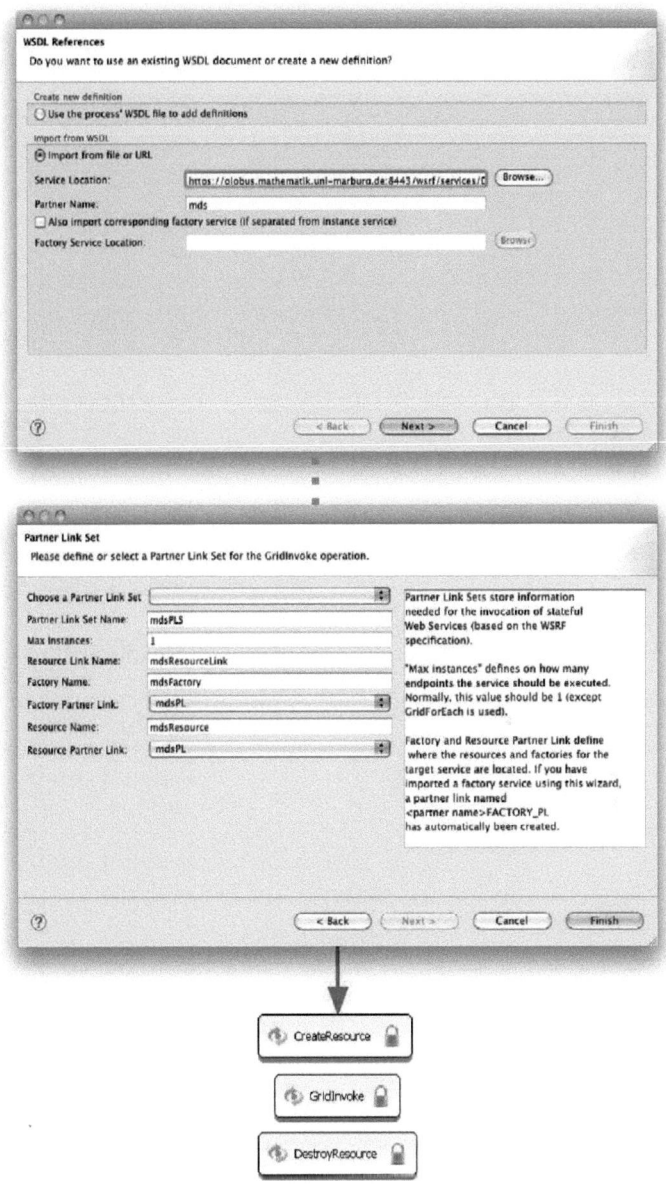

Figure 8.19: Wizard-based modeling of invoke operation on a stateful service.

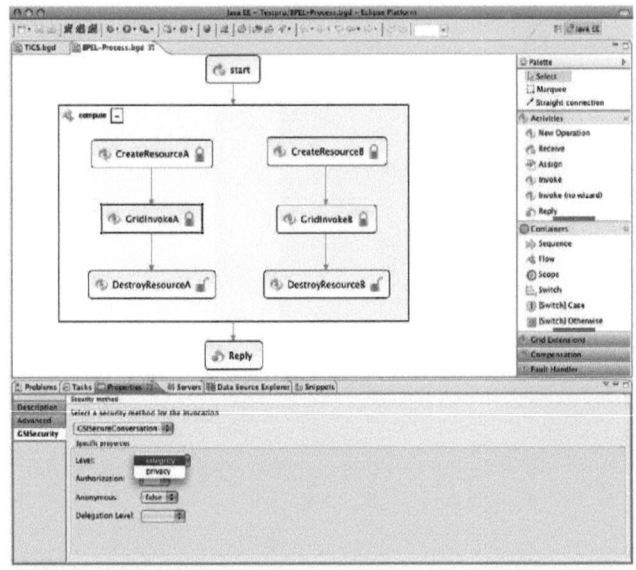

Figure 8.20: Modeling of a security-enabled Grid workflow with ViGO

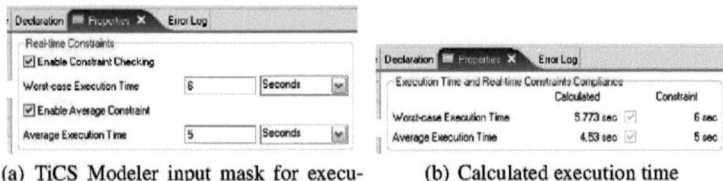

(a) TiCS Modeler input mask for execution time

(b) Calculated execution time

Figure 8.21: Input mask for execution time and an information view showing the results of the execution time calculation

Internally, the TiCS Modeler uses several formulas to compute the average (aet) and worst-case (wcet) execution time for a workflow (see Figure 8.21(b)), depending on the BPEL activities used. Consider, for example, the *flow* activity. The average/worst-case execution time of a *flow* with n independent activities is defined as the maximum average/worst-case execution time of all activities contained within the *flow*, as shown in Equation (8.1).

$$\text{aet}(\text{flow}) := \max_{i \in \{1,\dots,n\}} \{\text{aet}(\text{activity}_i)\}$$
$$\text{wcet}(\text{flow}) := \max_{i \in \{1,\dots,n\}} \{\text{wcet}(\text{activity}_i)\} \tag{8.1}$$

8.5.2.1 Implementation of the TiCS Extensions

This section exemplifies the realization of a plug-in for DAVO by means of the TiCS Modeler, since this is considered to be more interesting than the presentation of a bunch of screenshots and corresponding descriptions. The TiCS Modeler extends each BPEL activity with two properties: (1) `avgExecTime` and (2) `wcExecTime`. They store the average and worst-case execution time of that activity. For basic activities, the value of this property depends on the action realized by this activity. For a structured activity, on the other hand, the value of this property depends on the property values of the child activities contained in the structured activity and has to be calculated individually for different activities. Details of this calculation have been omitted to keep the example simple.

To be able to extend the data model, an implementation of the `IModelExtender` interface has to be provided by the TiCS Modeler. It is used to create the `ElementExtensions` for given `Elements` as shown in Listing 8.6. Like stated before, there are different properties for basic and structured activities, thus different `ElementExtensions` are used. For the basic activities, a further distinction is made between `ConnectedElements` related to a specific operation of a Web service and other `Elements`.

```
public class ModelExtender implements IModelExtender {
2    @Override
    public ElementExtension createExtension(
4      Element targetElement, ProcessContext context) {
        if (targetElement instanceof ContainerElement) {
6          return new ContainerElementExt();
        } else if (targetElement instanceof ↩
           ConnectedElement) {
8          return new ConnectedElementExt();
        } else {
10         return new ElementExt();
        }
12   }
}
```
Listing 8.6. The implementation of the `IModelExtender` interface

The three `ElementExtensions` are almost identical in this example, thus only one is exemplified in Listing 8.7. The most interesting method of this class is `applyExtension`, which modifies the actual element. In this case, it creates two new properties, instances of `ElementWCETProp` and `ElementAETProp`, adds the properties to a newly created `PropertyGroup`, which again is added to the `Element`. A `PropertyGroup` is merely a collection of properties to simplify their handling, which means that it is possible to remove multiple properties at once by the `removeExtension` method.

```
1  public class ElementExt extends ElementExtension {
       public ElementExt() {
3          super(Activator.PLUGIN_ID);
       }
5
       @Override
7      protected void applyExtension() {
           PropertyGroup group = new PropertyGroup(↩
               Activator.PLUGIN_ID);
9          group.add(new ElementWCETProp());
           group.add(new ElementAETProp());
11         getExtendedElement().addPropertyGroup(group);
       }
13
       @Override
15     protected void removeExtension() {
           getExtendedElement().removePropertyGroup(↩
               Activator.PLUGIN_ID);
17     }
   }
```

Listing 8.7: The `ElementExtender` for plain `Elements`, which are neither containers nor connected elements.

Listing 8.8 shows the worst-case execution time property in its simplest form. It has an ID to address it, a description and category used to identify it within the property view and is of the type Integer. After its creation, it is initialized with the value 0. By default, this value is editable in the property view.

```
   public class ElementWCETProp extends Property<Integer> ↩
       {
2      public static final String ID = "de.fb12.gdt.bpel.rt↩
           .wcet";
       public static final String DESCRIPTION = "worst-case↩
           execution time";
4      public static final String CATEGORY = "TiCS";

6      public ElementWCETProp() {
           super(ID, DESCRIPTION, CATEGORY, Integer.class);
8          setValue(0);
       }
10 }
```

Listing 8.8: The worst-case execution time property, which is applied to all `Elements` that are neither containers nor connected elements.

The `ConnectedElements` are extended with another property shown in Listing 8.9. Because the worst-case execution time of a `ConnectedElement` depends on the specific operation to which it is connected, this property is dependent on the *operation name* property (and therefore also transitively on the *port type* and *partner link* properties as stated in Section 8.3.1.1). This dependency is modeled by the implementation of the IPropertyValueDependent interface, which consists of the two public methods getPropertyValueDependencyIDs and relevantPropertyValueChange. The first method returns a list of the properties on which this property is depending. The second method is invoked when the value of one of the depending properties is changed. Since the value of the property is determined automatically, it is set to read-only in the constructor.

```
public class ConnectedElementWCETProp
  extends ElementWCETProp
  implements IPropertyValueDependent {

    public ConnectedElementWCETProp() {
        setEditable(false);
    }

    private final static String[] PROP_DEP_IDS =
        new String[] {ConnectedElement.OPERATION_NAME_PROP↩
        };

    @Override
    public String[] getPropertyValueDependencyIDs() {
        return PROP_DEP_IDS;
    }

    @Override
    public void relevantPropertyValueChange( ↩
        ValueChangeEvent event) {
        /* retrieve worst-case execution time */
    }
}
```

Listing 8.9: The worst-case execution time property that is applied to all ConnectedElements.

The ContainerElements are also extended with a specific property, which is shown in Listing 8.10. The worst-case execution time of a ContainerElement depends on the type of the container (e.g. *flow*, *sequence*, *switch*, etc.) and the worst-case execution times of its children (details have been described by Mathes et al. [103–105]). Consequently, this property does not depend on the values of other properties in the same Element, but on property values of other Elements. This is called an *external dependency* in DAVO and realized by implementing the interface IExternalEventDependent. This interface prescribes the methods getExternalEventDependencies and relevantExternalEvent. The first method returns a list of event classes about which this property needs to be notified. A ContainerChangeEvent is fired by a container when a child element is added or removed, whereas the property change in a child triggers a ContainerChildPropertyChangeEvent, which is a subclass of the ContainerChangeEvent. The latter method is invoked when such an event is fired. In this case, some further tests are necessary to determine whether the value of the property has to be updated. The actual calculation is done by implementing the IContainerCalculator interface, which is provided by a special factory (not shown here), depending on the type of the container.

```
1  public class ContainerElementWCETProp
       extends ElementWCETProp
3      implements IExternalEventDependent {

5      public ContainerElementWCETProp() {
           setEditable(false);
7      }

9      private IContainerCalculator getContainerCalculator() ↩
           {
           [...]
11     }

13     private ContainerElement getContainerElement() {
           [...]
15     }

17     @SuppressWarnings("unchecked")
       private final static Class<IExternalEvent>[]
19     EXT_EVT_DEP_CLS = (Class<IExternalEvent>[]) new ↩
           Class[] { ContainerChangeEvent.class };

21     @Override
       public Class<IExternalEvent>[] ↩
           getExternalEventDependencies() {
23         return EXT_EVT_DEP_CLS;
       }
25
       @Override
27     public void relevantExternalEvent(
           IExternalEvent event) {
29         ContainerChangeEvent ccEvent = (↩
               ContainerChangeEvent) event;
           boolean update = false;
31
           if (ccEvent.getType() == ContainerChangeEvent.↩
               Type.PROPERTY) {
33             if (((ContainerChildPropertyChangeEvent) ↩
                   event).getEvent()
                   .getPropertyName().equals(ID))
35                 update = true;
           } else {
37             update = true;
           }
39
           if (update) {
41             setValue(getContainerCalculator()
                   .calculateWCET(getContainerElement()));
43         }
       }
45 }
```

Listing 8.10: The worst-case execution time property, that is applied to all `ContainerElements`.

As an example of such a calculator, the `FlowCalculator` is shown in

Listing 8.11. This calculator calculates the worst-case execution time according to equation (8.1) in Section 8.5.2.

```java
public class FlowCalculator
    implements IContainerCalculator {

    @Override
    public Integer calculateWCET(
        ContainerElement containerElement) {
        Integer result = 0;
        for (Element child : containerElement.↩
            getChildren()) {
            Integer childWCET = (Integer) child.↩
                getPropertyValue(ElementWCETProp.ID);
            if (result < childWCET)
                result = childWCET;
        }
        return result;
    }
}
```

Listing 8.11: The calculator for flow activities.

8.5.3 SimpleBPEL

To demonstrate how SimpleBPEL actually eases the workflow development process, the medical use case (detection of respiration drop outs based on ECG analysis, see Section 2.2.2) is modeled using SimpleBPEL. The workflow can be summarized as follows:

- Input: record in European Data Format (EDF)

- In order to use with the Physio Toolkit, a conversion of the input to MIT format is required: *EDF2MIT*

- Subsequent services need data about special patterns in the heart beat signal (Q, S waves): *WQRS-Detection*

- Respiration dropouts are detected by the *Apnoea-Detection* function

- For beat detection, the binary output from the *WQRS-Detection* function needs to be converted into a plain text format: *Annotation-Reader*

- *R* peaks in the ECG wave-form are detected by *Beat-Detection* function

- Apnoea and beat detection may be executed in parallel

- Output: MIT-format file containing timestamps of respiration dropouts

Since *Beat-Detection* is the only function that requires a conversion (*Annotation-Reader*) of the results of *WQRS-Detection*, both steps have been combined into one SimpleBPEL fragment. However, this step is optional.[4]

Figure 8.22 depicts the modeling process of the *Annotation-Reader & Beat-Detection* function block in DAVO. The SimpleBPEL Profile Editor lists all functions blocks that have already been added to the profile on the bottom. When the BPEL expert has finished modeling all required function blocks, the profile may be exported into a ZIP file and passed to the domain expert.

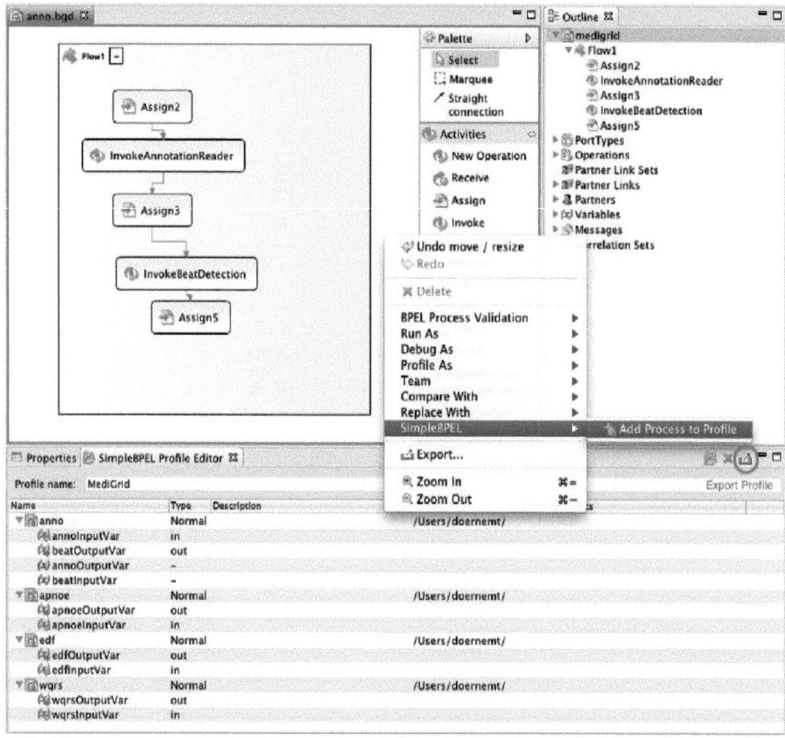

Figure 8.22: Modeling of function blocks with DAVO and SimpleBPEL Profile Editor

---

[4]The decision whether functions should be combined into a fragment depends on the required level of granularity. A high granularity (one function per function block as an extreme case) reduces the total number of function blocks (in the repository/editor palette), while the modeling complexity is increased since the SimpleBPEL process would contain exactly one function block per (web) service invocation. A low granularity, by contrast, reduces modeling complexity, since recurring sequences of invocations would be combined into function blocks. However, one would need to create a function block for each (reasonable) combination of services.

The domain expert has to carry out some steps to prepare the modeling process. First of all, he/she has to create a SimpleBPEL process. Thereby, the user is guided by a software "wizard" that interrogates some information about the process, such as the desired name. In the last step of the wizard, one can import domain profiles to work with. The imported profiles then populate the editor palette. The procedure is illustrated in Figure 8.23.

Afterwards, the SimpleBPEL fragments are available in the palette and may be added to the SimpleBPEL process by simply dragging them into the editor area. The user then has to connect the function blocks such that the desired flow of actions is achieved. The configured message compatibility mode thereby checks which connections are reasonable and prevents that the user makes invalid connections that would lead to a defective BPEL workflow. Finally, start and end points have to be added to the workflow and connected with the appropriate function blocks. Figure 8.24 shows the workflow in an almost complete state (the end point and two connections are missing). The screenshot was taken while the WQRS-Detection function block was being connected with the *Apnoea-Detection* block. All other input connectors are grayed-out, meaning that they cannot be used for this connection; the *Apnoea-Detection* input connector is only half-filled, indicating that it requires one further input.

As this example illustrates, modeling BPEL workflows using SimpleBPEL does not require a great deal knowledge in BPEL and related Web service specifications. The down side is that the expressiveness of SimpleBPEL is reduced. One can only define a flow of control between the function blocks. It is, for instance, impossible to repeat the invocation of a function block until a certain condition is met. While this would be possible to model based on the presented approach, it was an explicit and deliberate decision to keep the modeling approach simple for end users. Instead, loops have to be modeled within the function blocks.

8.6 Summary

The chapter was motivated by the need for development tool support that focusses on the needs of domain experts. Domain experts in this context refers to researchers from various scientific domains with no or little background in computer science. Therefore, tools that are tailored towards the needs of non-Web service experts are required. Hence, two development tools were introduced: (1) DAVO, Domain-adaptable Visual BPEL Orchestrator, and (2) SimpleBPEL.

DAVO is a domain-adaptable, graphical BPEL workflow editor. The key benefits that distinguish DAVO from other graphical BPEL workflow editors are the adaptable data model and user interface, which permit customization to specific domain needs.

SimpleBPEL subsumes the idea of separating workflow development into two distinct roles with clear areas of responsibility. Experienced users (BPEL experts) carry out the development of BPEL fragments for the needs of the given application domain. The second role is carried out by a domain expert

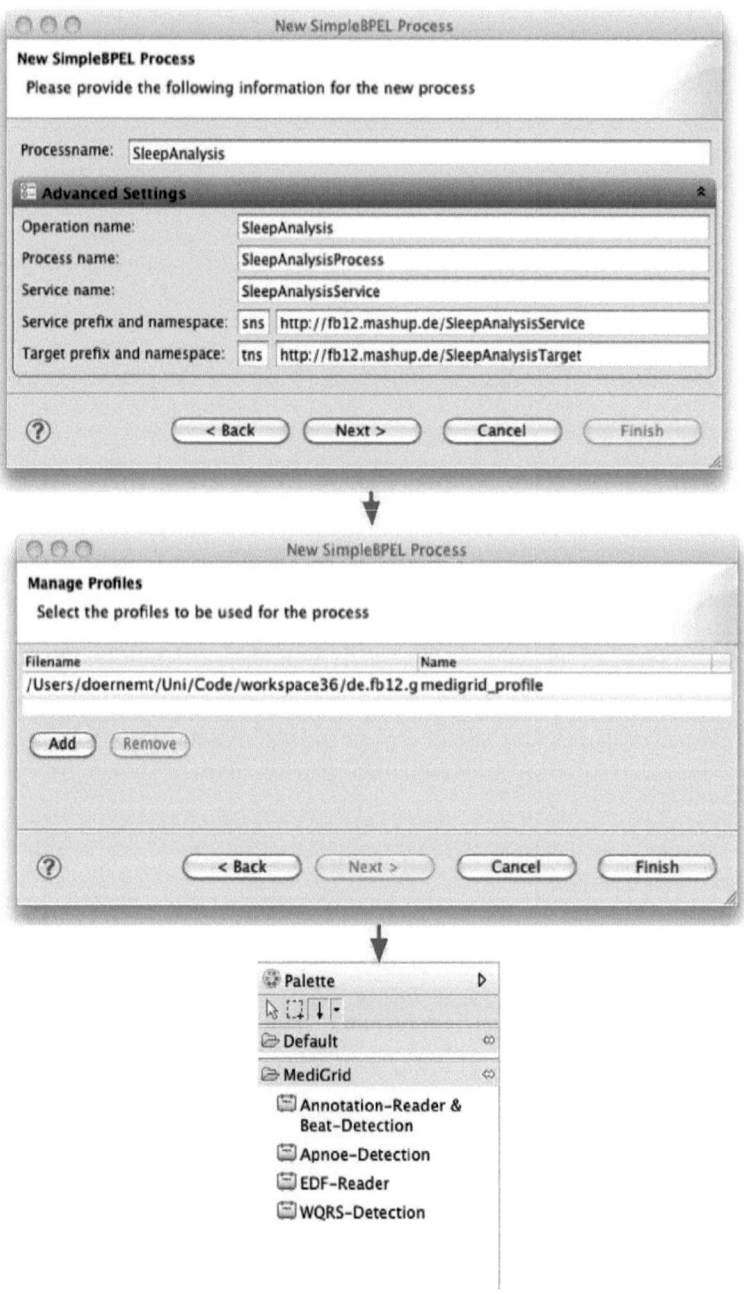

Figure 8.23: Wizard-assisted creation of a SimpleBPEL process

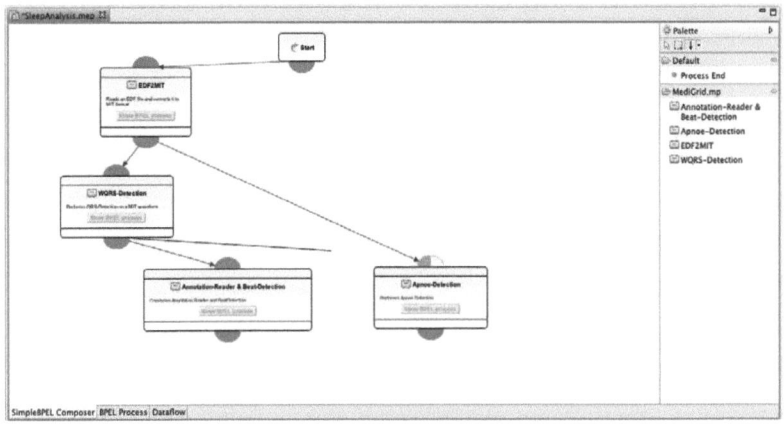

Figure 8.24: Simplified modeling of the medical use case with SimpleBPEL Composer

who simply has to combine the fragments, as required for his/her application.

The design and implementation of both tools were discussed. Due to the complex nature of the tools, only certain aspects were discussed in detail. Special focus was put on the adaptability of DAVO's data model; the validation and transformation process of SimpleBPEL fragments into executable BPEL workflows was also discussed.

Two use cases exemplified the adaptability of DAVO to specific domain needs: An extension for service-oriented Grid computing called Visual Grid Orchestrator (ViGO) and an extension for industrial automation called Time-Constrained Services (TiCS) Modeler were presented. The modeling abstractions introduced by SimpleBPEL were demonstrated by modeling the medical use case using SimpleBPEL fragments.

Chapter 9
Conclusions and Future Work

9.1 Summary

In this thesis, the design and implementation of a workflow management and development system tailored towards the needs of users from scientific domains has been presented. The majority of existing scientific workflow systems can be considered tailor-made for specific application domains and thus lack features that are required in other application domains. In contrast, the general idea behind this thesis is to build a general-purpose, domain-agnostic workflow system based on industry standards and to use existing software components wherever possible. The approach taken allowed to focus on implementing useful features rather than on developing such a system from scratch. As an introduction to the problems that have to be solved using such a workflow environment, three sample applications from medical research, systems biology and engineering were introduced. A number of (Quality of Service) requirements were deduced from these sample applications regarding the workflow execution environment as well as the development support tools that are required to ease workflow development. Since the system should not be tailored towards specific domains, emphasis was placed not on the "lowest common denominator" of all requirements, but on uniting all of the requirements that do not conflict with each other.

The requirements of the runtime environment include:

1. The underlying workflow language must be as powerful as possible. In particular, it must be possible to define *conditional* loops, i.e. the language must be *Turing-complete*.

2. Workflow components need a common interface.

3. The workflow system must be able to execute workflow activities on distributed resources, especially Grid and Cloud infrastructures.

4. The workflow engine must provide a load-independent *performance*, automatically scale in and out and perform advantageous resource assignment.

5. The workflow user should be able to influence workflow execution *cost*.

6. The workflow system must provide high *availability* and *reliability*.

7. The workflow system should take care of data *protection* and support access control mechanisms.

The following requirements for a user-friendly workflow development environment have been identified:

- Support for the graphical modeling of workflows that are to be executed on Grid and Cloud resources must be provided.

- The development tools should provide different levels of abstraction. A high degree of abstraction of technical details lowers the entry burden for non-IT experts, while IT-experts might wish to have full control when modeling workflows.

These requirements are reflected in the design and implementation of both the workflow execution system as well as the development tools. The developed workflow engine is based on BPEL (Business Process Execution Language), the de facto industry standard language for workflow modeling. It has been proven that BPEL is Turing-complete [47, 93], meaning that Requirement 1 is fulfilled; Requirement 2 is fulfilled by wrapping the workflow tasks with Web services. The ActiveBPEL workflow engine was used for the implementation. It was extended using several components to meet the given requirements.

One of the striking features of the presented extensions is that the workflow system has been enabled to automatically (without any user intervention) scale out and -in (Requirement 4) by provisioning resources from Cloud environments (Requirement 3). This idea, accompanied by a prototypical implementation, was first proposed in 2008 in several publications on which this thesis is based. Thus, the presented workflow system was the first workflow system with built-in support for Cloud infrastructures. Moreover, this feature cannot only be used to scale out an existing infrastructure within minutes, but is able to completely *replace* dedicated infrastructures. The advantage is twofold: (1) It allows even researchers with little or no computational resources to conduct workflow-support experiments, data analysis, and so forth; and (2) it relieves scientists from the burden of configuring and managing dedicated resources and thus helps them to focus on their *actual* profession: *research*.

To guarantee high availability and reliability (Requirement 6), the developed workflow system monitors the execution of workflow tasks and, if a failure occurs, applies user-defined fault handling policies. It utilizes the capabilities of IaaS-based Cloud infrastructures in a, for workflow systems, groundbreaking way: Faulty resources are automatically replaced (within 90 seconds) by newly provisioned machines from the Cloud. To guarantee the high availability of the workflow system, a deployment scenario has been developed and evaluated. In this scenario, the workflow engine itself is deployed in Amazon's Cloud infrastructure and monitored continuously. If the engine fails or becomes overloaded, it is replaced (or, in the latter case, availed) by another, newly provisioned resource hosting a workflow engine.

In addition, a multi-objective workflow scheduling algorithm as well as its implementation and integration into the workflow system has been presented. It is tailored towards the needs of Cloud-based workflow applications: in particular, if the workflow tasks are geographically distributed, data transmission can be the main bottleneck. The algorithm therefore takes data dependencies between workflow steps into account and schedules them to Cloud resources based on the two conflicting objectives of cost and execution time according to the preferences of the user (Requirements 4 and 5). Experimental results indicate that both the workflow execution times and the corresponding costs can be reduced significantly.

Furthermore, language extensions that allow workflow developers to integrate WSRF-based services (Requirement 3) into BPEL workflows were introduced. *gridInvoke*, *gridCreateResourceInvoke* and *gridDestroyResourceInvoke*) map the *factory pattern* of WSRF to BPEL. Moreover, it has been described how Grid Security Infrastructure (GSI) can be used within BPEL to provide security features like encryption and access control. Therefore, the language standard was further extended. The presented solution allows users to use all security mechanisms offered by Globus Toolkit 4 and also features certificate lifetime management.

Addressing sophisticated development support constitutes the final contribution of this thesis. This thesis presented DAVO, a domain-adaptable, graphical BPEL workflow editor. DAVO is tailored towards IT-savvy workflow developers and supports the entire BPEL standard. The key benefits that distinguish DAVO from other graphical BPEL workflow editors are the adaptable data model and user interface, which permit customization to specific domain needs. The cooperation with researchers from other disciplines has shown that further simplifications in workflow modeling are desirable. Thus, another modeling approach, coined SimpleBPEL, was proposed: separating workflow development into two distinct roles with clear areas of responsibility. Experienced users (BPEL experts) carry out the development of BPEL fragments for the needs of the given application domain. A domain expert who simply has to combine the fragments, as required for his or her application carries out the second role. The corresponding development tool, SimpleBPEL Composer, dramatically eases workflow development and lowers the entry burden for novice users.

9.2 Future Work

There a several areas for future work based on the workflow system and development tools presented in the previous chapters. At the present time, the software components are in a state of prototypical implementation and could be further stabilized as a reasonable first step. Moreover, the developed components are tailored towards the ActiveBPEL engine. It would be beneficial to explore the interfaces and extensibility mechanisms of other (open source) BPEL engines, such as Apache Ode [26], to enable users who prefer to use

other BPEL engines to benefit from the developed extensions.
Several areas for further research and development will be discussed briefly in the following.

Reproducibility The ability to reproduce scientific processes and analyses is an important requirement for scientists. Reproducibility implies that provenance data is available. However, the developed workflow system does not yet collect such data. According to Gil et al., this is the case for most scientific workflow systems: "Today, reproducibility is virtually impossible for complex scientific applications. First, because so many scientists are involved, the provenance records are highly fragmented, and in practice they are reflected in a variety of elements including emails, Wiki entries, database queries, journal references, codes (including compiler options), and others." [77] Therefore, a first step towards reproducibility could be to enable the workflow system to perform workflow execution tracing and logging combined with metadata extraction. Basically, this approach should enable the user to query a database containing all previously executed workflows for workflow runs with specific characteristics. Thus, users would be able to compare the results of different executions of the same workflow with different input data, which might be useful for the analysis of experimental series and other applications.

Workflow Security The security-related extensions that have been presented in Chapter 7 could be improved further. For instance, a workflow's structure (namely, the number of invocations per service) should be investigated in more detail to automatically select the security method fulfilling all requirements with the lowest performance overhead. Finally, performance measurements of previous workflow executions with different security mechanisms should be provided.

Development Tools GridFTP [9] is commonly used for data movement within service-oriented Grid environments. The ViGO extension for DAVO should be empowered with activities supporting the easy use of this technology, as the movement/transfer of data is important for scientific workflows. Furthermore, activities supporting the use of OGSA-DAI [12] to access databases within workflows would ease application development for Grid environments.

There are several possible improvements and further developments in SimpleBPEL. From an implementation perspective, profiles could be exchanged using a centralized database repository instead of file-based manual exchange. This would not only ease the process of sharing profiles with other researchers, but also allow users to quickly assemble workflows using the fragments other researchers (from the same domain) have completed. This, of course, only makes sense if the services used in the fragments would also be made available. A basic approach to semantic validation of SimpleBPEL fragment compositions has already been researched and developed by Harbach et al. [78]. The approach supports developers at the design time of a workflow by computing the semantics of a fragment from the semantic description of the enclosed services. Whenever the user wants to connect two fragments, it validates whether or not the fragments fit semantically. Thereby, the mechanism performs some basic mediation automatically if the semantic descriptions of fragments do not use the same ontology, but a translation is possible. Future work in this area includes a complex mediation scenario that allows arbitrarily complex mediator combinations, resembling a fully automatic composition. In addition, data level mediators could be hidden from the user and the system could create an optimal configuration automatically.

Scheduling One of the main weaknesses of the described workflow-based scheduling approach is that the user has to annotate expected data volumes and execution times at the workflow design time. To ease development and increase accuracy of workflow annotations, it would be beneficial to investigate how automatic assignment and determination of data flow graph annotations can be achieved. An interesting approach that should be further investigated has been described by Cardoso et al. [36] (see Section 3.2.2).

An interesting research topic is to integrate data caching mechanisms into the described service-oriented environment. If the same data is repeatedly requested by different workflow tasks, one could either transfer the data from the nearest neighboring node (in the same zone) or place the task on the node where the data is already present. Both approaches would save waiting time for data transfer and possibly costs.

List of Figures

1.1	Relationships between basic workflow terminology	2
2.1	Simplified representation of an ECG analysis	16
3.1	Graphical representation of the workflow taxonomy defined by Yu and Buyya	27
3.2	Overview of the development and runtime components of the proposed system	34
3.3	Extensions to the BPEL engine	37
3.4	Normal transfer of data using SOAP compared to the FlexSwA reference passing principle	38
3.5	Topology of on-demand provisioning component	40
3.6	Invocation of WSRF service using standard BPEL operations	43
4.1	Components of the Load Balancing Architecture	54
4.2	Sequence of calls to determine a dynamic endpoint	61
4.3	Workflow runtimes for all scenarios using static and load based allocation	66
4.4	Runtimes of workflow instances for scenario 1	67
4.5	Virtual machine and middleware boot times using Amazon's instance type High-CPU Medium	67
5.1	Bird's-eye view on the proposed fault handling architecture	75
5.2	Interaction of the sub-components of the Fault Tolerance Module	76
5.3	Chain of responsibility of the Load Balancer	84
5.4	Graphical configuration of ELB health check	85
5.5	Deployment scenario for the BPEL engine	87
5.6	Medical workflow. Screenshot taken from DAVO, the visual modeling tool	91
5.7	Runtimes of the workflow for $r = 0$	93
5.8	Runtimes of the workflow for $r = 1$	93
5.9	Runtimes of the workflow for $r = 3$	94
5.10	Runtimes of the workflow for $r = 3$ with Cloud-backed redundancy	95
6.1	Runtime decrease induced by opportune resource selection.	99
6.2	Runtime increase induced by unfavorable resource selection	100
6.3	Real-life measurements of data transfer speeds between different data centers of the Cloud provider Amazon	101

6.4	Control and data flow of the medical workflow	102
6.5	Architectural components of CaDaS from a birds-eye view	104
6.6	Internal representation of a Cloud topology and resources	105
6.7	Reservations for a single CPU core and data transfers	106
6.8	Fitness values of individuals and dominating ones (Pareto front).	109
6.9	Example of a Data Flow Invoke Handler String	110
6.10	Workflow runtimes for Scenario 2 with different user weights	119
6.11	Workflow runtimes for scenario 3	120
7.1	WSRF resource pattern	125
7.2	Invocation of WSRF service using standard BPEL operations	129
7.3	Execution chain of gridCreateResourceInvoke, gridInvoke and gridDestroyResourceInvoke	132
7.4	Schematic workflow incorporating Web and secure Grid services	134
7.5	Schematic sequence of a workflow execution with automatic proxy management	136
7.6	Automatic Security Configuration using Globus MDS	138
7.7	Logical components of the ActiveBPEL engine	140
7.8	Process lifecycle and its implementing classes	141
7.9	Duration of service invocation using different security mechanism and message sizes	150
8.1	Conceptual overview of the core components of DAVO	158
8.2	A simplified `Element` class hierarchy.	159
8.3	Relationship between EditParts, Figures and the data model in GEF	160
8.4	Main functional areas of DAVO's user interface.	161
8.5	Modeling of the medical use case in SimpleBPEL Composer using SBFs defined in DAVO	163
8.6	Data model of the Domain Profile	164
8.7	Data model of the SimpleBPEL Composer	165
8.8	Bijective mapping between two messages	166
8.9	Integration of process fragments into a BPEL workflow	166
8.10	The property model of DAVO	168
8.11	The Element extension mechanism	169
8.12	The `EditPart` type hierarchy	170
8.13	State change of a property in DAVO	170
8.14	The Property adapter model	171
8.15	A BPEL translation process using the shadow model	172
8.16	Profile Editor	173
8.17	Visual representation of SimpleBPEL fragments	177
8.18	Graphical representation of the message compatibility check	177
8.19	Wizard-based modeling of invoke operation on a stateful service	181
8.20	Modeling of a security-enabled Grid workflow with ViGO	182
8.21	TiCS input mask and execution time calculation view	182

8.22 Modeling of function blocks with DAVO and SimpleBPEL Profile Editor 188
8.23 Wizard-assisted creation of a SimpleBPEL process 190
8.24 Simplified modeling of the medical use case with SimpleBPEL Composer 191

List of Tables

3.1	Mapping of workflow systems to the workflow taxonomy	29
4.1	Amazon instance types and prices for region EU and Linux operating system	52
5.1	Sample mappings of individual faults to groups	82
5.2	Theoretical and empirical workflow fail ratios	92
6.1	Results for Scenario 1 (50 x 1 workflow)	118
6.2	Results for scenario 2 (25 x 2 workflows in parallel)	119
7.1	Experimental results in milliseconds for GSITransport using encryption and integrity.	148
7.2	Experimental results in milliseconds for GSISecureMessage using encryption and integrity.	148
7.3	Experimental results in milliseconds for GSISecureConversation using encryption and integrity.	148
7.4	Experimental results in milliseconds using pure HTTP.	149

Listings

3.1	A sample fault handling policy	41
3.2	Integration of a custom invoke handler into ActiveBPEL engine	41
4.1	Manual runtime setting of an service endpoint in BPEL	50
4.2	Integration of a custom invoke handler (load balancer) into a workflow	59
4.3	Excerpt of the custom invoke handler (dynamic resolver)	59
4.4	Source code excerpt of the load-based scheduling algorithm	63
5.1	Manual fault handling in BPEL	71
5.2	Schema-like Definition of a Policy	77
5.3	Example of global policy rules	78
5.4	Integration of a the fault tolerant invoke handler and two policies into ActiveBPEL engine	79
5.5	Excerpt of the fault handling mechanism in Fault Tolerant Invoke Handler	80
5.6	Parsing and instantition of fault handling policies	82
5.7	Configuration steps required to run the BPEL engine on an Amazon-provided AMI	87
5.8	Configuration of Amazon's Elastic Load Balancer service	88
5.9	Configuration steps to set up Amazon EC2 auto-scaling service	89
5.10	Amazon CloudWatch configuration for auto-scaling and fault tolerance	89
6.1	Pseudo-code for a multi-objective genetic scheduling algorithm	107
6.2	Format of Data Flow Invoke Handler String	110
6.3	Excerpt of the generation of the data flow graph	111
6.4	Check for the validity of resource reservations and backfilling mechanism	113
6.5	Addition of candidate resources to the initial population	114
6.6	Calculation of the data transfer delay between two workflow steps	115
6.7	Excerpt of class SchedulerTimer	116
7.1	Example response containg a resource identifier	125
7.2	Invocation of WSRF service with plain BPEL	130
7.3	Grid-specific extensions for the invocation of stateful WS	131
7.4	Syntax of the security settings for invocation	135
7.5	Excerpt of class de.fb12.soap.proxyCert.SOAPHandler: handling of proxy information	142
7.6	Except of class org.activebpel.rt.axis.bpel.AeInvokeHandler: addition of security settings to SOAP call	143

7.7	Extract of the client API	145
7.8	Additions to server-config.wsdd configuration file	145
7.9	Verification of security configuration using automatic determination of settings	146
7.10	Actual automatic selection of security method during execution time	147
8.1	Validation of SimpleBPEL fragments	173
8.2	Schema definition of domain profiles	174
8.3	Addition of SimpleBPEL fragments to the editor palette . . .	175
8.4	Instantiation of SimpleBPEL fragments	175
8.5	Validation of connection requests in `ConnectionCreate-Command`.	176
8.6	The implementation of the `IModelExtender` interface . .	183
8.7	The `ElementExtender` for plain `Elements`, which are neither containers nor connected elements.	184
8.8	The worst-case execution time property, which is applied to all `Elements` that are neither containers nor connected elements.	184
8.9	The worst-case execution time property that is applied to all `ConnectedElements`.	185
8.10	The worst-case execution time property, that is applied to all `ContainerElements`.	186
8.11	The calculator for flow activities.	187

Bibliography

[1] Active Endpoints, ActiveBPEL.
`http://www.activevos.com/community-open-source.php`.

[2] Amazon Web Services LLC, Amazon Elastic Compute Cloud (EC2).
`http://aws.amazon.com/ec2/`.

[3] Amazon Web Services LLC, Amazon Simple Storage Service (S3).
`http://aws.amazon.com/s3/`.

[4] Eclipse Draw2D, Project Homepage.
`http://www.eclipse.org/gef/overview.html`.

[5] Eclipse Graphical Editing Framework (GEF), Project Homepage.
`http://www.eclipse.org/gef/`.

[6] Eclipse, Project Homepage. `http://www.eclipse.org/`.

[7] EGEE – Enabling Grids for E-Science, Project Homepage. `http://glite.web.cern.ch/glite/`.

[8] Globus Toolkit, Project Homepage. `http://www.globus.org/toolkit/`.

[9] GridFTP, Project Homepage. `http://www.globus.org/grid_software/data/gridftp.php`.

[10] Grimoires, Project Homepage. `http://www.grimoires.org`.

[11] OASIS: Web Services Resource Framework 1.2 (WSRF). `http://www.oasis-open.org/committees/tc_home.php?wg_abbrev=wsrf`.

[12] OGSA-DAI, Project Homepage. `http://www.ogsadai.org.uk/`.

[13] Subversive - SVN Team Provider. `http://www.eclipse.org/subversive/`.

[14] Typica, Project Homepage.
`http://code.google.com/p/typica/`.

[15] UNICORE, Project Homepage. http://www.unicore.eu/.

[16] XLANG: Web Services for Business Process Design. http://www.xml.com/pub/r/1153.

[17] IBM: Web Services Flow Language (WSFL) v1.0, May 2001. http://www-4.ibm.com/software/solutions/webservices/pdf/WSFL.pdf.

[18] W3C: SOAP Message Transmission Optimization Mechanism, January 2005. http://www.w3.org/TR/soap12-mtom/.

[19] W3C: SOAP Version 1.2 Part 1: Messaging Framework (Second Edition), April 2007. http://www.w3.org/TR/soap12-part1/.

[20] Active Endpoints, ActiveVOS. http://activevos.com/, 2010. http://activevos.com/.

[21] B. Allcock, J. Bester, J. Bresnahan, A. Chervenak, C. Kesselman, S. Meder, V. Nefedova, D. Quesnel, S. Tuecke, and I. Foster. Secure, efficient data transport and replica management for high-performance data-intensive computing. In *Proceedings of the 18th IEEE Symposium on Mass Storage Systems and Technologies (MSS)*. IEEE Press, 2001.

[22] G. Allen, K. Davis, T. Goodale, A. Hutanu, H. Kaiser, T. Kielmann, A. Merzky, R. Van Nieuwpoort, A. Reinefeld, F. Schintke, et al. The Grid Application Toolkit: Toward Generic and Easy Application Programming Interfaces for the Grid. *Proceedings of the IEEE*, 93(3):534–550, 2005.

[23] P. Amnuaykanjanasin and N. Nupairoj. The BPEL Orchestrating Framework for Secured Grid Services. In *International Conference on Information Technology: Coding and Computing*, volume 1, pages 348–353, Los Alamitos, CA, USA, 2005. IEEE Computer Society.

[24] T. Andrews, F. Curbera, H. Dholakia, Y. Goland, J. Klein, F. Leymann, K. Liu, D. Roller, D. Smith, S. Thatte, I. Trickovic, and S. Weerawarana. Business Process Execution Language for Web Services – Version 1.1, 2003. http://www.ibm.com/developerworks/library/specification/ws-bpel/.

[25] Apache Foundation. Apache Axis. http://ws.apache.org/axis/.

[26] Apache Foundation. Apache Ode (Orchestration Director Engine). http://ode.apache.org/, 2011.

[27] M. Armbrust, A. Fox, R. Griffith, A. Joseph, R. Katz, A. Konwinski, G. Lee, D. Patterson, A. Rabkin, and I. Stoica. Above the Clouds: A Berkeley View of Cloud Computing. *EECS Department, University of California, Berkeley, Tech. Rep. UCB/EECS-2009-28*, 2009.

[28] A. Barker and J. van Hemert. Scientific Workflow: A Survey and Research Directions. In R. Wyrzykowski, editor, *Proceedings of Seventh International Conference on Parallel Processing and Applied Mathematics*, LNCS 4967, pages 746–753. Springer-Verlag, 2007.

[29] J. J. Barton, S. Thatte, and H. F. Nielsen. SOAP Messages with Attachments. W3C Note, 2000.

[30] J. Basney, M. Humphrey, and V. Welch. The MyProxy Online Credential Repository. In *Software, Practice and Experience*, volume 35, pages 801–816, 2005.

[31] F. Berman, G. Fox, and T. Hey. *Grid Computing: Making the Global Infrastructure a Reality*. Wiley, 2003.

[32] D. Box, E. Christensen, F. Curbera, D. Ferguson, J. Frey, M. Hadley, C. Kaler, D. Langworthy, F. Leymann, B. Lovering, S. Lucco, S. Millet, N. Mukhi, M. Nottingham, D. Orchard, J. Shewchuk, E. Sindambiwe, T. Storey, S. Weerawarana, and S. Winkler. Web Services Addressing. http://www.w3.org/Submission/ws-addressing/, August 2004.

[33] T. D. Braun, H. J. Siegel, N. Beck, L. L. Bölöni, M. Maheswaran, A. I. Reuther, J. P. Robertson, M. D. Theys, B. Yao, D. Hensgen, and R. F. Freund. A Comparison of Eleven Static Heuristics for Mapping a Class of Independent Tasks onto Heterogeneous Distributed Computing Systems. *J. of Parallel and Distributed Computing*, 61(6):810 – 837, 2001.

[34] G. Canfora, M. D. Penta, R. Esposito, and M. Villani. An approach for qos-aware service composition based on genetic algorithms. *Proceedings of the 2005 conference on Genetic and evolutionary computation*, pages 1069–1075, 2005.

[35] J. Cardoso. Stochastic workflow reduction algorithm. *LSDIS Lab, University of Georgia*, 2002.

[36] J. Cardoso, A. Sheth, J. Miller, J. Arnold, and K. Kochut. Quality of Service for Workflows and Web Service Processes. *Web Semantics: Science, Services and Agents on the World Wide Web*, 1(3):281–308, 2004.

[37] K. S. M. Chan, J. Bishop, J. Steyn, L. Baresi, and S. Guinea. A Fault Taxonomy for Web Service Composition. In *Proceedings of the 3rd International Workshop on Engineering Service Oriented Applications (WESOA07), Springer LNCS*, 2007.

[38] K. Chao, M. Younas, N. Griffiths, I. Awan, R. Anane, and C. Tsai. Analysis of Grid Service Composition with BPEL4WS. In *Proceedings of 18th International Conference on Advanced Information Networking and Applications*, pages 284–289. IEEE Press, 2004.

[39] E. Christensen, F. Curbera, G. Meredith, and S. Weerawarana. Web Services Description Language, 2001. http://www.w3.org/TR/wsdl.

[40] P. Couvares, T. Kosar, A. Roy, J. Weber, and K. Wenger. Workflow management in condor. *Workflows for e-Science*, pages 357–375, 2007.

[41] D-Grid Community Project. InGrid - Innovative Grid Technology in Engineering. http://www.ingrid-info.de, 2007.

[42] D-Grid Initiative. Project Website. http://www.d-grid.de.

[43] T. Dalman, T. Dörnemann, E. Juhnke, M. Weitzel, M. Smith, W. Wiechert, K. Nöh, and B. Freisleben. Metabolic Flux Analysis in the Cloud. In *Proceedings of IEEE eScience 2010*, pages 57–64. IEEE Press, 2010.

[44] T. Dalman, E. Juhnke, T. Dörnemann, M. Weitzel, K. Nöh, W. Wiechert, and B. Freisleben. Service Workflows and Distributed Computing Methods for 13C Metabolic Flux Analysis. In *Proceedings of 7th EUROSIM Congress on Modelling and Simulation*, pages 1–7. , 2010.

[45] K. Deb, A. Pratap, S. Agarwal, and T. Meyarivan. A Fast Elitist Multi-Objective Genetic Algorithm: NSGA-II. *IEEE Transactions on Evolutionary Computation*, 6:182–197, 2000.

[46] E. Deelman, J. Blythe, Y. Gil, C. Kesselman, G. Mehta, S. Patil, M. Su, K. Vahi, and M. Livny. Pegasus: Mapping scientific workflows onto the grid. In *Grid Computing*, pages 131–140. Springer, 2004.

[47] E. Deelman, D. Gannon, M. Shields, and I. Taylor. Workflows and e-Science: An overview of workflow system features and capabilities. *Future Generation Computer Systems*, pages 524–540, Jan 2009.

[48] E. Deelman, G. Singh, M. Su, J. Blythe, Y. Gil, C. Kesselman, G. Mehta, K. Vahi, G. Berriman, and J. Good. Pegasus: A framework for mapping complex scientific workflows onto distributed systems. *Scientific Programming*, 13(3):219–237, 2005.

[49] A. Dennis. Active Endpoints Announces Open Source BPEL Initiative. http://www.activevos.com/content/blog/active_endpoints_announces_open_source_bpel_initiative.pdf, July 2004.

[50] M. Di Penta, R. Esposito, M. L. Villani, R. Codato, M. Colombo, and E. D. Nitto. WS Binder: a Framework to Enable Dynamic Binding of Composite Web Services. In *Proceedings of the 2006 International Workshop on Service-oriented Software Engineering*, pages 74–80. ACM, 2006.

[51] T. Dörnemann, T. Friese, S. Herdt, E. Juhnke, and B. Freisleben. Grid Workflow Modelling Using Grid-Specific BPEL Extensions. In *Proceedings of German e-Science Conference (GES)*, 2007.

[52] T. Dörnemann, S. Heinzl, K. Dörnemann, M. Mathes, M. Smith, and B. Freisleben. Secure Grid Service Engineering for Industrial Optimization. In *Proceedings of the 7th International Conference on Optimization: Techniques and Applications (ICOTA)*, pages 371–372. , 2007.

[53] T. Dörnemann, E. Juhnke, and B. Freisleben. On-Demand Resource Provisioning for BPEL Workflows Using Amazon's Elastic Compute Cloud. In *Proceedings of the 9th IEEE/ACM International Symposium on Cluster Computing and the Grid (CCGrid '09)*, pages 140–147. IEEE Press, 2009.

[54] T. Dörnemann, E. Juhnke, T. Noll, D. Seiler, and B. Freisleben. Data Flow Driven Scheduling of BPEL Workflows Using Cloud Resources. In *Proceedings of 3rd IEEE International Conference on Cloud Computing (IEEE CLOUD)*, pages 196–203. IEEE Press, 2010.

[55] T. Dörnemann, M. Mathes, R. Schwarzkopf, E. Juhnke, and B. Freisleben. DAVO: A Domain-Adaptable, Visual BPEL4WS Orchestrator. In *Proceedings of the 23rd IEEE International Conference on Advanced Information Networking and Applications (AINA)*, pages 121–128. IEEE Press, 2009.

[56] T. Dörnemann, M. Smith, and B. Freisleben. Composition and Execution of Secure Workflows in WSRF-Grids. In *Proceedings of the 8th IEEE International Symposium on Cluster Computing and the Grid (CCGrid)*, pages 122–129. IEEE Press, 2008.

[57] Eclipse.org. BPEL Project. http://www.eclipse.org/bpel/.

[58] H. El-Rewini, T. Lewis, and H. Ali. *Task Scheduling in Parallel and Distributed Systems*. Prentice Hall, 1994.

[59] J. Elson and J. Howell. Handling Flash Crowds from your Garage. In *ATC'08: USENIX 2008 Annual Technical Conference*, pages 171–184, Berkeley, CA, USA, 2008. USENIX Association.

[60] O. Ezenwoye and S. M. Sadjadi. TRAP/BPEL: A Framework for Dynamic Adaptation of Composite Services. In *Proceedings of the International Conference on Web Information Systems and Technologies (WEBIST 2007)*, 2007.

[61] T. Fahringer, A. Jugravu, S. Pllana, R. Prodan, C. Seragiotto Jr, and H. Truong. Askalon: a tool set for cluster and grid computing. *Concurrency and Computation: Practice and Experience*, 17(2-4):143–169, 2005.

[62] M. Ferber, S. Hunold, and T. Rauber. Load Balancing Concurrent BPEL Processes by Dynamic Selection of Web Service Endpoints. In *Proceedings of 9th International Conference on Parallel Processing Workshops*, pages 290–297. IEEE Press, Sept. 2009.

[63] J. L. R. Filho, P. C. Treleaven, and C. Alippi. Genetic-Algorithm Programming Environments. *Computer*, 27:28–43, June 1994.

[64] H. Foster, S. Uchitel, J. Magee, and J. Kramer. Leveraging Eclipse for Integrated Model-Based Engineering of Web Service Compositions. In *Proceedings of the International Conference on Object-Oriented Programming, Systems, Languages, and Applications (OOPSLA), Workshop on Eclipse Technology eXchange (ETX)*, pages 95–99. ACM Press, 2005.

[65] I. Foster. What is the grid? a three point checklist. *GRID today*, 1(6):32–36, 2002.

[66] I. Foster. Globus Toolkit Version 4: Software for Service-Oriented Systems. In *IFIP International Conference on Network and Parallel Computing*, pages 2–13. Springer-Verlag, 2006.

[67] I. Foster, D. Berry, A. Djaoui, A. Grimshaw, B. Horn, H. Kishimoto, F. Maciel, A. Savvy, F. Siebenlist, R. Subramaniam, J. Treadwell, and J. V. Reich. The Open Grid Services Architecture, Version 1.0. Whitepaper GGF, 2004.

[68] I. Foster, T. Freeman, K. Keahy, D. Scheftner, B. Sotomayor, and X. Zhang. Virtual Clusters for Grid Communities. In *Proceedings of the Sixth IEEE International Symposium on Cluster Computing and the Grid*, pages 513–520. IEEE Computer Society, 2006.

[69] I. Foster and C. Kesselman. *The Grid 2: Blueprint for a New Computing Infrastructure*. Morgan Kaufmann, 2003.

[70] I. Foster, C. Kesselman, J. Nick, and S. Tuecke. The Physiology of the Grid: An Open Grid Services Architecture for Distributed Systems Integration. In *Open Grid Service Infrastructure WG, Global Grid Forum*, pages 1–31, 2002.

[71] I. Foster, C. Kesselman, and S. Tuecke. The Anatomy of the Grid: Enabling Scalable Virtual Organizations. In *International Journal of High Performance Computing Applications*, volume 15, pages 200–222, 2001.

[72] I. Foster, J. V "ockler, M. Wilde, and Y. Zhao. Chimera: A Virtual Data System for Representing, Querying, and Automating Data Derivation. In *Proceedings of the 14th Conference on Scientific and Statistical Database Management*. IEEE Press, 2002.

[73] I. Foster, Y. Zhao, I. Raicu, and S. Lu. Cloud Computing and Grid Computing 360-Degree Compared. *Grid Computing Environments Workshop*, Jan 2008.

[74] J. Frey, T. Tannenbaum, M. Livny, I. Foster, and S. Tuecke. Condor-g: A computation management agent for multi-institutional grids. *Cluster Computing*, 5(3):237–246, 2002.

[75] T. Friese, M. Smith, and B. Freisleben. GDT: A Toolkit for Grid Service Development. In *Proceedings of the 3rd International Conference on Grid Service Engineering and Management*, pages 131–148, 2006.

[76] E. Gamma, R. Helm, and R. E. Johnson. *Design Patterns. Elements of Reusable Object-Oriented Software*. Addison-Wesley, 1995.

[77] Y. Gil, E. Deelman, M. Ellisman, T. Fahringer, G. Fox, D. Gannon, C. Goble, M. Livny, L. Moreau, and J. Myers. Examining the challenges of scientific workflows. *Computer*, pages 24–32, 2007.

[78] M. Harbach, T. Dörnemann, E. Juhnke, and B. Freisleben. Semantic Validation of BPEL Fragment Compositions. In *Proceedings of the fourth IEEE International Conference on Semantic Computing (ICSC2010)*, pages 176–183. IEEE Press, 2010.

[79] S. Hastings, S. Oster, S. Langella, D. Ervin, T. Kurc, and J. Saltz. Introduce: An Open Source Toolkit for Rapid Development of Strongly Typed Grid Services. *Journal of Grid Computing*, 5(4):407–427, 2007.

[80] S. Heinzl, M. Mathes, T. Friese, M. Smith, and B. Freisleben. FlexSwA: Flexible Exchange of Binary Data Based on SOAP Messages with Attachments. In *Proceedings of the IEEE International Conference on Web Services*, pages 3–10, Chicago, USA, 2006. IEEE Press.

[81] M. Held and W. Blochinger. Collaborative BPEL Design with a Rich Internet Application. In *Proceedings of the 8th IEEE International Symposium on Cluster Computing and the Grid (CCGrid)*, pages 202–209. IEEE Press, 2008.

[82] I. Ivanov. Utility Computing: Reality and Beyond. In J. Filipe and M. S. Obaidat, editors, *Proceedings of $4^{t}h$ International Conference on E-business and Telecommunications (ICETE)*, pages 16–29. Springer, 2007.

[83] E. Juhnke, T. Dörnemann, D. Böck, and B. Freisleben. Multi-Objective Scheduling of BPEL Workflows in Geographically Distributed Clouds. In *Proceedings of the 4th IEEE International Conference on Cloud Computing (IEEE CLOUD)*, pages 412–419. IEEE Press, 2011.

[84] E. Juhnke, T. Dörnemann, and B. Freisleben. Fault-Tolerant BPEL Workflow Execution via Cloud-Aware Recovery Policies. In *Proceedings of 35th Euromicro Conference on Software Engineering and Advanced Applications (SEAA)*, pages 31–38. IEEE Press, 2009.

[85] E. Juhnke, T. Dörnemann, S. Kirch, D. Seiler, and B. Freisleben. SimpleBPEL: Simplified Modeling of BPEL Workflows for Scientific End Users. In *Proceedings of the 36th EUROMICRO Conference on Software Engineering and Advanced Applications (SEAA)*, pages 137–140. IEEE Press, 2010.

[86] E. Juhnke, T. Dörnemann, R. Schwarzkopf, and B. Freisleben. Security, Fault Tolerance and Modeling of Grid Workflows in BPEL4Grid. In *Proceedings of Software Engineering 2010, Grid Workflow Workshop (GWW-10)*, pages 193–200. , 2010.

[87] E. Juhnke, D. Seiler, T. Stadelmann, T. Dörnemann, and B. Freisleben. LCDL: An Extensible Framework for Wrapping Legacy Code. In *Proceedings of 11th International Conference on Information Integration and Web-based Applications & Services (iiWAS2009)*, pages 646–650. ACM, 2009.

[88] G. Juve, E. Deelman, K. Vahi, G. Mehta, B. Berriman, B. Berman, and P. Maechling. Scientific workflow applications on amazon ec2. In *Proceedings of 5th IEEE International Conference on E-Science, Workshops*, pages 59–66. IEEE Press, 2009.

[89] D. Karastoyanova, A. Houspanossian, M. Cilia, F. Leymann, and A. Buchmann. Extending BPEL for Run Time Adaptability. In *EDOC '05: Proceedings of the Ninth IEEE International EDOC Enterprise Computing Conference*, pages 15–26. IEEE Computer Society, 2005.

[90] J. Kim, M. Spraragen, and Y. Gil. An Intelligent Assistant for Interactive Workflow Composition. In *Proceedings of the 9th International Conference on Intelligent User Interfaces*, pages 125–131. ACM, 2004.

[91] J. D. Knowles and D. W. Corne. The Pareto Archive Evolution Strategy: A New Baseline Algorithm for Multi-Objective Optimization.

In *Proc. of the IEEE Congress on Evolutionary Computation (CEC)*, pages 98–105. IEEE, 1999.

[92] Y. Kwok and I. Ahmad. Static Scheduling Algorithms for Allocating Directed Task Graphs to Multiprocessors. *ACM Computing Surveys (CSUR)*, 31(4):406–471, 1999.

[93] K. Lassen and W. van der Aalst. WorkflowNet2BPEL4WS: A Tool for Translating Unstructured Workflow Processes to Readable BPEL. *On the Move to Meaningful Internet Systems 2006: CoopIS, DOA, GADA, and ODBASE*, pages 127–144, 2006.

[94] G. Lee, N. Tolia, P. Ranganathan, and R. Katz. Topology-aware Resource Allocation for Data-Intensive Workloads. In *Proceedings of the 1st ACM Asia-Pacific Workshop on Systems*, volume 41, pages 1–6. ACM, 2010.

[95] K. Lee, J. Jeon, W. Lee, S.-H. Jeong, and S.-W. Park. QoS for Web Services: Requirements and Possible Approaches. http://www.w3c.or.kr/kr-office/TR/2003/ws-qos/, 2003.

[96] F. Leymann. Choreography for the Grid: Towards Fitting BPEL to the Resource Framework. In *Concurrency and Computation: Practice and Experience*. John Wiley & Sons, Ltd., 2005 (online).

[97] Y. Liu, A. Ngu, and L. Zeng. Qos computation and policing in dynamic web service selection. *Proceedings of the 13th international World Wide Web conference on Alternate track papers & posters*, pages 66–73, 2004.

[98] R.-Y. Ma, Y.-W. Wu, X.-X. Meng, S.-J. Liu, and L. Pan. Grid-Enabled Workflow Management System Based On BPEL. *International Journal of High Performance Computing Applications*, 22(3):238–249, 2008.

[99] S. Majithia, M. S. Shields, I. J. Taylor, and I. Wang. Triana: A Graphical Web Service Composition and Execution Toolkit. In *Proceedings of the IEEE International Conference on Web Services (ICWS'04)*, pages 514–524. IEEE Press, 2004.

[100] A. Martinez, M. Patino-Martinez, R. Jimenez-Peris, and F. Perez-Sorrosal. ZenFlow: A Visual Web Service Composition Tool for BPEL4WS. In *Proceedings of the IEEE Symposium on Visual Languages and Human-Centric Computing (VL/HCC)*, pages 181–188. IEEE Computer Society Press, 2005.

[101] M. Mathes. *Time-Constrained Web Services for Industrial Automation*. PhD thesis, University of Marburg, Department of Mathematics and Computer Science, 2009.

[102] M. Mathes, S. Heinzl, and B. Freisleben. Towards a Time-Constrained Web Service Infrastructure for Industrial Automation. In *Proceedings of the 13th IEEE International Conference on Emerging Technologies and Factory Automation (ETFA)*, pages 846–853. IEEE Computer Society Press, 2008.

[103] M. Mathes, R. Schwarzkopf, T. Dörnemann, S. Heinzl, and B. Freisleben. Orchestration of Time-Constrained BPEL4WS Workflows. In *Proceedings of the 13th IEEE International Conference on Emerging Technologies and Factory Automation (ETFA)*, pages 1–4. IEEE Computer Society Press, 2008.

[104] M. Mathes, R. Schwarzkopf, T. Dörnemann, S. Heinzl, and B. Freisleben. Composition of Time-Constrained BPEL4WS Workflows using the TiCS Modeler. In *Proceedings of the 13th IFAC Symposium on Information Control Problems in Manufacturing (INCOM)*, pages 892–897. Elsevier, 2009.

[105] M. Mathes, C. Stoidner, R. Schwarzkopf, S. Heinzl, T. Dörnemann, B. Freisleben, and H. Dohmann. *Time-constrained Services: A Framework for Using Real-Time Web Services in Industrial Automation*, volume 3. Service Oriented Computing and Applications. Springer London, 2009.

[106] A. McGough and D. Colling. The GRIDCC Project. In *Proceedings of the 1st International Conference on Communication System Software and Middleware (Comsware)*, pages 1–4, 2006.

[107] MediaGrid Community, D-Grid Initiative. GDI-Grid – Geodateninfrastruktur-Grid Project Web Site. http://www.gdi-grid.de/.

[108] MediaGrid Community, D-Grid Initiative. MediaGrid – Verteilte Analyse und Nutzung von Multimediadaten. http://www.mediagrid-community.de/.

[109] R. Mietzner and F. Leymann. Towards Provisioning the Cloud: On the Usage of Multi-Granularity Flows and Services to Realize a Unified Provisioning Infrastructure for SaaS Applications. In *Proceedings of IEEE Congress on Services - Part I*, pages 3–10, Los Alamitos, CA, USA, 2008. IEEE Computer Society.

[110] S. Modafferi, E. Mussi, and B. Pernici. SH-BPEL: A Self-healing Plug-in for WS-BPEL Engines. In *MW4SOC '06: Proceedings of the 1st Workshop on Middleware for Service Oriented Computing (MW4SOC 2006)*, pages 48–53. ACM, 2006.

[111] D. Mukherjee, P. Jalote, and M. G. Nanda. Determining qos of ws-bpel compositions. *Service-Oriented Computing–ICSOC 2008*, pages 378–393, 2008.

[112] OASIS. Web Services Resource Framework, 2004. http://www.oasis-open.org/committees/tc_home.php?wg_abbrev=wsrf.

[113] OASIS. Web Services Security: SOAP Message Security 1.1. http://,http://www.oasis-open.org/committees/tc_home.php?wg_abbrev=wss, February 2006.

[114] T. Oinn, M. Addis, J. Ferris, D. Marvin, M. Senger, M. Greenwood, T. Carver, K. Glover, M. Pocock, A. Wipat, et al. Taverna: a tool for the composition and enactment of bioinformatics workflows. *Bioinformatics*, 20(17):3045, 2004.

[115] Oracle Inc. Oracle Process Manager. http://www.oracle.com/technetwork/middleware/bpel/overview/index.html, October 2010.

[116] C. Ouyang, M. Dumas, A. ter Hofstede, and W. van der Aalst. From BPMN Process Models to BPEL Web Services. *Proceedings of the 4th International Conference on Web Services (ICWS), IEEE Computer Society, Chicago IL, USA*, pages 285–292, 2006.

[117] M. Papazoglou and W. V. D. Heuvel. Service-oriented design and development methodology. *International Journal of Web Engineering and Technology*, 2(4):412–442, 2006.

[118] PhysioNet. PhysioToolkit. http://www.physionet.org/physiotools/.

[119] R. Prodan and T. Fahringer. *Grid Computing: Experiment Management, Tool Integration, and Scientific Workflows*. Springer, 2007.

[120] J. Salas, F. Perez-Sorrosal, M. Patiño Martínez, and R. Jiménez-Peris. WS-Replication: A Framework for Highly Available Web Services. In *Proceedings of the 15th International Conference on World Wide Web*, WWW '06, pages 357–366, New York, NY, USA, 2006. ACM.

[121] J. Schad, J. Dittrich, and J. Quiane-Ruiz. Runtime Measurements in the Cloud: Observing, Analyzing, and Reducing Variance. *Proceedings of the VLDB Endowment*, 3(1), 2010.

[122] A. Slomiski. On Using BPEL Extensibility to Implement OGSI and WSRF Grid Workflows. *Concurrency and Computation: Practice and Experience*, 18(10):1229–1241, 2006.

[123] M. Smith, M. Schmidt, N. Fallenbeck, T. Dörnemann, C. Schridde, and B. Freisleben. *Secure On-Demand Grid Computing*. Journal of Future Generation Computer Systems. Elsevier, 2008.

[124] J. Stankovic. Misconceptions About Real-Time Computing: A Serious Problem for Next-Generation Systems. *Computer*, 21(10):10–19, 1988.

[125] A. Streule. Abstract Views on BPEL Processes. Master's thesis, Institute of Architecture of Application Systems, University of Stuttgart, Germany, 2009.

[126] S. Subramanian, P. Thiran, N. C. Narendra, G. K. Mostefaoui, and Z. Maamar. On the Enhancement of BPEL Engines for Self-Healing Composite Web Services. In *Proceedings of IEEE/IPSJ International Symposium on Applications and the Internet*, volume 0, pages 33–39, Los Alamitos, CA, USA, 2008. IEEE Computer Society.

[127] K. L. L. Tan and K. J. Turner. Orchestrating Grid Services using BPEL and Globus Toolkit. In *Proceedings of the 7th PGNet Symposium*, pages 31–36, Liverpool, 2006.

[128] Y. J. Tang, H. G. Martin, S. Myers, S. Rodriguez, E. E. K. Baidoo, and J. D. Keasling. Advances in analysis of microbial metabolic fluxes via ^{13}C isotopic labeling. *Mass Spectrometry Reviews*, 28(2):362–375, 2009.

[129] I. Taylor, M. Shields, I. Wang, and A. Harrison. The triana workflow environment: Architecture and applications. *Workflows for e-Science*, pages 320–339, 2007.

[130] I. Taylor, M. Shields, I. Wang, and R. Philp. Grid enabling applications using triana. In *Workshop on Grid Applications and Programming Tools*. Citeseer, 2003.

[131] M. ter Linden, H. de Wolf, and R. Grim. GridAssist, a User Friendly Grid-Based Workflow Management Tool. In *ICPP Workshops*, pages 5–10. IEEE Computer Society, 2005.

[132] The World Wide Web Consortium. Simple Object Access Protocol (SOAP), 2003. http://www.w3.org/TR/soap/.

[133] L. Vaquero, L. Rodero-Merino, J. Caceres, and M. Lindner. A Break in the Clouds: Towards a Cloud Definition. *ACM SIGCOMM Computer Communication Review*, 39(1):50–55, 2008.

[134] B. Venners. Designing Distributed Systems, A Conversation with Ken Arnold.
http://www.artima.com/intv/distrib.html.

[135] L. Wang, H. J. Siegel, V. R. Roychowdhury, and A. A. Maciejewski. Task Matching and Scheduling in Heterogeneous Computing Environments Using a Genetic-Algorithm-Based Approach. *J. of Parallel and Distributed Computing*, 47(1):8–22, 1997.

[136] X. Wang, R. Buyya, and J. Su. Reliability-Oriented Genetic Algorithm for Workflow Applications Using Max-Min Strategy. In *Proceedings of the 9th IEEE/ACM Intl. Symp. on Cluster Computing and the Grid (CCGrid '09)*, pages 108–115. IEEE, 2009.

[137] B. Wassermann, W. Emmerich, B. Butchart, N. Cameron, L. Chen, and J. Patel. *Workflows for e-Science*, chapter Sedna: A BPEL-Based Environment for Visual Scientific Workflow Modeling, pages 428–449. Springer, 2007.

[138] M. Weitzel. *High Performance Algorithms for Metabolic Flux Analysis*. PhD thesis, University of Siegen, Germany, 2009.

[139] W. Wiechert. ^{13}C Metabolic Flux Analysis. *Metababolic Engineering*, 3(3):195–206, 2001.

[140] W. Wiechert, M. Möllney, S. Petersen, and A. A. de Graaf. A Universal Framework for ^{13}C Metabolic Flux Analysis. *Metabolic Engineering*, 3(3):265–283, 2001.

[141] Workflow Management Coalition. Workflow Management Coalition Terminology & Glossary. http://www.wfmc.org/standards/docs/TC-1011_term_glossary_v3.pdf, 1999.

[142] J. Yu and R. Buyya. A novel architecture for realizing grid workflow using tuple spaces. In *Proceedings of the 5th IEEE/ACM International Workshop on Grid Computing*, pages 119–128. IEEE Computer Society, 2004.

[143] J. Yu and R. Buyya. A Taxonomy of Scientific Workflow Systems for Grid Computing. *ACM SIGMOD Record*, 34:44–49, 2005.

[144] J. Yu and R. Buyya. A Taxonomy of Scientific Workflow Systems for Grid Computing. Technical Report GRIDS-TR-2005-1, Grid Computing and Distributed Systems Laboratory, University of Melbourn, Australia, 2005.

[145] J. Yu, M. Kirley, and R. Buyya. Multi-objective Planning for Workflow Execution on Grids. In *Proceedings of the 8th IEEE/ACM International Conference on Grid Computing*, GRID '07, pages 10–17. IEEE, 2007.

[146] M. Zager. Business Process Orchestration with BPEL: BPEL supports time critical decision making. *SOA World*, 5(11), Dec. 2005.

[147] E. Zitzler, M. Laumanns, and L. Thiele. SPEA2: Improving the Strength Pareto Evolutionary Algorithm. Technical Report 103, ETH Zurich, May 2001.

[148] E. Zitzler and L. Thiele. An Evolutionary Algorithm for Multiobjective Optimization: The Strength Pareto Approach. Technical Report 43, ETH Zurich, May 1998.

i want morebooks!

Buy your books fast and straightforward online - at one of world's fastest growing online book stores! Environmentally sound due to Print-on-Demand technologies.

Buy your books online at
www.get-morebooks.com

Kaufen Sie Ihre Bücher schnell und unkompliziert online – auf einer der am schnellsten wachsenden Buchhandelsplattformen weltweit! Dank Print-On-Demand umwelt- und ressourcenschonend produziert.

Bücher schneller online kaufen
www.morebooks.de

VDM Verlagsservicegesellschaft mbH
Heinrich-Böcking-Str. 6-8   Telefon: +49 681 3720 174   info@vdm-vsg.de
D - 66121 Saarbrücken   Telefax: +49 681 3720 1749   www.vdm-vsg.de

Printed by Books on Demand GmbH, Norderstedt / Germany